# English Catholic Books 1641-1700:

## *A Bibliography*

Thomas H. Clancy, S.J.

**LOYOLA UNIVERSITY PRESS**
Chicago   60657

LIBRARY OF CONGRESS
CATALOGING IN PUBLICATION DATA

Clancy, Thomas H.
  *English Catholic books, 1641-1700.*

  1. Catholic literature—Bibliography.
2. Theology, Catholic—Bibliography.   I. Title.
Z7837.C53        016.23'02        74-704

ISBN 0-8294-0231-4

# PREFACE

It is now seventeen years since the appearance of <u>A</u> <u>Catalogue</u>
<u>of</u> <u>Catholic</u> <u>Books...1558-1640</u> by A. F. Allison and D. M.
Rogers. At the Second Oxford Conference on Post-Reformation
Catholic History in 1959 I heard Dr. Rogers issue a call for
volunteers to help him in the preparation of another catalog
which would cover the years 1641-1700.

At that time I had little taste for the project, but my
mind returned to it five years later. With the help of two
student assistants, Walter Sagrera and Kathleen Sullivan, I
began to comb the catalogs. The first library I searched was
the Folger. During the academic year 1965-1966 I was able,
through a grant from the Society of Religion in Higher Education, to spend a year at Oxford which was devoted mainly to
bibliographical research. Up to that time I was still thinking
of contributing to the projected "Catholic Wing," but it soon
became apparent that many who were better suited than I to
direct this project were otherwise occupied and I became the
principal compiler by default.

Dr. David Rogers had been collecting material on
seventeenth century Catholic books for many years and gave
me complete access to his files. Much of what is valuable in
the present list is due to his researches.

In England most of my work was done at the Bodleian
and the British Museum with shorter visits to Oscott, Ware,
Heythrop, Cambridge and other libraries in Oxford and London.
On my return to America I worked in the libraries of Yale,
Union Theological Seminary, Georgetown and Duke University, with many return trips to the Folger. Several provisional
and partial versions of the present list have been circulated to
scholars. Among many who have sent me corrections and ad-
ditions I must single out Dr. James Molloy.

In the summer of 1968 I was received most cordially at
Yale by the late Donald Wing who opened his files and his im-
mense knowledge to me. Up to his death in October of 1972

iii

we frequently exchanged information with most of it coming from him. It is to this unselfish scholar that I owe the discovery of the recent massive acquisitions of recusant works by the University of Texas at Austin and the Newberry Library and I was received graciously in both places. This list has profited enormously from the meticulous bibliographical work of Mr. Bernard Wilson at the latter institution.

It should be noted that Mr. Wing was engaged at the time of his death in a revision of his valuable work. As these pages go to press I have only seen Vol. I of the second edition. Many of the omissions noted here will probably be corrected in the remaining volumes of the revised edition of Wing's catalog. Indeed many of them have been drawn from his files. It did not seem desirable, however, to wait any longer to publish what must remain for some time to come a provisional listing of Catholic books.

In the final editorial work I have been assisted by Miss Patricia Marshall, a trained librarian, whose knowledge of bibliography and English history as well as the refinements of proofreading have been of inestimable assistance. Carol Gaddis and Cheryl Tregle typed the manuscript. I am also indebted to the Faculty Research Fund of Loyola University, New Orleans for supporting me partially during two summers of research on this project.

It only remains to say that none of the persons or institutions mentioned above should be held accountable for the deficiencies of the present work. The author is acutely aware of his shortcomings as a bibliographer and is only emboldened to publish by the thought that this list may be the building stone for a better and more complete "Catholic Wing."

T. H. C.

August, 1973
Loyola University
New Orleans

# TABLE OF CONTENTS

# INTRODUCTION

The aim of this catalog is to give abridged entries of all
"English" books written by Roman Catholics and published in
the Roman Catholic interest between 1641 and 1700 inclusive.
Books which are known--or are thought--to have existed at
one time, but which have now apparently perished are not included. The extension of the word "English" is that adopted
by Allison and Rogers[1]: "For our purposes the word 'English'
covers the four languages of the British Isles: English, Irish,
Scots and Welsh. Service books in Latin printed abroad for
use in England are included, but other works in foreign
languages written by English[2] Catholics are included only if
they were printed--or if they claim to be printed--in England. "

By "Catholic" is meant that the work was written by a
Roman Catholic[3] and published in the Catholic interest. Purely
literary efforts are not included nor are books written on non-
religious topics except where they bear an imprimatur or
other sign of official Church approval.[4] Books written by
Catholics on political topics are included if they plead the
Catholic interest or defend Catholic doctrine.[5]

Catholic books issued by a notoriously Protestant
publisher or edited in a Protestant sense are not included.[6]
But Catholic books of devotion printed by a neutral publisher
without comment are included.[7] The criterion for inclusion,
therefore, is not typography, as it was for Allison and Rogers,
but rather the content of the book. This has involved a number
of conjectures. Anonymous pleas for toleration, e. g., from
Catholics and dissenters are sometimes very similar. I have
been liberal in including books of this type.

None of the numerous publications of the Catholic Confederation of Kilkenny are included. These are mostly broadsides and it was thought that their inclusion would radically
alter the character of this list. The items I have come across
in this category are listed in Appendix I.[8]

## Description

Each book is entered under the author if his name is known. If the book is signed by initials and the author is not known, it is entered under the last initial. When an author uses a pseudonym or name in religion, the book is entered under his true name, but a cross-reference is given. If the author is not known, the book is entered under the first word of the title, excluding the article.

The order of entry is as follows:

1. Author's name (if known) or initial. In the absence of both, the title is given.
2. The short title of the entry or, where there is no title, the first words of the text.
3. Place of publication. If none is given, this is signified by n. p. (= no place).
4. Publisher and/or printer. If none is given, no notation is made.
5. Date as it appears on tp. If none is given, this is signified by n. d. (= no date).
6. Format, if known.
7. After the format, the number of paginated pages of the principal part of the work is given in cases where the book has less than 100 p.
8. Locations, with the shelf-mark. Where the library symbol is underlined, this signifies that the copy has been examined by the author. These are generally the only locations given except where a location is derived from a library catalog or an unusually reliable source.
9. Wing number.

Matter in parentheses anywhere in the description is added by the compiler. I have been less austere than Allison and Rogers in adding material which I think will be helpful to the researcher.

It should be noted that the absence of a Wing number does not necessarily mean that the item is not in Wing, simply that I have not been able to find it there. Where Wing has a mistaken date, title or format I have silently changed it in the description. Where I have split a Wing item into two or more entries, the Wing number is placed after the first entry only.

I have used the Wing symbols for libraries wherever possible and invented my own or borrowed from Allison and Rogers where the library is not listed in Wing's original edition. These symbols are listed below. It will be noted that copies are located in only 50 libraries, a third of which I have not visited in the preparation of this bibliography. This calls to mind the necessity of two cautions which should be expressed.

First, Allison and Rogers visited hundreds of libraries and made a real census of copies so that a paucity of locations in their catalog signified a rare book. I have visited comparatively few libraries and have not listed the complete holdings of any except accidentally. The result is that some fairly common items have only one or two locations. In many cases further copies can be located in Wing.

Second, Allison and Rogers have shown that many works unlisted in the standard catalogs turn up in small collections. This is especially true of devotional books. Since most of my work has been done in the larger collections one would expect to find many more hitherto unknown books and editions in the smaller libraries. It will be noted that I have visited no libraries in Scotland, Ireland or Wales.

For the larger libraries I have given the shelf-mark of the copies examined. This has not made for a neat page but the thought of other researchers being forced to spend the hours I sometimes spent tracking an item down in a huge catalog led me to add this feature. For some libraries a shelf-mark is not always necessary, e.g., the Folger uses the Wing number for cataloged items. The six digit figure added after FSL refers to a provisional listing. In other libraries it has not always been possible to list the shelf-mark since the items had not been cataloged when I examined the copies in question.

I have insisted on the provisional nature of this list. In order to speed up the revision process I have listed in Appendix I books left out of the main list. These fall into six categories:

1   Publications of the Catholic Confederation of Kilkenny which I have discovered.
2   Ghosts which appear in standard sources but which do not apparently exist today.
3   Books by Catholic authors published under Protestant auspices.
4   Books of doubtfully Catholic origin. Most of these I have not seen, but their existence is attested to by good sources.
5   Works by English Catholics in Latin and languages other than the four languages of the British Isles noted above.
6   Works falsely attributed to Catholic authors.

## Survey of Catholic Books

This catalog furnishes one more indication that English Catholics had moved in the mid-17th century from their golden age to a silver one. Even though the dismantling of censorship during the Civil War and Interregnum and later on a more tolerant atmosphere made it easier for them to publish books more or less openly in England their books did not approach the quality or quantity of the former age.

In the period 1615-1640 Catholics published 481 items or an average of 96 books each five-year period. In the next 60 years they published roughly 1144 books which averages out to 95 each five-year period. But almost a third of these were published in the four years from 1685 through 1688 when Catholic publishing was open and even officially encouraged. If we disregard these years the average annual yield from 1641 to 1700 was something like 13 books.

As in the reign of James I and Charles I the annual crop of Catholic books fluctuates widely in quantity. If we were to plot the raw total of items published in five-year periods between 1616 and 1700 we would get a graph that corresponds to other indicators we have of Catholic fortunes.

The volume is high in the last years of James I when Gondomar's influence was felt. Then comes the Anglo-Spanish war and a great decline in 1626-1630. The steady fall that sets in after 1632 is due in part to the disappearance of John Heigham from the publishing scene in that year. The English College Press at St. Omers also slows down in the 1630's and from 1642 to 1692 published very few books.

In the 1640's Catholic publishing is reduced almost to the vanishing point by the ravages of Civil War. Then the curve begins to rise again as hopes brighten for some rapprochement with the Independents. Cromwell's 1655 tightening up of press control is reflected in a sharp drop in the number of books published in the following year, but after that there is a fairly steady rise coming to a peak in 1662 when hopes for toleration were strong. Once those hopes are dashed volume goes down during the next five-year period. The Oates Plot and the Exclusion crisis are reflected in the low totals for 1676-1685. Then comes the cloudburst of James II's reign followed by very low yield the last decade of the century.

The raw totals do not tell the whole story, since there are a far greater proportion of pamphlets, broadsides and sermons and a smaller proportion of "stout books" in the

2nd half of the 17th century than earlier. This is especially true of the years of James II when most of the Catholic sermons were published.

Where do the books come from? There are during our period four sorts of printers/booksellers that produce Catholic books:

1   Foreign presses. By 1641, as noted above, two of the big presses of St. Omers, John Heigham and the English College Press, had dropped out of the field, but a small trickle of English Catholic books still come from publishers in Antwerp, Bruges, Douai, Paris and other cities.

2   Neutral London publishers. The rise of the Salesian school of spirituality leads to the production of a new kind of spiritual book whose message is more generally Christian and less specifically Roman Catholic. St. Francis de Sales himself is a good example of this. His "Boswell," Jean-Pierre Camus, wrote edifying romances that appealed to a class of readers who would be repelled by the more traditional spiritual treatises. The best seller in this class was Nicholas Caussin whose Holy Court, though frankly Catholic, enjoyed wide popularity in 17th century England. These books rarely had to be bowdlerized in a Protestant sense, but some of the non-Catholic versions of these and other Catholic spiritual writers are listed in Appendix I.

3   As in the last years of Elizabeth and the early years of James I, there were some unfriendly publishers who were willing to publish Catholic books if they thought they would increase tensions in the English Catholic community. These books come within our terms of reference because they were written by Catholics who considered their publication to be in the Catholic interest, even though the intention of the printer or bookseller might have been the opposite. Many of Peter Walsh's books fall into this category.

4   During the reign of James II three publishers dominate the Catholic trade: Matthew Turner, Henry Hills and the Thompsons (Mary and Nathaniel). There were besides several other smaller publishers willing to publish Catholic books.

Finally, the publishers of fully one third of the books listed are unknown. For reasons listed above I have not been able to identify the origin of the vast majority of books which bear the name of no printer or bookseller.

In many cases Catholic authors wrote anonymous or pseudonymous books adopting the disguise of a reasonable Protestant or a neutral observer in order to be read by a wider audience. One of the outstanding writers in this class was John Austin who wrote his pleas for toleration under the pseudonym of Will Birchley and posed as a reasonable Protestant.

Later on some Catholic author, probably Ignatius Brown, S. J., used the same device to criticize some of the assumptions of Protestant belief in his highly successful, Pax Vobis. Catholics also used misleading titles to trap unsuspecting Protestants into reading their pleas for toleration, e. g., A dialogue or discourse between a parliament-man and a Roman Catholic touching the present state of the recusants in England and showing how from time to time they have always maintained their religion by treasons and conspiracies (1641). John Huddleston, alias Dormer, S. J., or some other clever Catholic adopted the same six first words of a popular Protestant pamphlet, The new plot of the papists, to make a sober plea for the innocence of the Jesuits who were executed in the Oates plot. Works with such deceiving titles are very common in the reign of James II. Andrew Pulton entitles one of his tracts: A full and clear exposition of the protestant rule of faith laying forth the large extent of true protestant charity against the uncharitable papists. At the end he appends the following note: "I have been obliged to prefix different titles to this short discourse, by reason of the Endeavors I have experienced to be used by Protestant Ministers to keep out of the Peoples hands all books and papers which might contribute to the dis-abusing a Nation. ..." In such cases to reveal the name of the printer and/or bookseller might have revealed the artifice of the author.

Of the authors cataloged only two, Richard Crashaw and John Dryden, each represented by two minor works, have gained entrance into the canon of 17th century literature. Along with Kenelm Digby there are the only ones who have been the subject of serviceable biographies.[9] Among the top two dozen authors in productivity are certain translated authors. Most popular are Caussin and Bossuet. In general the English Catholics who had read Spanish and Italian authors in the STC period switched to French authors in our period. This reflects the growing influence of French culture, but it also reflects the more eirenic stance of English Catholicism in the latter period.

Certain hardy perennials continue to sell: St. Augustine, Thomas a Kempis, the Manual of Prayers (originally adapted from the work of Vorepius, a Dutch priest, in 1583), and the Primer to the Blessed Virgin (introduced to English readers by Richard Verstegan in 1599). Of the native English authors few are well known. John Gother's life is largely a mystery[10] but his writing career falls neatly into two parts: controversial tracts during the reign of James II and devotional and moral treatises in the last decade of the century. Thomas White, alias Blacklo, enjoys the distinction of provoking Thomas Hobbes into writing his first piece of polemic.[11] White wrote works of controversy against both Protestants and his fellow Catholics. His work also contains systematic philosophy and theology, devotional books and one startling invasion in the field of political philosophy.[12] John Sergeant was a disciple of White's and like his master engaged in numerous literary battles, one of them with John Locke. Abraham Woodhead was a prolific translator and controversialist. Many of his books were published on the famous Oxford press of Obadaiah Walker.

What strikes us as we survey the list of the most productive identifiable authors is the preponderance of secular priests. Of the 18 most published English authors five are secular priests. Besides White, Gother, and Sergeant there are Sylvester Jenks and Henry Turberville. There are also a surprising number of lay authors on the list. Besides John Heigham, whose best-selling Touchstone was reprinted repeatedly during the 17th century, we have Woodhead, Austin, and Thomas Vane. Franciscans (Peter Walsh, J.V. Canes) and Benedictines (Serenus Cressy, Philip Ellis, John Maurice Corker) are also prominent.

Some of the absences are also noteworthy. There are many English Jesuit authors such as John Warner, John Huddleston, Lewis Sabran and James Mumford, but most of them published in short bursts only. Jesuits do not have the prominence in this list they enjoyed in that of Allison and Rogers. It is also curious to remark how few of the Elizabethan Catholic leaders are reprinted. Not a single work of Cardinal Allen is republished. Of Robert Persons' work only his Christian Directory and Three Conversions are reprinted. There is only a single reprint of Edmund Campion's Ten Reasons.

In reviewing the list of the most prolific authors it becomes apparent that to be a much-published writer one needed a steady income from an outside source. Thomas White had a reliable patron in Sir Kenelm Digby. John Sergeant found time to do a good deal of writing while serving as secretary of the Chapter of the English clergy. Later on he had an annuity left to him by Thomas White,[13] and found a patron in the Duke of Perth. Peter Walsh received a pension from the Marquess of Ormonde. The religious orders for their part seemed less willing to subsidize writers and presses than they did in the beginning of the 17th century.

What we have then as far as volume is concerned is a body of writings that constitutes less than 2% of the "English" books issued during these years. Even so as a sectarian corpus it far surpasses in size the much better known Baptist and Quaker writings and is second in size only to that of the Established Church.

What about quality? The remarks of Macaulay about the less than third rate quality of Roman Catholic writers of the Jacobean interlude is well known.[14] We may concede that the literary quality of the books we have cataloged is less than distinguished. It compares very favorably, however, to that of the Church of England literature these books provoked and answered.

But it is unsafe to make any generalizations about this literature until it is studied. Victor Hamm has found many of the books we list helpful in understanding John Dryden, the dominant writer of the age.[15] They are necessary too for the understanding of the ecclesiastical history of the 17th century. One of the most striking facts about that history is the extent to which the Anglican and Roman Catholic writers are obsessed with each other. Each side seems honor bound to produce an answer to every book of controversy the other side puts out. Even during the Interregnum when Anglicans might have been expected to direct their fire to the Puritans practically all of their energies were devoted to contending against the Papists. John Hammond, who was the spiritual and intellectual leader of the Laudian exiles even though he remained in England, compiled lists of Catholic controversial works and assigned various Anglican writers to answer them.[16]

In political life too the subject of Popery was a topical one especially during the exclusion crisis of 1679-1681 and the reign of James 1685-1689. The mythical history of Popery and its influence on life and politics in the 17th century is often referred to. These books give us a chance to examine the real intellectual life of the English Catholic body.

Their influence spread beyond England. Books from our list were among the first imported by the New World's tiny Catholic body in Maryland. Mumford, Barry, Rodriguez, Turberville, Gother, Persons: these are among the books read by America's earliest English speaking Catholics.[17]

Their influence spread too among the non-Catholics of England. As the century wore on the Protestants appropriated for their own use many authors first published by English Catholics: Verstegan, Rodriguez, Herman Hugo, Blosius, Bernard, Bona, Bouhours and many others. It was principally through Catholic books that English readers satisfied their keen interest in European intellectual movements such as Jansenism, Cartesianism and the Westernization of the world that was just beginning.

For all these reasons, therefore, these books are worthy of study. They show us a side of English life that has been sorely neglected in our intellectual histories. It will be many years before we have a complete map of English Catholic literature in the 17th century. In the meantime we offer this imperfect guide to those dark thickets.

# NUMBER OF CATHOLIC BOOKS
published by years and five-year
period subtotals
1641-1700

| 1616 | 22 | 1641 | 14 | 1661 | 24 | 1681 | 13 |
|------|----|------|----|------|----|------|----|
| 1617 | 16 | 1642 | 11 | 1662 | 29 | 1682 | 11 |
| 1618 | 23 | 1643 | 2 | 1663 | 18 | 1683 | 5 |
| 1619 | 16 | 1644 | 5 | 1664 | 7 | 1684 | 19 |
| 1620 | 26 | 1645 | 7 | 1665 | 19 | 1685 | 32 |
|      | 103 |     | 39 |     | 97 |      | 80 |

| 1621 | 25 | 1646 | 4 | 1666 | 6 | 1686 | 104 |
|------|----|------|----|------|----|------|-----|
| 1622 | 27 | 1647 | 8 | 1667 | 11 | 1687 | 148 |
| 1623 | 34 | 1648 | 14 | 1668 | 9 | 1688 | 93 |
| 1624 | 26 | 1649 | 9 | 1669 | 13 | 1689 | 7 |
| 1625 | 20 | 1650 | 14 | 1670 | 16 | 1690 | 4 |
|      | 132 |     | 49 |     | 55 |      | 356 |

| 1626 | 14 | 1651 | 11 | 1671 | 13 | 1691 | 4 |
|------|----|------|----|------|----|------|----|
| 1627 | 8 | 1652 | 28 | 1672 | 24 | 1692 | 5 |
| 1628 | 5 | 1653 | 14 | 1673 | 29 | 1693 | 4 |
| 1629 | 4 | 1654 | 23 | 1674 | 30 | 1694 | 5 |
| 1630 | 32 | 1655 | 18 | 1675 | 23 | 1695 | 9 |
|      | 63 |     | 94 |     | 119 |      | 27 |

| 1631 | 22 | 1656 | 5 | 1676 | 13 | 1696 | 9 |
|------|----|------|----|------|----|------|----|
| 1632 | 34 | 1657 | 24 | 1677 | 7 | 1697 | 8 |
| 1633 | 26 | 1658 | 20 | 1678 | 15 | 1698 | 14 |
| 1634 | 18 | 1659 | 20 | 1679 | 25 | 1699 | 11 |
| 1635 | 20 | 1660 | 23 | 1680 | 15 | 1700 | 14 |
|      | 120 |     | 92 |     | 75 |      | 56 |

| 1636 | 11 |
|------|----|
| 1637 | 7 |
| 1638 | 18 |
| 1639 | 16 |
| 1640 | 11 |
|      | 63 |

(1641-1700 figures do not include
5 items to which no date has been
assigned)

xvi

# ABBREVIATIONS AND REFERENCES

| | |
|---|---|
| A&R | A. F. Allison and D. M. Rogers, A catalogue of catholic books in English printed abroad or secretly in England 1558-1640. Bognor Regis. 1956 |
| Birrell | T. A. Birrell's list of the works of John Warner S. J. in his edition of The history of English persecution of Catholics and the Presbyterian plot, Publications of the Catholic Record Society Vols. 47 & 48 |
| B. S. | Biographical Studies. After Vol. 4 this review is known as Recusant History |
| CRS | Publications of the Catholic Record Society |
| D-K | Godfrey Davies and Mary Frear Keeler (eds.), Bibliography of British History, Stuart Period. 2nd ed. Oxford. 1970 |
| DNB | Dictionary of National Biography |
| Dodd | C. Dodd, The church of England chiefly with regard to Catholics, 3 vols. Brussels. 1737-1742 (D-K # 1458) |
| ECP | Press of the English College at St. Omer |
| Fry and Davies | Mary Isobel Fry and Godfrey Davies, "Supplements to the Short-Title Catalogue 1641-1700," excerpted from Huntington Library Quarterly Vol. 16, No. 4 (1953) |
| Gibson | R. W. Gibson, St. Thomas More, a preliminary bibliography, New Haven. 1961 |

| | |
|---|---|
| Gillow | Jos. Gillow, A literary and biblio-graphical history or bibliographical dictionary of the English Catholics. 5 vols. London and New York. 1885-1902 |
| Hiscock | W. G. Hiscock, The Christ Church supplement to Wing's Short Title catalogue. Oxford. 1956 |
| Hoskins | Edgar Hoskins: Horae beatae Mariae virginis... or Sarum and York primers. London. 1901 |
| JAM | James A. Molloy |
| Macdonald | Hugh Macdonald, John Dryden. A bibliography. Oxford, 1939 |
| Madan | F. Madan, Oxford Books. 3 vols. Oxford 1895-1931 |
| Newdigate | Notes of C. A. Newdigate S. J. at Farm St. Library, London |
| N&Q | Notes and Queries |
| OS | G. F. Pullen, Recusant Books at St. Mary's Oscott, Parts I & II, New Oscott, 1964, 1966 |
| PMLA | Publications of the Modern Language Association |
| RH | Recusant History |
| STC | A. W. Pollard, G. R. Redgrave, et. al.: A short-title catalogue of books printed in England, Scotland and Ireland... 1475-1640. London, 1956 |
| Thomason | George Thomason whose collection of pamphlets and tracts is in the British Museum. See the catalogue of the collection edited by G. K. Fortes-cue, 2 vols. London, 1908 |
| Walsh | M. O'N. Walsh, "Irish books printed abroad 1475-1700" in The Irish Book, Vol. 2, No. 1 (1963) entire issue |
| Wing | Donald G. Wing: Short title catalogue of books printed in England, Scotland, Ireland... 1641-1700. New York, 1945-1951. 3 vols. Revised edition Vol. I. New York. 1972. When an item is proper to the first or second edition of Volume I, the ordinal 1 or 2 is prefixed to signify the edition |

|              | referred to.                           |
|--------------|----------------------------------------|
| Wing: Ghosts | Donald Wing: A gallery of ghosts.      |
|              | New York, 1967                         |
| Wood         | Anthony à Wood                         |

# NOTES

1     A&R, p. iii.

2     Irish, Welsh, Scottish and foreign writers are included here if they were closely connected to the English scene or living in England at the time their books were published.

3     The term "Catholic" is preferred to the more cumbersome and not unneutral term, "Roman Catholic," throughout.

4     e. g. #602.

5     e. g. #317, 320, 1078, 1079.

6     See category W in Appendix I.

7     Almost all the works of Camus and Caussin fall in this category.

8     A more complete listing can be found in E. A. Clough's very helpful A short-title catalogue arranged geographically (London, 1969), pp. 85-86.

9     In addition J. B. Dockery's Christopher Davenport (London, 1960) is very useful.

10    But see Sister Marion Norman's "John Gother and the English way of spirituality" in 11 RH 306.

11    Jean Jacquot: "Notes on an unpublished work of Thomas Hobbes," 9 Notes and Record of the Royal Society (1952) 188-195.

12    #1078

13    See T. A. Birrell's Introduction to R. Pugh: Blacklo's Cabal (Westmead, 1970).

14    See the comments of Victor Hamm in "Dryden's The Hind and the Panther and Roman Catholic apologetics," 83 PMLA (1968) p. 400. Cf. T. A. Birrell, Catholic allegiance and the Popish plot (Nijmegen, 1950) p. 15.

15    Art. cit. and "Dryden's Religio Laici and Roman Catholic Apologetics," 80 PMLA (1965) 190-8. Sanford Budick has been kind enough to acknowledge the help he received from a MS version of this bibliography in his Dryden and the Abyss of Light (New Haven, 1970).

16    Robert S. Bosher: The making of the restoration settlement (New York, 1951) p. 36 ff.

17    Thomas Hughes, The History of the Society of Jesus in North America, Text Vol. 2 (New York, 1917) p. 517 n. 7.

# LIBRARY SYMBOLS

| | |
|---|---|
| BN | Bibliotheque Nationale, Paris[1] |
| BUTE | Marquess of Bute[2] |
| C | Cambridge University Library |
| CE | Emmanuel College, Cambridge |
| CGC | Gonville & Caius College, Cambridge[3] |
| CHEL | Sepulchrine Convent, New Hall, Chemlsford[3] |
| CN | Newberry Library, Chicago |
| CS | St. John's College, Cambridge |
| DAI | Douai Abbey, Woolhampton, Berkshire[2] |
| DE | Downside Abbey, Bath[3] |
| DMR | David M. Rogers |
| DN | National Library of Ireland, Dublin[3] |
| DT | Trinity College, Dublin[3] |
| DUC | Durham Cathedral |
| EC | Eton College |
| EN | National Library of Scotland, Edinburgh[3] |
| FSL | Folger Shakespeare Library, Washington |
| HP | Heythrop College, London[4] |
| KNY | Franciscans, Killeney, Eire[3] |
| L | British Museum, London |
| Lanherne | Carmelite Convent, Lanherne, Cornwall[3] |
| LC | Library of Congress, Washington |
| LFS | Farm St. Library, Jesuit Church, London |
| LGL | Gillow Library, Farm St. London |
| LIL | Law Society Library, London |
| LL | Lincoln's Inn, London |
| LSC | Sion College, London |
| LW | Dr. Williams' Library, London |
| MH | Harvard University[3] |
| NCD | Duke University Library, Durham, N. C. |
| NC | Columbia University, New York |
| NF | Fordham University, New York |
| NN | New York Public Library |

| | |
|---|---|
| NU | Union Theological Seminary, New York |
| O | Bodleian Library, Oxford |
| OB | Balliol College, Oxford |
| OC | Christ Church, Oxford |
| OM | Magdalen College, Oxford[3] |
| OME | Merton College, Oxford[3] |
| OS | St. Mary's Seminary, Oscott, Warwickshire |
| PFOR | Pforzheimer Library, New York City |
| SN | Syon Abbey, South Brent, Devon[3] |
| ST | Stonyhurst College, Lancashire[5] |
| THC | Thomas H. Clancy |
| TMTH | St. Scholastica's Abbey, Teighmouth, Devon[2] |
| TU | University of Texas, Austin |
| WARE | St. Edmund's College, Ware |
| WCL | Chapin Library, Williams College, Williamstown, Mass.[3] |
| WGT | Georgetown University, Washington |
| Y | Yale University, New Haven, Conn. |

1 Books located through catalogs only.
2 All references to these libraries derived from David M. Rogers.
3 All references to these collections derive from correspondence with the librarians.
4 I examined most of these books at the old location at Oxfordshire.
5 All locations to this collection are taken from the notes of Fr. C.A. Newdigate, S.J. at Farm St.

A., J.: A vindication of the roman catholics. See Caron (R.)

1   (Abbot, John):  Devout rhapsodies in which is treated of the excellencie of divine scripture. By J.A. Rivers (Pseud.) London. Thomas Harper f. Daniel Frere. n.d. (Thomason gives 11 Nov. 1647) 4to. 80 p. O Mal 297 (ii). Wing A 67

2   (Abbot, John):  Devout rhapsodies. By J.A. Rivers. London. Thomas Harper f. Daniel Frere. 1647. 4to. 80 p. FSL A 67 a

3   (Abbot, John):  Devout rhapsodies. By J.A. Rivers. London. Thomas Harper f. Daniel Frere. 1648. 4to. 80 p. O Ashm. 1032 (2)

4   (Abbot, John):  Devout rhapsodies. By J.A. Rivers. London. Thomas Harper f. Daniel Frere. 1648. 4to. 2 parts 80 + 48 p. (See 1 BS 30-1)

5   (Abbot, John):  Ka mee and I'le ka thee, or a dialogue. n.p. 1649. 4to. 34p. FSL 154791. (See 1 BS 31 f. for evidence of authorship.) Wing K 28

6   (Abbot, John):  The sad condition of a distracted kingdom expressed in a fable of Philo the Jew. London. Printed by B.A. 1645. 4to. 31 p. L 11626 d. 66; OS # 1137 (See 1 BS 247). Wing P 2130

Abercrombie:  see Con (Alexander)

Abridgement of Christian doctrine: see Turberville (Henry)

Abridgement of the life of S. Francis Xavierus: See B, (W).

7   An abstract of the Douay catechism. (Ware copy is lacking tp. hence n.d.p. but approbation is dated 17 Dec. 1672)

8   An abstract of the Douay catechism. Douay. 1682. Sixes. 72 p. CN Case 3 A 1866. 2 Wing A 131A

9   An abstract of the Douay catechism. London. 1688. Sixes. 63 + 5 p. Ware; YM. 2 Wing A 131B

10   An abstract of the Douay catechism. Douay. M. Mairesse. 1697. Sixes. Ware; OS #1503. Wing A 132

An account of Dr. Still's late book: see Canes (J. V. )

An account of the Jesuites life: See Grene (M)

11    Actes of the general assembly of the clergy of France.
n. p. Printed by J. R. 1682. 4to. 36 p.
OS #1148. Wing A 457

12    Acts of the general assembly of the French clergy. London. 1685. 4to. 43p. O G. Pamph. 1055
(3); NU 1685 + C 363; OS #1149. Wing
A 458

13    An address presented to the reverend and learned
ministers of the Church of England.
(Coloph. ) London f. Randall Taylor.
1688. 4to. 4 p. Cap. title. NC. Wing
A 559

14    An address presented to the reverend and learned
ministers. (Coloph. ) Reprinted at
Holy Rood House. 1688. 4to. Cap.
title. Wing A 560

15    Advice to the confuter of Bellarmine. London. Henry
Hills. 1687. 4to. 12 p. LW P. P. 7:48:
4 (18); TU; L 3936 c 31. Wing A 653

Agreement between the Church of England: see Gother
(John)

Afternoon instructions for the whole year: See Gother
(John)

16    (Alanson, John): Seasonable address of the Church of
England to both houses of Parliament.
n. p. d. (St. Omer. ECP) 4to. 32 p. DE

17    (Alanson, John): Seasonable address. n. p. (St. Omer.
ECP) 1677. 4to. 31 p. LFS

18    Albertus Magnus, St.: The paradise of the soul. Trans.
N. N. n. p. (London) f. William Brooks.
1682. 12mo. L 528 b 23; CN Case 3 A
1802; Fry & Davies A 875 +; LGL. 2
Wing A 875H

19    Albertus Magnus, St.: A treatise of adhering to God.
Trans. Sir Kenelm Digby. London f.
Henry Herringman. 1654. 12mo. L 3833
a 61; LW 1049 N 2. (This also includes
Digby's A conference with a lady. See
A &R 270 for earlier ed. ) Wing A 876

Albis, Thomas de: see White (Thomas), alias Blacklo

20    (Alonso de Madrid): The wise Christian's study...from
the Spanish of Alphonsus by J. M. (trans. )
Douay. M. Mairesse. 1680. BUTE. 2

2

Wing A 2900A

Alphonsus: See Alonso de Madrid

An amicable accomodation: see Gother (John)

21    Amydenus, Theodorus: Pietas romana et parisiensis or a faithful relation. Oxford. 1687. 8vo in 4s. 2 parts, the second of which is by Miles Pinckney. WGT; Ware; OS #3228. Wing A 3033/W3450

22    (Anderton - or Anderdon, Christopher): A catechism for the use of his royal highness, the prince of Wales. Paris to be sold by Thomas Moette. 1692. 4to. Wing A 3077

23    (Anderton, Lawrence): The english nunne. n. p. (S. Omer. ECP) 1642. 8vo. L 853 d. 4. Wing A 3109

24    (Anderton, Thomas): The history of the iconoclasts. n. p. 1671. 8 vo. O 8º R 124 Th BS; DAI; Ware; L 699 b.15. Wing A 3110

25    (Andries, Jodocus): The perpetual crosse or passion of Jesus Christ. Antwerp. Cornelius Wooks. 1649. 24º. L 555 a 18 (1). Wing P 1581

Animadversions by way of answer to...Kenne: see Reed (F.J.)

Annat, Francois: joint author of An Answer (1659), see Nouet.

26    The answer of the new converts of France to a pastoral letter. London. Henry Hills. 1686. 4to. 17p. OS #1176; HP; NU 1687 H 52; NN CI p. v. 22 (18). Wing A 3297

An answer to a discourse against transubstantiation: see Gother (John)

An answer to a little book: see Con (Alexander)

An answer to Dr. Sherlock's: see Sabran (Lewis)

An answer to M. de Rodon's funeral of the Mass: see N. N.

27    An answer to Monsieur Talon's plea. London. Randall Taylor. 1688. 4to. 37p. OS #1178; TU. Wing A 3365

28    An answer to the city-conformists letter. n. d. p. (1688) Wing A 3399A

29    An answer to the city-conformists letter. London. Mary Thompson. 1688. 4to. Hiscock A 3399A+

An answer to the declaration of the house: see Digby
　　　　　(Kenelm)
　　　　An answer to the query of a deist: See C. (J.)
30　　　An answer to the reflections of the five Jesuits speeches.
　　　　　　　　　n. d. p. Cap. title. fol. 4 p. O Wood 424
　　　　　　　　　(6) (On this copy Wood has noted "Aug.
　　　　　　　　　1679.") Wing A 3441
　　　　An answer to three treatises: see Walsh (Peter)
31　　　(Antoine,　　　　): Vindication of the Roman Catholiks.
　　　　　　　　　London f. John & Thos. Lane. 1688.
　　　　　　　　　4to. 15 p. O Z Jur. 33.4; Ware. Wing
　　　　　　　　　A 3517
32　　　Antonio, Don (prior of Crato): The royal penitent or
　　　　　　　　　the psalmes of. Trans. Fr. Ch. (i.e.
　　　　　　　　　Francis Chamberleyne) London. Printed
　　　　　　　　　by R. D. f. John Dakins. 1659. 12mo. L
　　　　　　　　　1361 a 62. Wing A 3518
33　　　Archdekin, Richard: A treatise of miracles. Lovanii.
　　　　　　　　　Typis Andreae Bouvet. 1667. 8vo in 4s.
　　　　　　　　　L 3932 aaa 6; WGT. 2 Wing A 3605A
34　　　(Arnauld, Antoine, the younger): The faith of the Catholic
　　　　　　　　　church. (Edinburgh) Holy Rood house.
　　　　　　　　　1687. 12mo. WCL. 2 Wing B 5241A =
　　　　　　　　　F260
35　　　(Arnauld, Antoine, the younger): The new heresie of
　　　　　　　　　the Jesuits. London. 1662. 4to. 23 p.
　　　　　　　　　O B.6. 11 Linc.; L 3938 aaa 61. Wing
　　　　　　　　　A 3730
　　　　Articles proposed to the Catholics: see H. (T.)
36　　　Articles to unite Catholicks and Evangelicks. n.p. 1661.
　　　　　　　　　4to. 5p. O Firth e 2 (10); L E 1055 (5)
　　　　　　　　　where Thomason dates it Dec. 1660.
　　　　　　　　　(Newdigate thinks this was translated
　　　　　　　　　from a Dutch original) Wing A 3888
37　　　Arundell, Henry: Poems written by. (coloph.) London.
　　　　　　　　　1679. brds. O Vet A 3 c 26 (1); CN Case
　　　　　　　　　6 A 158. Wing A 3896
38　　　Arundell, Henry: Poems written by. (coloph.) London 1679
　　　　　　　　　"By a copy under his own hand." brds.
　　　　　　　　　MH. Wing A 3897
39　　　Arundell, Henry: Verses made by the honorable Lord
　　　　　　　　　Arundell of Warder. n. d. p. brds. (1679);
　　　　　　　　　TU .Wing A 3898
40　　　(Augustine, St.): Digitus Dei, or God appearing. n.p.d.
　　　　　　　　　(1672) 8vo. TU, FSL (Only the first

third of this work is taken up by the translation of one chapter of Augustine's De Civ. Dei. ) Wing A 4208

41 (Augustine, St. ): Digitus Dei, or God appearing. London f. D. M. 1677. 8vo. Wing A 4209

42 Augustine, St.: The life of.. the first part, written by himself. London by J. C. f. John Crook. 1660 8vo. O Wood 435 (2). Wing A 4211

43 Augustine, St.: The meditations, soliloquia and manual. Second edition. Paris. Mrs. Blagaert. 1655. 12mo. LFS; TU (imp. ) CN Case 3 A 1803. (This is the Floyd trans. See A&R 50). Wing A 4212

44 Augustine, St.: The meditations, soliloquia, and manual. London f. Matthew Turner. 1686. 12mo. LFS; Ware; DE; CN 3 A 1804. 2 Wing A 4212A

45 Augustine, St.: The profit of believing. London. R. Daniel. 1651. 12mo. CN 3 A 1805. Wing A 4213

46 Augustine, St.: Saint Austins care of the dead. Second edition. n.p. (London. R. Daniel). 1651. 12mo. Wing A 4205

47 Augustine, St.: S. Augustine's confessions. n.p. 1679. 8vo. FSL; Ware; DE, TU Wing A 4207

48 Augustine, St.: Vive Jesus. The rule of St. Austin. Paris f. Rene Guignard. 1678. 12mo. L C. 111 b.3; DE

49 (Austin, John): The catholiques plea or an explanation. London f. H.J. n.d. (1652) 8vo. 2 parts. Part I signed at the end "John Birchley" (Pseud. ). Ware. (This is the same as A 4245 in all details except for tp. ) 2 Wing A 4242B

50 (Austin, John): The Christian moderator. n. p. (London) f. H.J. 1651. 4to. 28p. Signed at the end "William Birchley." L E 640 (1); NU 1651 + A 93. Wing A 4243

51 (Austin, John): The christian moderator. Second edition. London. By N. T. f. H.J. 1652. 4to. Signed "William Birchley." FSL (one part of 38, i.e. 30p. ); NU 1652 + A 93. Wing A 4244

52 (Austin, John): The Christian moderator. Fourth edition. London f. H.J. 1652. 8vo.

5

2 parts. Part I signed at end "Will. Birchley." L E 1313; Ware; CN Case 3 A 1808. Wing A 4245

54   (Austin, John):   The christian moderator. Second part. London by M. H. f. W. C. 1652. 4to. 34p. Signed at end "Will. Birchley." FSL; NU; OS #1222. Wing A 4247

55   (Austin, John):   The christian moderator. The third part. London by J. G. f. Richard Lowndes. 1653. 4to. 30 p. FSL; OS #1223. Wing A 4248

     (Austin, John):   The christian moderator. Part IV: see Cressy (S. P.)

56   (Austin, John):   Devotions in the ancient way of offices. Paris. 1668 8vo. O Vet E 3 f. 6; Ware; TU; Hoskins #256; CN 3A1809. Wing A 4248A

57   (Austin, John):   Devotions. First part in the ancient way of offices. Second edition. Roan. 1672. 12mo. (Dedication signed "J. S.") FSL 181266; Hoskins #256B; NU VT 25 A 93 d 1672. Wing A 4249

58   (Austin, John):   Devotions. First part. Third edition. Roan. 1685. 12mo. Hoskins #256D; C G. 16. 13 (This ed. has 584 p.). Wing A 4250A

59A  (Austin, John):   Devotions. First part. Fourth edition. Roan. 1685. 12mo. CN Case 3A 1811 (This ed. has 654p.)

60   (Austin, John):   Devotions. Second part. The four gospels in one. n. p. (Paris) 1675. 8vo. O 138 g. 169; Ware; CN Case 3A 1810 (variant). Wing A 4251

61   (Austin, John):   Devotions in the ancient way. Fifth edition. Roan. 1687. 12mo. OS #724

62   Avila, Juan de:   Certain selected spiritual epistles. Rouen. John le Cousturier. 1631. 8vo. (The original sheets of the first part of this work were reissued with the remainder reprinted c. 1650. See A&R 58). 2 Wing A 4274

63   Ayray, James:   A sermon preached at Welde house. London f. William Grantham. 1686. 4to. 24 p. L 693 d 1 (14); O Sermons 23 (4); OS #1229. 2 Wing A 4297A

64      Ayray, James:  A sermon preached before her majesty
                        the queen dowager.  London f. John &
                        Thomas Lane. 1687. 4to. 31 p. L 114
                        f. 26; TU. 2 Wing A 4297B
65      B., A.:  A letter to the honourable Collonel Okey.
                        London. 1659. 4to. 11p. Y Brit. Tracts
                        1659 L 57. 2 Wing B 20
        B., J.:  See Belson (John)
        B., L.:  See P. (L.)
        B., M.:  See Corker (James Maurice)
        B., N.:  See Bacon (Nathaniel)
        B., T.:  See Bayly (Thomas) & I., P.
66      B., W.:  An abridgement of the life of S. Francis
                        Xavierus. S. Omers. Thomas Geubels.
                        1667. 8vo. 60 p. L G 14366. Wing B
                        205A
67      B., W.:  A seasonable discourse shewing. n.p. 1679.
                        4to. 40 p. O Pamphl. 144 C (12); Ware;
                        OS #1231. Wing B 227
68      (Bacon, Nathaniel):  A journal of meditations..written
                        by N. B. n.p. 1669. 8vo. Trans. E.M.
                        (i.e. Edward Mico). Ware ( - tp); WGT;
                        TU; CN 3 a 1812.  Wing B 352
69      (Bacon, Nathaniel):  A journal of meditations. Written
                        by N. B. Trans. E. M. (ico). Second
                        edition. n.p. (St. Omer. ECP) 1674.
                        8vo. O Vet E 3 f. 149; TU; CN Case 3
                        A 1813.  Wing B 353
70      (Bacon, Nathaniel):  A journal of meditations. Written
                        by N. B. Trans. E. M. (ico). Third
                        edition. London. Henry Hills f. him
                        and Matthew Turner. 1687. 8vo. Ware
                        ( - tp); TU; CN Case 3 A 1814; OS
                        #1232a.  Wing B 354
        Baker, David Austin: The holy practices, see More
                        (Gertrude)
71      Baker, (David) Austin:  Sancta Sophia or directions for
                        the prayer of contemplation. Doway.
                        John Patte & Thomas Fievet. 1657.
                        8vo. 2 vols. Ed. Serenus Cressy. OS
                        #42; WGT; TU; LW 1001 L. 1.; CN
                        Case 3 A 1815. Wing B 480/S570
72      Baker, Austin:  Sancta Sophia. Doway. John Patte &
                        Thomas Fievet. 1667. DAI

73     Barclay, John: His defence of the most holy sacrament. London. Mary Thompson.. & sold by Matthew Turner and John Lane. 1688. 4to. 21 p. L T 1012 (6); O Z Jur. 33. 4º. Wing B 715

74     Barclay, John: His vindication of the intercession of saints. London. Mary Thompson.. and sold by Matthew Turner. 1688. 4to. 20 p. L 702 h. 36. Wing B 716

75     Barry, Paul de: Devotions to Saint Joseph. n.p. (St. Omer. ECP) 1663. 16º. ST (imp); HP; LFS

76     (Barry, Paul de): Devotions to Saint Joseph. n.p. (St. Omer. ECP) Printed by T. F. 1700. 18mo. FSL B 973. 5; TU. 2 Wing D 1242

77     (Barry, Paul de): Pensez-y bien or thinke well on it. Trans. Francis Chamberleyne. Gante. Bauldwin Manilius. 1665. 12mo. L 699a35; NU. Wing P 1432

78     (Barry, Paul de): Pious remarkes upon the life of S. Joseph. Second edition. n.p. Printed by T.F. 1700. 18mo. FSL B 973. 5; TU (This work is usually found with Devotions, #76 supra., FSL and BN make them one item with two parts. Pagination and signatures are distinct. Wm. Warren seems to have been the editor of the 1700 editions). 2 Wing B 973A

79     Barzia y Zambrana, Joseph de: A discourse on the excellency of the soul. London. f. Matthew Turner. 1685. 4to. 34 p. O Ashm. 745 (10); TU. Wing B 1011

80     (Basset, Joshua): Reason and authority or the motives. London. Henry Hills. 1687. 4to. FSL; O Vet A 3 e 473 (3); LW P.P. 7:48:4; NN C I p.v. 10; OS #1267. Wing B 1042

81     Batt, Antonie: A hidden treasure of holie prayers. Paris. Wil: Baudry. 1641. Sixes. O Don F. 42; L 3129 df 59. Wing B 1142

82     (Batt, Antony): A poor man's mite. n.p. 1674. 8vo. 45p. Ware (This is a close reprint of the 1639 ed. See A&R 74)

83     (Bayly, Thomas): An end to controversie.. By T. B.

Doway. 1654. 4to. FSL; TU; CN Case
3A 1820; OS #52. Wing B 1510

84   (Bayly, Thomas): A legacie left to protestants. Dowa.
     1654. 4to. Preface is signed T. B.
     Ware; OS #53. Wing B 1512

85   Bayly, Thomas: The life and death of that renowned
     John Fisher. London. 1655. 8vo. O
     Wood 307; TU; CN 3 A 1821; OS #54;
     (Bayly was an editor rather than the
     author of this biography. See P. Hughes:
     St. John Fisher - London, 1935 - and
     references there cited. ). Wing B 1513

     Becatelli, Ludovico: See Joyner

86   Bede, Venerable: England's old religion. Antwerp.
     1658. 4to. FSL; Ware; CN 3A 1822.
     (Editor signs himself H. B. which is
     usually taken to mean Henry Harcourt,
     alias Beaumont, S. J.  But the DNB
     s. v. Harcourt contends that the editor
     was Henry Harcourt of Leicestershire. )
     2 Wing B 1659

87   The belief of praying for the dead.  London.  Matthew
     Turner. 1688. 4to. 62 p. Ware; TU.
     Wing B 1787

88   Bellarmine. (St. ) Robert: Christian doctrine composed
     by. The last edition. n. p. Printed f.
     A. L. 1676. 12mo. 70p. O 8° C 437
     Linc. Wing B 1822

89   Bellarmine, (St. ) Robert: The mourning of the dove.
     Trans. A. B. (i. e. Thomas Everard).
     n. p. (St. Omer. ECP) 1641. 12mo.
     (see 2 B. S. 207)

90   Bellarmine, St. Robert: A short christian doctrine.
     n. p. 1688. 12mo. 48 p. O Vet A 3 g. 67

     (Bellarmine, St. Robert): The use & great moment,
     see title

91   (Belson, John): Tradidi vobis, or the traditional con-
     veyance of faith. By J. B. Esq. n. p.
     1662. 12mo. OS #69; WGT; TU; CN
     Case 3 A 1824 (In the preface signed
     S. W. the editor says he published this
     without the author's consent. ) Wing
     B 1861

92   Benedict, St. : Rule of the holy father. Douay. 1700.
     Sixes. L 4071 a. 2

9

Bernard, Francis: see Eyston

93     Bernieres-Louvigny, Jean de: The interior christian.
Antwerp. 1684. 8vo. Trans. A. L. O
Vet B 3 e 103; TU; CN 3 A 1825; DAI.
Wing B 2045

94     Betham, John: A sermon of the Epiphany. London f.
Matthew Turner. 1687. 4to. 34p. FSL
B 2509 g. 2 Wing B 2059A

95     Betham, John: A sermon preach'd before the King.
London. Henry Hills. Sold by Matthew
Turner. 1686. 4to. 32 p. Ware; OS
#1320; NU 1686 E 47; TU; CN Case 3
A 1826. Wing B 2060

96     Bettam, John: A brief treatise of education. Paris.
P. Laurens. 1693. 12mo. 22 p. O
Vet E 3 g 3; L 8309 a 3

97     (Binet, Etienne): Purgatory survey'd. Paris. 1663.
8vo. Trans. R. T. HP; TU; CN Case 3
A 1823. Wing B 2915

Bible: see Psalms

98     (Biondo, Giusseppe): The penitent bandito. n. p. 1663.
12mo. in 6s. Preface signed T. M.
(i. e. Tobie Matthew who translated
1620 ed. See A&R 112. ) FSL; L 865
a 8; CN 3 A 1835. 2 Wing B 2936B

Birchley, Will(iam): see Austin (John)

99     Bix, Angelus: Sermon on the passion. London by J.
G. n. d. (1688). DE. 2 Wing B 3035A

100    Blake, James: Applausus in honorem...Jacobi II.
Londini. Typis Nat. Thompson. 1685.
4to. 8 p. Y Brit. Tracts 1685 B 58.
Wing B 3131

101    Blake, James: A sermon of the blessed sacrament.
London. Henry Hills. 1686. 4to. 38p.
L 111 a 20; TU; OS #1349. Wing B 3132

Bleeding Iphigenia: see French (Nich. )

Blind obedience of an humble penitent: see Jenks (Sylv. )

102    Blosius, Lewis, Certaine devout prayers. Doway. B.
Bellere. 1662. Lanherne

102A   Blosius, Ludovicus: The Furnace of divine love.
London. f. M. Turner. 1686. 12mo.
Trans. R. F. LFS

103    Blosius, Franciscus Ludovicus: A mirrour for monkes.
Paris. 1676. 12mo. Ware (This edition

has a dedication signed I S S I, i. e.,
John Strange S. J.) Wing B 3203

104 Blosius, Franciscus Ludovicus: A mirrour for monkes.
Paris. 1676. 12mo. L 1412 a 28; TU;
CN Case 3 A 1836 (This edition does
not have the dedication. )

105 Blosius: Seven exercises. London f. Matthew Turner.
1686. 24º. L 4402 aa 3. Wing B 3204

106 (Blount, Thomas): Calendarium catholicus. n. p. 1661.
12mo. O Wood 4. Wing A 1321

107 (Blount, Thomas): Calendarium catholicum. London.
Henry Hills. 1689. 8vo. Unpaginated.
L PP 2465 (2). 2 Wing A 1323/1386E

(Blount, Thomas): A catalogue of lords, see title.

108 (Blount, Thomas): Kalendarium catholicum. n. p. (London) 1686. 8vo. Unpaginated. Ware;
EC. Wing A 1322

109 (Blount, Thomas): A new almanack after the old fashion.
n. p. (London) 1663. 12mo. O Wood 6.
Wing A 1324

Blount, Walter Kirkham: The spirit of Christianity, see
title

110 Bona, John: A guide to heaven. n. p. 1672. 12mo. in
6s. Trans. T. V. (i. e. Thomas Vincent
Sadler). O Vet A 3 f. 980; BN.Wing B
3549

111 Bona, J.: A guide to heaven. Roan. 1673. 12mo. Trans.
James Price. O Vet E 3 g 9 & Vet E 3
f. 1142; OS #89; Ware; CN 3 a 1839
Wing B 3550

112 Bonaventure, St.: The soliloquies. London f. H. Twyford & R. Wingate. 1655. 24º in 12s.
L 4404 aa 27; DAI Wing B 3555

Bonaventure, St.: Short treatise, see Following collections.

113 Bonaventure, St. (? ?): Stimulus divini amoris, that is
the goade of divine love. Doway. Widow
of Mark Wyon. 1642. 12mo. Trans. B.
Lewis A. (i. e. Lewis Palgrave, alias
East) FSL 203059; O Vet E 3 f. 18; Y;
TU; CN Case 3 A 1840 (This work is
probably not by St. Bonaventure. )
Wing B 3556

114 Bonilla, Juan de: A short treatise of the quiet of the
soul. By Fr. John de Bovilla (sic),

|       |                                                                                                                                                                                                     |
|-------|-----------------------------------------------------------------------------------------------------------------------------------------------------------------------------------------------------|
|       | n. p. 1700. Sixes. 58 p. CN 3 A 1845                                                                                                                                                                 |
| 115   | Bossuet, Jacques Benigne: A conference with Mr. Claude. London f. Matthew Turner. 1687. 4to. L T 1838; OS #96 & 1367; Y; NN C I p. v. 10. Wing B 3780                                                 |
| 116   | Bossuet, J. B.: A discourse on the history of the whole world. London f. Matthew Turner. 1686. 8vo. Ware. Wing B 3781                                                                                 |
| 117   | Bossuet, J. B.: An exposition of the doctrine of the catholique church. Trans. Wat Montague. Paris. Vincent du Moutier. 1672. 12mo. O Mason AA 216; HP; TU; CN 3 A 1861. Wing B 3782                  |
| 118   | Bossuet, J. B.: An exposition of the doctrine of the Catholic church. London. 1685. 4to. 2 parts 22 + 48 p. FSL; L 222 d. 8; TU; CN Case 4 A 1849. Wing B 3783                                        |
| 119   | Bossuet, J. B.: An exposition of the doctrine of the Catholic church. London. 1685. 4to. 3 parts 24 + 51 + 16 p. LFS; FSL B 3783a; OS #1369; TU; CN Case 64. 75 v. 3; NN C I p. v. 25                 |
| 120   | Bossuet, J. B.: An exposition of the doctrine of the Catholic church. London. Henry Hills. 1686. 4to. 55 p. OS #1370; Ware; O C. 11. 3 Linc.; L 3901 a 13. Wing B 3784                                |
| 120A  | Bossuet, J. B.: An exposition of the doctrine. London. Henry Hills. 1686. 4to. 2 parts. 20 + 55 p. NU 1686 B 74                                                                                       |
| 121   | Bossuet, J. B.: An exposition of the doctrine. Second edition. London. 1686. 12mo. 190 p. Ware. 2 Wing B 3784A?                                                                                       |
| 122   | Bossuet, J. B.: An exposition of the doctrine. Second edition. London. 1686. 8vo. 90p. Council House, Shewsbury.                                                                                      |
| 123   | Bossuet, Jacques B.: An exposition of the doctrine. n. p. 1687. 8vo. 2 parts 204 + 33 p. L 1471 e 8. 2 Wing B 3785?                                                                                   |
| 124   | Bossuet, J. B.: A pastoral letter from the Lord bishop of Meaux. London. Henry Hills. 1686. 4to. 37p. L T 1887 (1); NU 1686 B 74; OS #1374; TU; NN C. I. p. v. 22, Wing B 3787                        |

125 Bossuet, J. B.: A pastoral letter. n. p. 1686. 4to.
   37 p. NU; TU. Wing B 3788

126 Bossuet, J. B.: Quakerism a la mode. London f.
   John Harris & A. Bill. 1698. 8vo. L
   856 f. 18 (7). Wing B 3789

127 Bossuet, J. B.: A sermon preached at the funeral
   of Mary Therese. London. By J. C.
   and F. C. f. H. R. and are sold by
   Samuel Crouch. 1684. 4to. 31 p. FSL;
   NU 1684 B 74; Y Brit. Tracts. Wing B
   3791

128 Bossuet, J. B.: A sermon preached at the funeral
   of a person of the highest quality.
   London. I. V. 1686. 4to. 31 p. Y
   Brit. Tracts 1686 B 86; OS #1378
   (Anr. ed. of preceding) 2 Wing B 3791
   A

129 Bossuet, J. B.: A treatise of communion under
   both kinds. n. p. (London) f. Matthew
   Turner. 1687. 4to. Dedication signed
   "Jo. Davis" (John Davis of Kidwelly,
   trans? ) FSL; OS #1377; TU; NU 1686
   B 74. Wing B 3793

130 Bossuet, J. B.: A treatise of communion under
   both species. Paris. Cramoisy. 1685.
   12mo. Ware; L 1020 c. 21; CN 3 A 1842.
   Wing B 3792

131 (Boudon, Henri-Marie): The wayes of the crosse.
   Paris. 1676. 12mo. Dedication signed
   I. S. S. I. (i. e. John Strange S. J.,
   trans.) Ware; NU; CN Case 2 A 117.
   Wing W 1176

132 Bouhours, Dominic: The life of St. Francis Xavier.
   London f. Jacob Tonson. 1688. 8vo.
   Trans. (John) Dryden. Macdonald #134;
   OS #99; WGT; O 8° X 18 Art BS; Ware
   ( - tp); TU; CN Case 3 A 1843. Wing B
   3825

133 Bouhours, Dominic: The life of St. Ignatius. London. Henry Hills. 1686. 8vo. Mac-
   donald #151; Ware; NF; TU; CN Case
   3 A 2097; NU Wing B 3826

134 (Boutauld, Michel): The counsels of wisdom or a
   collection of the maxims of Solomon.
   London. J. Shedd f. M. Turner. 1680.

12mo. Y Has 44 677 bg; O Wood 845
(on this copy Wood writes that Edward
Sheldon was the translator.) 2 Wing
B 3860A

135 (Boutauld, Michel): A method of conversing with
God. (London) Mary Thompson. 1688.
12mo. Trans. Clare, S.J.) This edition is dedicated to the Queen Dowager.
Ware; O Antiq. f. E 1688.2; DAI; HP.
2 Wing B 3860D

136 (Boutauld, Michel): A method of conversing with
God. London. Thomas Hales (vere St.
Omer. ECP) 1692. 12mo. Trans. I.
W. of the Society of Jesus (i.e. Sir
John Warner, alias Clare, S.J.) This
edition is dedicated to Ann Bedingfield,
Abbess of Gravelines. L 4403 aaa 30;
HP; WGT; CN Case 3 A 1844. 2 Wing
B 3860E

Bovilla, Juan de: see Bonilla
Brereley, John: see Wilson (Matthew)

137 (Bridget, St.): The most devout prayers of St.
Brigitte. Antworp. 1659. 12mo. 22 p.
FSL; O l.g. 134. Wing B 2958

138 (Bridget, St.): The most devout prayers of. Antworp. 1659. 12mo. anr. ed. BUTE

139 (Bridget, St.): The most devout prayers of. Doway.
Balthazar Bellere 1663. 8vo. 77p. O
(Uncatalogued March 1966) 2 Wing B
2958A

140 (Bridget, St.): The most devoute prayers of St.
Brigitte. Antworp f. T.D. 1686. 12mo.
22 p. L 3456 aa 74 Wing B 2959

A brief account of the ancient church government:
see Woodhead (A.)

141 Brief and devout method or manner of hearing
masse. n.p. 1669. 12mo. Ware

A brief answer to... Dr. Henry More: see Walton

142 A brief relation to the order and institute of the
English religious women at Liege.
n.d.p. (Liege, 1652?) 12mo. 57 p.
O Vet B 3 f. 116. Wing B 4627

A brief survey of the Lord of Derry his treatise:
see Smith (Richard)

143      Bristow, Richard: Motives inducing to the Catholike
                 faith. n. p. (St. Omer) 1641. 12mo. OS
                 #107; L 3935 aa 13. Wing B 4802

        Brontius, Adolphus: see Cary (Edward)

144      (Broughton, Richard): Monastichon Brittanicum or a
                 historical narration. By R. B. London f.
                 Henry Herringman. 1655. 8vo. (Posthumous
                 work published by G. S. who signs dedica-
                 tion) L G 20169 & E 1461 (2). Wing B
                 5000

145      Broughton, Richard: A true memorial of the ancient...
                 state of Great Britain. n. p. (London)
                 1650. 8vo. (Editor signs himself G. S.
                 P. of which P. stands for Priest. Hence
                 same editor as preceding item. ) O Gough
                 Eccles. top. 6; WGT; OS #1417; NN ZDV
                 1650; TU; CN Case D 245. 1218 & 3 A
                 1849 one of which is an important variant.
                 Wing B 5001

        Brown, Ignatius: Pax Vobis, see G. (E. )

146      (Brown, Ignatius): An unerrable church or none. By
                 J. S. n. p. 1678. 8vo. Walsh #68; O 130
                 g. 169. Wing B 5021

147      (Brown, Ignatius): The unerring and unerrable church.
                 By J. S. n. p. 1675. 8vo. Walsh #67; TU;
                 Ware; CN Case 3 A 1850. Wing B 5022

148      (Brown, Stephen): Jesu, Maria, Joseph, Teresa. The
                 soul's delight. By Paul of St. Ubald
                 (name in religion) Antworp. William
                 Lesteens. 1654. 12mo. 3 parts. Ware;
                 HP ( - 3rd part); CN Case 3 A 1851
                 (Elsewhere in the book the author signs
                 himself S. B. native of Dublin. Brown
                 was an Irish Carmelite. )

        Bruzeau, Paul: The faith of the Catholic Church, see
                 Arnauld (A. )

        C., A.: See Crowther (Arthur Anselm)

149      C., J.: An answer to the query of a deist. n. d. p.
                 (c. 1682?) 4to. 12 p. OS #1475; NU
                 1687 C 10 ( - tp) Wing C 51

150      C., J.: A sermon preached upon the feast of the
                 most holy sacrament of the Eucharist.
                 n. p. D. Edwards. 1695. 12mo. 26p.
                 OS #1476

C., J.: John Cross, i.e. religious name of John
   Moor, q.v.

C., J.V.: see Canes

151 C., N.: A modest and true account of the chief
   points. Antwerp. 1696. 8vo. <u>Ware</u>.
   Wing C 5422

C., R.: see Smith (Richard)
   see Crashaw (Richard)

C., S.: see Cressy

C., T.: see Carwell (Thomas)

C., W.: see Clifford (Wm.)

Calendarium catholicus: see Blount (T.)

152 Campion, Ed.: Reasons of a challenge. London f.
   Matthew Turner. 1687. 4to. 32 p. <u>HP</u>;
   <u>TU</u>. Wing C 407

Campion, William: see Wigmore (Wm.)

153 Camus, J.P.: Diotrephe or an history of Valentines.
   London f. Th. Harper. 1641. 12mo.
   Dedication signed S. du Verger (i.e.
   trans.?) <u>O</u> Wood 275. Wing C 412

154 Camus, J.P.: Forced marriage. Second edition.
   London f. W. Jacob. 1678. 8vo. L 12510
   b 4 Wing C 414

155 Camus, J.P.: The loving enemie. London. Printed
   by J. G. and are to be sold by John
   Dakins. 1650. 8vo. <u>0</u> Douce C 66.
   Wing C 415

156 Camus, J.P.: The loving enemie. Second edition.
   London f. Thomas Rooks. 1667. 12mo.
   L 12510 a 6. Wing C 416

157 Camus, J.P.: Nature's paradox. London by J. G.
   f. Edwin Dods and Nath. Ekins. 1652.
   4to. 0 Bliss A 39. Wing C 417

158 (Canes, John Baptist Vincent): An account of Dr.
   Still.'s late book. n.p. 1672. 8vo.
   64 (i.e. 76) p. (Anr. issue of C 433)
   <u>HP</u>; <u>TU</u>; <u>CN</u> Case 3 A 1857. 1 Wing C
   426

159 (Canes, J.B.V.): Diaphanta..three attendants on
   Fiat Lux. n.p. 1665 8vo. OS #134;
   <u>FSL</u> 150443; <u>O</u> 8° B 317 Linc. <u>TU</u>;
   <u>CN</u> 3 A 1855. Wing C 427

160 (Canes, J.B.<u>V</u>.): An epistle to the authour of the
   animadversions upon Fiat Lux. n.p.
   1663. 8vo. <u>0</u> 8° Z 193 Th; OS #136;

CN Case 3 A 1853 & Case C 64.1438
(one of which is an important variant).
Wing C 429

162 C(anes), J(ohn) V(incent): Fiat Lux. Second edition.
n.p. 1662. 8vo. OS #137; FSL 137831;
HP; TU; CN 3 A 1854. Wing C 430

163 C(anes), J(ohn) V(incent): Fiat Lux. Third edition.
n.p. 1665. 8vo. FSL 146569; 0 Antiq.
f. U 1665/1. Wing C 432

164 (Canes, J. B.): Infallibility. n.p.d. (1662) 4to. 27p.
(This was left out of the 1st ed. of Fiat
Lux and included in the second edition).
CS A.3.53; Ware; OS #138. 2 Wing C
432 A

165 (Canes, J. B.): The reclaimed papist. n.p. (London)
1655. 8vo. FSL. Wing C 435

166 C(anes), J.V.: Three letters declaring the...pro-
ceedings. n.p. 1671. 8vo. 0, TU; Ware
(imp.). Wing C 436

167 C(anes), J.V.: (In Greek majuscules) TW KATHOLIKW
STILLINGFLEETON. or an account given
to a Catholick friend. Bruges. Luke
Kerchove. 1672. 8vo. 4 parts. OS #139;
0 8° B 289 Linc. WGT; TU; CN Case 3
A 1856. Wing C 433

168 Carier, Benjamin: A missive to his majesty. Paris.
1649. 8vo. 54p. (New material added in
this edition by the editor who signs the
preliminaries, "N. Strange.") FSL
189909; 0 Wood 869. Wing C 572

169 Carier, Benjamin: A missive to his majesty. London
f. Matthew Turner. 1687. 12mo. 29 +
(8) + 54p. (This ed. includes material
by Strange.) L 4402 e 5; TU. Wing C
573

Carisbrick: see Scarisbrick

170 Caron, R.: Loyalty asserted. London. T. Mabb.
1662. 4to. 63 p. L G 5509 (1); CN Case
3 A 1859. Wing C 609

171 Caron, R.: Remonstrantia hibernorum contra lou-
vaienses. n.p. (London) 1665. 4to. 3
parts. 0 K 120 Th. Wing C 610

172 (Caron, R.): A vindication of the roman catholicks.
(By) J.A. n.p. 1660 4to. 22p. L G
5509 (2). Wing C 611

Carre or Car, Thomas/Miles: see Pinckney (Miles)

173 (Carwell, Thomas): Labyrinthus cantuariensis or Doctor Laud's labyrinth. By T. C. Paris. John Billaine. 1658. fol. TU; FSL; WGT; CN Case 5 A 413 (According to Stillingfleet writing in preface to S 5625, this work came out in 1664) Wing C 721

174 (Cary, Edward): The catechist catechiz'd or loyalty asserted. By Adolphus Brontius (pseud.) n. p. 1681. 8vo.

Castaniza, Juan de: see Scupoli

175 (Castlemaine, Roger Palmer, earl of): The catholique apology with a reply to the answer. Third edition. n. p. 1674. 8vo. OS #155; 0 8° A 104 Linc.; WGT; CN Case 3 A 1864 (Robert Pugh is supposed to have aided Castlemaine in the writing of, or to have largely written, this series of books beginning with Nos. 181-2 and continued through #180, #179, & #175.) Wing C 1240

176 (Castlemaine): The catholique apology. Third edition. n. p. 1674. Hiscock C 1240 + . OC Allestree 0. 6. 9

177 (Castlemaine): The compendium or a short view of the late tryals. n. p. 1674. 4to. 88 p. 0C Pamph. 7 a 217; OS #1502. Wing C 1241

178 (Castlemaine): The earl of Castlemain's manifesto. n. p. 1681. 8vo. Ware; TU; CN Case 3 A 2096. Wing C 1245

179 (Castlemaine): A full answer and confutation. n. p. (Antwerp) 1673. 4to. 0 4° E 33 Th & other copies in Pamph. C 131, etc.; FSL 181147; OC Pamph. G. 6. 3. 10 (The place of printing is derived from the fact that there is a prefatory letter from M. Cnobbaert, an Antwerp printer, but this may well be a blind.) 2 Wing C 1244

180 (Castlemaine): A reply to the answer to the catholique apology. First edition. n. p. 1666. 4to. FSL 181150; 0 8° B 2 Linc.; TU; CN Case 3 A 1865. Wing C 1246

181 (Castlemaine): To all the royalists that suffered... The humble apologie of all the English

Catholics. n.p. 1666. 4to. 14p. Hiscock
C 1249 +; OC Pamph. G. 3. 6. 10

182 (Castlemaine): To all the royellists that suffered. n.p.
1666. 4to. 14p. FSL 168728. Wing C
1249

183 A catalogue of lords, knights, and gentlemen of the
catholick religion. n. d. p. Brds. O Wood
276a (83). Wing C 1383

184 The catechism for the curats compos'd by the decree
of the council of Trent. London. Henry
Hills f. him and Matthew Turner. 1687.
8vo. OS #162 (4 copies); L 3558 aaa 27;
O Antiq. e E 1687/4; ND Div S. 238. 2 C
363 CF; WGT; TU; CN 3A1867. Wing C
1472

Catechism for the use of his royal highness: see
Anderton (Chris. )

185 A catechism of pennance, guiding sinners. Trans. W.
B. n. p. (London) f. M. T. 1685. 12mo.
Ware; Y Mgv55; TU; CN Case 3 A 1868.
1 Wing C 1475A

186 The catechism or christian doctrine. n. d. p. (1700?)
Sixes. 36p. Y Mhc5 K 288 T 6. Wing C
1478

The Catholic representer: see Gother (J. )
Catholick theses: see Woodhead (A. )
The catholick answer to the seekers request: see N.
N.
The catholick letter to the seeker: see N. N.

187 The catholick mirrour or a looking glasse for
protestants. Paris (vere England) 1662.
8vo. HP; TU; CN Case 3 A 1869. 2 Wing
C 1494 A

Catholicks no idolaters: see Godden (T. )

187A The catholike younger brother. n. p. (St. Omer. ECP)
1642. 8vo. DUC. Wing C 1496

The catholique apology: see Castlemaine
The catholiques plea: see Austin (J. )

188 Caussin, Nich.: The angel of peace. n.p. 1650. 12mo.
O 8° C 21 TH BS; CN Case J 22.382.
Wing C 1541

189 Caussin, N.: The christian diary. Cambridge. R.
Daniel. 1648. 12mo. C 7.42. 63 Sel. e.
Wing C 1542

190 Caussin, N.: The christian diary. London f. John

Williams. 1649. 12mo. <u>L</u> 4409 aa 1; CGC.
2 Wing C 1542 A

191    Caussin, N.: The christian diary. London. R. Daniel
f. John Williams. 1650. 12mo. <u>CS</u> Oo
14. 18. 2 Wing C 1542B

192    Caussin, N.: The christian diary. London f. John
Williams. 1652. 12mo. <u>O</u> 8° C 21 Th
BS; <u>Ware.</u> Wing C 1543

193    Caussin, N.: The christian diary. London f. John
Williams. 1662. 32°. MH. 2 Wing C 1544

194    Caussin, N.: The christian diurnal. Trans. S. T. H.
(i. e. Sir Thomas Hawkins) Third edition.
1686. 12mo. <u>C</u> 1. 51. 80; <u>TU</u>; <u>CN</u> 3 A 1871.
2 Wing C 1544A

195    Caussin, N.: Entertainments for Lent. 8vo. <u>C</u> CCE
6. 29 (This copy is missing everything
before A. The trans. is the same as
that of the 1649 ed. See #207 infra. This
ed. has 272 p. 8vo. )

196    Caussin, N.: Entertainments for Lent. . by the R. F. N.
Causni (sic). Trans. Sir B. B(rook).
London f. John Dakins. 1661. 12mo. <u>O</u>
Vet A 3 f. 1015; CN. 2 Wing C 1545A

197    (Caussin, N. ): Entertainments for Lent. Trans. Sir
B. B. London. Printed for I. W. and are
to be sold by Philemon Stephens the
younger. 1661. 12mo. <u>CN</u> Case 3 A 1871
(imp. ). 2 Wing C 1544B

198    Caussin, N.: Entertainments for Lent. Trans. Sir
B. B. London f. John Williams. 1672.
12mo. L 4408 b. 49. Wing C 1546

199    Caussin, N.: Entertainments for Lent. Trans. Sir
B. B. London f. John Williams to be
sold by R. Moore. 1682. 12mo. <u>FSL</u>;
DE (imp. ) 2 Wing 1546A

200    Caussin, N.: Entertainments for Lent. Trans. Sir
Basil Brook. London f. John Williams..
to be sold by Matt. Turner. 1607 (Mistake for 1687) 12mo. <u>C</u> U* 7 138; <u>WGT</u>.
Wing C 1545

201    Caussin, N.: Entertainments for Lent. Trans. Sir
B. B. London f. John Williams and are
to be sold by Matth. Turner. 1687.
12mo. <u>TU.</u> 2 Wing C 1546B or C

202     Caussin, N.: The holy court. Trans. Sir T. H(awkins)
        & others. London. William Bentley to be
        sold by John Williams. 1650. fol. 3 parts.
        L 4375 h 5; OS #170; WGT; NN ZIL + 1650.
        Wing C 1547

203     Caussin, N.: The holy court. Trans. Sir T.H. &
        others. Third edition. London f. John
        Williams. 1663. fol. in 4s. NN Stuart
        1936; Y Me 65 C 312 + C 836; 2 Wing C
        1548A

204     Caussin, N.: The holy court. Third ed. London. By
        J.W. and are to be sold by Thomas
        Rookes. 1664. fol. L 4375 h. 6; TU.
        Wing C 1549

205     Caussin, N.: The holy court. Trans. Sir T.H. &
        others. (London) f. John Williams.
        1678. fol. OS #171; Ware; TU. Wing C
        1550

206     Caussin, N.: The holy history. (London) f. W. Crook
        and Jo. Baker. 1653. 4to. Wing C 1551

207     Caussin, N.: The penitent or entertainments for
        lent. Trans. Sir Basil Brook. 1649.
        n. p. 1649. 12mo. Ware (There are two
        imperfect copies of this work, both
        minus tp. at L 4409 aai and C S 100
        e. 64. 2. They might well be different
        editions. )

208     Caussin, N.: A short treatise of the church militant.
        Trans. C. M. n. p. 1661. O Vet (Uncata-
        logued further in March 1966) 82 p. 2
        Wing C 1551A

209     Caussin, N.: The unfortunate politique. Trans. Sir
        I. H. London f. William Sheares. 1653.
        8vo. CN Case Y 1565. C 29. 2 Wing C
        1551B

210     The ceremonies for the healing of them.. with the
        king's evil. London. Henry Hills. 1686.
        12mo. 20p. O Wood 893; TU

211     The ceremonies us'd in the time of King Henry VII
        for the healing of... the king's evil.
        London. Henry Hills. 1686. 4to. 12p.
        Ware. Wing C 1675

212     (Ceriziers, Rene): Innocency acknowledg'd in life
        and death of S. Genovesa. Trans. J.
        T(assburgh). Gaunt. John vanden

Kerchove. 1645. 8vo. L; <u>CN</u> Case Y
1565. C 328. Wing C 1678

213    Ceriziers, Rene: The triumphant lady or the crowned
          innocence. Trans. Sir William Lower.
          London f. Ga. Bedell and Tho. Collins.
          1656. 8vo. <u>FSL</u>. Wing C 1682

214    Charles II: Copies of two papers written by. n. d. p.
          (London. c. 1686) s. sh. <u>L</u> 816 m 2 (7*);
          <u>TU</u>

215    Charles II: Copies of two papers written by.n. d. p.
          (London. c. 1686) F'cap fol. 2 parts 8+7p.
          (The second part is "A copie of a paper
          by the late duchess of York." Note that
          the next four items all contain this paper.
          I have not examined C 2945-6) <u>FSL</u> C
          2942a

216    Charles II: Copies of two papers. London. Henry
          Hills. 1686. F'cap fol. 11 p. <u>FSL</u>; <u>L</u>
          515 1. 18 (50); <u>NN</u> *KC p. v. 26; <u>NC</u>
          Spec. Coll. B 936 C 38 cap. 2. Wing C
          2943

217    Charles II: Copies of two papers. London. H. Hills.
          1686. 4to. 14p. <u>FSL</u>. Wing C 2944

218    Charles II: Copies of two papers. London. H. Hills.
          1686. 4to. 14p. OS #1548a (tp is slightly
          different from C 2944)

219    Charles II: Copies of two papers. n. d. p. (1686?)
          F'cap fol. 7 p. <u>FSL</u> 2944a

220    Charles II: Copies of two papers. Dublin, reprinted
          for Robert Thornton. 1686. 4to. 8 p.
          <u>NU.</u> Wing C 2945

221    Charles II: Copies of two papers. London. Henry
          Hills. 1687. brds. 2 Wing C 2946A
       Charles II: Eikon basilike, see title
       The childes catechism: see Sadler (T. V.)
       The christian directory, see Persons (R.)
       The christian education of children, see Varet (A. L.)
       The christian moderator, see Austin (J.)
       Christian rules proposed, see Clifford (W.)
       Church government, see Woodhead (A.)

222    The church of England truly represented. London f.
          the author & sold by Matthew Turner.
          1686. 4to. 18p. <u>NU</u> 1686 S 41; OS
          #1555. Wing C 4192

223    Clare, St.: The first rule of the glorious virgin S.
Clare. Rouen. 1658. 12mo. 2 parts.
O CUP 403 1 i

224    Clare, St.: The first rule. Audomari. Typis Thomae
Geubels. 1665. 12mo. CN Case 3 A 1873

Clare, St.: Rule, see Following collections

225    A clear proof of the certainty and usefullness of the
protestant rule of faith. London. Henry
Hills. 1688. 4to. 12 p. TU; FSL. Wing
C 4620

A cleare vindication of the roman catholicks, see
Davenport

226    (Clenche, William): St. Peter's supremacy faithfully
discuss'd. Henry Hills to be sold by
Matthew Turner. 1686. 4to. FSL 147078;
OS #185; TU. Wing C 4640

227    C(lifford), W(illiam): Christian rules proposed to a
vertuous soule. Paris. 1655. 8vo. (? ?).
Ware; BUTE

228    (Clifford, Wm.): Christian rules. By W. C. n. p.
(Paris) 1659. 12mo. NN *KC 1659; TU.
Wing C 4710

229    (Clifford, William): Christian rules. By W. C. Third
edition. n. p. 1665 8vo. FSL 137845;
HP; OS #189; TU. Wing C 4711

230    (Clifford, Wm.): The little manual of the poore mans
dayly devotion. By W. C. Paris. Vincent
du Moutier. 1669. 12mo. Wing C 4712

231    (Clifford, Wm.): The little manuel of the poor man's
daily devotion. By W. C. Second edition.
Paris. Vincent du Moutier. 1670. 12mo.
Ware; OS #190; BN. Wing C 4713

232    (Clifford, Wm.): The little manuel of the poore man's
daily devotion. By W. C. Third edition.
London. 1682. 12mo. Wing C 4714

233    (Clifford, Wm.): A little manual. The fourth edition.
By W. C. London f. Matthew Turner.
1687. 12mo. Ware; DE

234    (Codrington, Thomas): Constitutiones clericorum
saecularium in commune viventium.
n. p. (London. Ralph Metcalf) 1697.
12mo. 48p. TU; CN Case 3 A 1880

235    Codrington, Thomas: A sermon preach'd before
their majesties. London. Nathaniel
Thompson. 1687. 4to. 48p. TU;

OS #1588b; <u>NU</u> 1687 t. C 671. Wing C
4879A

236 Codrington, Thomas: A sermon preached before the
Queen dowager. London f. Wm. Grant-
ham. 1687. 4to. 32 p. OS #1588 a; <u>Ware</u>;
<u>TU NU</u> 1686 E 47. Wing C 4880

237 A collection of prayers. London f. Mat. Turner. 1688.
DMR

A collection of several treatises: see Cressy.
Collette, St.: Declarations, See Following Collections.

238 (Collins, Wm.): Missa triumphans or the triumph of
the mass. By F. P. M. O. P. Louain.
1675. 8vo. 2 parts. (This edition is
dedicated to the Duchess of York.) <u>L</u>
3936 a 20; Walsh #130. Wing C 5389

239 (Collins, Wm.): Missa triumphans or the triumph.
By F. P. M. O. P. Louain. 1675. 8vo.
2 parts. (This edition is dedicated to
the Queen). Walsh #131; <u>FSL</u> 181140;
<u>TU; CN</u> 3 A 1878

A compendious discourse, see Woodhead (A.)
The compendium or a short view, see Castlemaine

240 Compleat office of the holy week. Trans. W. K. Blount.
London f. Matthew Turner. 1687. 8vo.
2 parts. (This is a later ed. of O 150).
OS #723; <u>Ware</u>; <u>LFS</u>. Wing C 5648

241 (Con, Alexander): An answer to a little book. n. p.
1682. 12mo. (The only Wing location
for this is ON but it was not discoverable
there in March 1971.) Wing C 5681

242 (Con, Alexander): An answer to a little book. n. p.
1686. 12mo. <u>TU;</u> BUTE. Wing C 5682

243 (Con, Alexander): Scolding no scholarship. n. p.
Printed f. the author 1669. 8vo. <u>L</u> 857
e. 27; NU 1669 A 144; <u>TU.</u> Wing A 87

Concerning the congregation of the Jesuits, see
Warner (J.)

244 A conference between two protestants and a papist.
n. p. 1673. Sixes. 33p. <u>OC</u> Pamph.
G. 3. 6. 10; <u>Y</u> Mhc 8. 9. Wing L 2675

Considerations on the council of Trent: see Wood-
head (A.)
A contemplation of heaven: see White (Thomas)
A contrite and humble heart: see Jenks (Sylv.)
Controversial discourses relating to the Church:

see D. (B. )

245 (Corker, James Maurice): A rational account given
by a young gentleman. By M. B. n. p. d.
(c. 1690) 4to. Cap. title. 8 p. <u>LFS</u>;
OS #1618. 2 Wing C 6300

246 (Corker, J. M. ): A remonstrance of piety and innocence. London. 1682. 12mo. Wing C
6301

247 (Corker, J. M. ): A remonstrance of piety and innocence. London. 1683. 12mo. OS #542;
<u>Ware</u>; <u>TU</u>; <u>CN</u> 3 A 1881; <u>O</u> Wood 830
(On the flyleaf of this copy Wood notes
that this was published November, 1682).
2 Wing C 6301A

248 (Corker, J. M. ): Roman-Catholick principles. By
M. B. London. 1680. 4to. 12 p. OS
#1619; <u>O</u> Wood B 40 (3). Wing C 6302

249 (Corker, J. M. ): Roman-Catholick principles by
M. B. Third edition. n. p. 1680. 4to.
20 p. <u>O</u>. Wing C 6303

250 (Corker, J. M. ): Roman Catholick principles. n. p. d.
(1683) brds. <u>O</u> C. 10. 3 Linc. (15) (Date
derived from MS note on this copy).
Wing C 6304

251 (Corker, J. M. ): Roman Catholick principles. n. p. d.
(c. 1685) 4to. Cap. title. 8 p. <u>FSL</u>.
Wing C 6305

252 (Corker, J. M. ): Stafford's memoires or a brief
and important account. n. p. 1681. fol.
76 p. OS #1260; <u>O</u> Wood 427 (11). Wing
C 6306

253 (Corker, J. M. ): Stafford's memoires. London. 1682.
12mo. <u>Ware</u> copy has 126 p. Copies at
<u>TU</u> & <u>CN</u> E 5. 57805 have last page
numbered 216. 2 Wing C 6307

Counsels of wisdom: see Boutauld (M. )

Covent., Franc.: see Davenport (C. )

254 (Crashaw, Richard): Carmen deo nostro... sacred
poems. By R. C. Paris. Peter Targa.
1652. 4to. OS #203; <u>L</u> E 1598; WCL.
Wing C 6830

255 Crashaw, Richard: A letter from Mr. Crashaw to
the countess of Denbigh n. p. d. (London,
1653). 4to. 3 p. <u>L</u> E 220 (2). Wing C
6833

256    Crasset, Jean: A new form of meditations for every
day in the year. London. 1685. 8vo.
Hiscock C 6851+; <u>CS</u> Oo 12. 8; <u>L</u> 3457
h. 8; <u>CN</u> Case 3 A 1882. 2 Wing C 6851

257    Cressy, Serenus: The church history of Brittany.
n. p. (Rouen) f. the author. 1668. Fol.
<u>FSL</u> 160858

258    Cressy, Serenus: The church history of Brittany.
n. p. (Rouen). Printed 1668. Fol. His-
cock C 6890+; <u>OC</u> W. T. 2. 12. (Main);
<u>O</u> Douce C. Substit. 248; <u>WGT</u>; <u>TU</u>;
CN Case 6 A 333. 2 Wing C 6890

259    (Cressy, S. ): Collections of several treatises in
answer to Dr. Stillingfleet. n. p. 1672.
8vo. 4 parts. <u>O</u> Antiq. e U. 6; <u>NU</u> 1672
C 92; <u>FSL</u> 189512; <u>WGT</u>; <u>TU</u>; <u>CN</u> Case
3 A 1891 (Contains C 6898, W 3454, W
3455, C 6892). Wing C 6891

        Cressy, S. : Dr. Stillingfleet's principles, see
Woodhead (A. )

260    (Cressy, S. ): An epistle apologetical of S. C. n. p.
1674. 8vo. <u>L</u> 698 b. 35; <u>Ware;</u> <u>CN</u> Case
3 A 1886. Wing C 6893

261    Cressy, Hugh Paulin de (Serenus): Exomologesis
or a faithful narration. Paris. 1647.
12mo. <u>FSL;</u> <u>TU</u>; <u>CN</u> Case 3 A 1883.
Wing C 6894

262    Cressy: Exomologesis. Paris. Jean Billaine. 1653.
12mo. <u>Ware</u>; <u>TU</u>; LC BX 4668 C 8 1653;
<u>CN</u> Case 3 A 1884. Wing C 6895

263    Cressy: Exomologesis. Paris. Jean Billaine. 1659.
12mo. <u>LC</u> BX 4668 C 8 1659. Wing C
6896

264    (Cressy, S. ): Fanaticism fanatically imputed. By
S. C. n. p. 1672. 8vo. <u>FSL</u> 137817
(This ed. has 198p. ) Wing C 6898

265    (Cressy, S. ): Fanaticism fanatically imputed. By
S. C. n. p. 1672. 8vo. <u>CN</u> Case 3 A
1887 (This ed. has 179p. then 2 blank
leaves then pp. 181-188 which contains
a postscript. )

266    (Cressy, S. ): I question. Why are you a Catholique?
n. p. 1673. 8vo. <u>CS</u> Tt 11. 27; OS #211;
<u>TU</u>; <u>CN</u> Case 3 A 1888

267    (Cressy, S. ): I question. Why are you a Catholic?

n. p. d. (1688) 12mo. <u>L</u> 3932 aa 14. 2
Wing C 6901A (misplaced)

269   (Cressy, S. ): A non est inventus returned. n. p. 1662.
8vo. <u>FSL</u> bd. w. STC 3603; <u>TU</u>; <u>CN</u>
Case 3 A 1885

270   (Cressy, S. ): Q. Why are you a Catholick? n. p.
1672. 8vo. 87 p. <u>CS</u> Tt 13. 12; <u>O</u> Crynes
918 (3) Wood 869 (4) (This is the first
ed. of No. 266 supra. ) Wing C 6899

271   (Cressy, S. ): Reflexions upon the oathes of supremacy
and allegiance by a catholick gentleman.
n. p. 1661. 8vo. 96p. <u>O</u> 8° B 285 Linc.;
<u>TU</u>; <u>CN</u> Case 3 A 1889. 2 Wing C 6901
(Cressy claims authorship on p. 64 of C 6893)

272   (Cressy, S. ): Reflexions upon the oathes of supremacy
and allegiance or the christian modera-
tor. The fourth part. By a Catholick
gentleman. n. p. 1661. 8vo. 96p. OS
#212

273   (Cressy, S. ): Roman-Catholick doctrines no novelties.
By S. C. n. p. 1663. 8vo. <u>O</u> Mar 303;
OS #799; <u>WGT</u>; <u>TU</u>; <u>CN</u> Case 3 A 1890.
Wing C 6902

274   (Croiset, Jean): A spiritual retreat for one day in
every month. n. p. 1698. 12mo. <u>O</u> Vet
E 3 f. 154; <u>TU</u>; Y. 2 Wing C 7007 C

275   (Croiset, J. ): A spiritual retreat. London (<u>ve</u>re St.
Omer) Printed by T. F. 1700. 12mo.
<u>Ware</u>; <u>CN</u> Case 3 A 1893. 2 Wing C 7007
D

Cross, John: see Moor (J. )

276   (Cross, Nich. ): Cynosura, or the saving star.
London. I. Redmayne f. Thos. Rookes.
1670. fol. OS #215; <u>FSL</u>; <u>NU</u> 1679 C 95;
<u>CN</u> Case 5 A 414. Wing C 7252

277   (Cross, Nich. ): The Cynosura. London. J. Redmayne
f. Thomas Rooke. 1679. Fol. <u>NU</u>. Wing
C 7253

278   (Cross, N. ): Pious reflections and devout prayers.
Doway. M. Mairesse. 1695. 8vo. OS
#1639

279   Cross, Nicholas: A sermon preach'd before her
sacred majesty the queen. . 21st. .
April 1686. London. Nathaniel Thomp-
son. 1687. 4to. 31 p. <u>L</u> 114 f. 37; <u>NU</u>

1686 E 47. Wing C 7254

Crowther, Anselm & Sadler, Thomas Vincent: The Christian pilgrim, see Scupoli.

280  (Crowther, Arthur Anselm & Sadler, Thomas Vincent): The dayly exercise of the devout christian. Published by A. C. & T. V. New edition. n. p. 1662. 12mo. FSL C 7409. 2; WGT (imp. ); CN 3 A 1895 (First edition was C 7409). 2 Wing C 7409A

281  (Crowther-Sadler): A dayly exercise of the devout christian. Published by T. V. Third edition n. p. 1673. 12mo. Ware; LFS, DAI, TU. 2 Wing C 7409B

282  (Crowther-Sadler): A dayly exercise of the devout christian. Fourth edition. n. p. 1685. 12mo. HP, DE (imp. ); LFS; Ware; TU. 2 Wing C 7409B

283  (Crowther-Sadler): The dayly exercise of the devout christian. Published by T. V. Fifth edition. London f. Matthew Turner. 1688. 8vo. FSL C 7409. 3; BUTE; DE; Ware; TU; CN 3 A 2027. 2 Wing C 7409E

284  (Crowther-Sadler): The dayly exercise of the devout rosarists. Published by A. C. & T. V. Amsterdam. 1657. 12mo. FSL; TU. Wing C 7409

285  (Crowther-Sadler): Jesu, Maria, Joseph, or the devout pilgrim. Published by A. C. & T. V. Amsterdam. 1657. 12mo. OS #217; FSL 181141; TU. Wing C 7410

286  (Crowther-Sadler): Jesus, Maria, Joseph, or the devout pilgrim. Published by A. C. & T. V. Amsterdam. 1663. 12mo. L C 53 i. 22. Wing C 7411

287  (Crowther-Sadler): The spiritual conquest. Paris. 1651. 8vo. O Douce C 403; TU. 1 Wing C 1220

288  Cyprien de Gamaches: The christian that would be saved. Trans. Richard Cartor. Doway. Baltassar Bellere. 1662. 12mo. LFS

289  (Cyprien de Gamaches): Heaven opened and the pains of purgatory avoided. n. p. 1663. 8vo. O Antiq. f. U 1662/1. Wing C 7715

290        Cyprien de Gamaches: Sure characters. Reprinted
                      at Holy Rood House. 1687. 8vo. TU.
                      Wing C 7716

291        D., B.: Controversial discourses relating to the
                      church. Doway. (Vere St. Omer. ECP)
                      1697. 8vo. O Vet E 3 f. 53; Ware; DAI;
                      CN Case 3 A 2082; LGL (Attributed to
                      John Wilmot, earl of Rochester. Trans.
                      W. Darrell). Wing R 1741

        D., J.: see John Huddleston S.J. whose alias was
                      John Dormer.

        D., J.: see Dymock (James)
                see Duns

        D., N.: see Persons (R.)

        D., W.: see Darrell (W.)

        Daily exercises of a christian life: see Nepveu (F.)

292        (Daniel, Ed.): Meditations collected and ordered for
                      the use of the English college of Lisbo.
                      Lisbo. Paul Crasbeeck. 1649. 8vo. OS
                      #218; Ware ( - tp.); CN Case 3 A 1896

293        (Daniel, Ed.): Meditations collected. Second edition.
                      Doway. Baltazar Bellere. 1663. 12mo.
                      in 6s. OS #219; O Antiq. f. F 1663.1; TU;
                      CN Case 3 A 1897. 2 Wing D 200A

294        (Daniel, Gabriel): The discourses of Cleander and
                      Eudoxus. Cullen (Vere St. Omer. ECP)
                      1694. 8vo. CE; (Trans. W. Darrell)

295        (Darrell, Wm.): The layman's opinion. Signed on p.
                      8 "W. D." n. p. 1687 4to. 8p. OS #1655;
                      O Ashm. 1018 (18); NN C.I. p.v. 19;
                      NU. Wing D 266

296        (Darrell, Wm.): A letter to a lady. n. p. d. (London.
                      1688) s. sh. L 3939 dd 4 (2) Wing D 267

297        (Darrell, Wm.): A letter to the author of the reply.
                      (Coloph.) By W. D. London. Henry Hills.
                      1687. Cap. title. 4to. 8 p. OS #1666;
                      O Pamph. G 141 (4); L 4106 bb(1); NU.
                      Wing D 268

298        Entry cancelled

299        Darrell, Wm.: The vanity of human respects. London
                      f. John Tottenham. 1688. 4to. 25p. L
                      1021 d. 23 (10)

300        Darrell, Wm.: The vanity of human respects. Lon-
                      don f. John & Thomas Lane. 1688. HP.
                      2 Wing D 269A

301 Darrell, Wm.: A vindication of St. Ignatius. London
f. Anthony Boudet. 1688. 4to. 40 p. OS
#1667; L T 1847 (3); TU. Wing D 270

302 (Davenport, Christopher): A cleare vindication of
roman catholicks. n. p. 1659. 4to. 6p.
OS #1670; O Linc B. 2. 4. Wing D 351

303 (Davenport, C. ): Enchiridion of faith. By Fran:
Covent. Douay. 1654. 8vo. L 1412 c
28. 2 Wing D 350

304 (Davenport, C. ): Enchiridion of faith. Second ed.
By Fran. Covent. Douay. 1655. 8vo.
L 857 a. 22; OS #223; Ware; TU; CN
Case 3 A 1898. 2 Wing D 350A

305 (Davenport, C. ): An explanation of roman catholic
belief. n. p. 1656. 4to. 9 p. O 8° P
254 Th (The text of this statement had
appeared earlier in A 4247. It is often
attributed to Thomas Blount. ) Wing D
352

306 (Davenport, C. ): An explanation of the roman
catholick's belief. Fourth edition.
n. p. 1670. 8vo. 11p. O 8° c 716 Linc.
Wing D 353

307 (Davenport, C. ): An explanation of the roman
catholikes belief. n. p. d. brds. O Wood
276a (111) (On this copy Wood has noted
"Given to me by Mr. Tho. Blount 26
Oct. 1673. ") OS #1669. 2 Wing D 354

308 (Deane, Thomas): The religion of Mar. Luther.
Oxon. Henry Cruttenden. 1688. 4to.
24p. L 3935 c 10; TU. Wing D 499

309 (Dechamps, Etienne Agard): The secret policy of
the Jansenists. Troyes. Christian
Roman (blinds? ? ) 1667. 8vo. 72p. L
3900 a 59

310 (Dechamps, Etienne Agard): The secret policy of the
jansenists. Second edition. Troyes.
Christian Roman. 1667. 8vo. HP

311 Declaration of the daily grievances of the Catholiques
recusants of England. London f. John
Turner. 1641. 4to. 7p. FSL. Wing D
663

312 A declaration of the principall pointes of the christian
doctrine. Paris. Sebastien Cramoisy.
1647. 4to. FSL; O 1362 f 2; TU; CN

Case 3 A 1902. Wing D 742
A defence of the doctrin: see Warner (J. )
A defence of the innocency: see Warner (J. )
A defence of the papers: see Dryden (J. )
Devotions in the ancient way of offices: see Austin
        (J. )
Devout and godly petitions: see Jesus psalter

313      A dialogue between a new catholic convert and a
            protestant. London. Henry Hills. 1686.
            4to. 6 p. OS #1700; O Vet A 3 a 473 (6);
            HP; TU. Wing D 1297

314      A dialogue between two church of England-men. n. p. d.
            (c. 1687) 18°. 12 p. Cap. title. TU. 2
            Wing D 1339A

315      A dialogue or discourse between a parliament-man
            and a roman catholick. n. p. (London)
            1641. 4to. 8 p. L 8122 d 77. Wing D
            1368?

316      A dialogue or discourse between a parliament-man
            and a roman catholike. n. p. 1641. 4to.
            22p. O B 23. 7 Linc. (14)
Diaphanta or three attendants: see Canes

317      (Digby, Kenelm): An answer to the declaration of the
            house. n. p. (Paris) 1648. 4to. 42 p.
            (? ?) (Anr. ed. of D 1447) FSL D 1447a.
            2 Wing D 1420A

318      (Digby, Kenelm): A discourse concerning infalli-
            bility. Paris. Peter Targa. 1652. 12mo.
            L C 46 a 30. Wing D 1431

319      (Digby, Kenelm): A discourse concerning infallibility.
            Amsterdam. 1652. 8vo. O Vet B 3 f.
            130. Wing D 1430

320      (Digby, Kenelm): The royall apologie. Paris. 1648.
            4to. 42p. FSL;NN *KC 1648. Wing D
            1447

321      Digby, Kenelm: Two treatises. Paris. Gilles Blaizot.
            1644. Fol. O Ashmol. H 25; OS #229;
            NN *KC + 1644. Wing D 1448

322      Digby, Kenelm: Two treatises. London f. John
            Williams. 1645. 8vo. 2 parts. CN
            Case B 79. 242. Wing D 1449

323      Digby, Kenelm: Two treatises. London f. John
            Williams. 1658. 8vo. LGL. Wing D
            1450

324     Digby, Kenelm:  Two treatises. London f. John
                Williams. 1665. 8vo. C̲N̲ B 79.243.
                Wing D 1451
        Digby, Kenelm:  Conference with a lady, see Albert,
                St.
        Digitus Dei:  see Augustine
        Discourse concerning infallibility: see Digby (K. )
        Discourse concerning the foundation: see Maimbourg
                (L. )
        Discourse on miracles: see Worsley (E. )
        Discourse on the necessity of church guides: see
                Woodhead (A. )
        Discourse on the use of images: see Gother (J. )
        Discourses of Cleander and Eudoxus: see Daniel (G.)
        Dr. Sherlock's preservative: see Sabran (L. )
        Dr. Sherlock sifted: see Sabran (L. )
        Dr. Stillingfleet against Dr. Stillingfleet: see Warner
                (J. )
        Dr. Stillingfleet's principles (1673): see Warner (J. )
        Dolefal fall of Andrew Sall: see French (N. )
        Dormer, John: see Huddleston (J. )
325     Drexel, Hieremy: A pleasant and profitable treatise
                of Hell. n.p. 1668. 8vo. W̲a̲r̲e̲; L. 2
                Wing D 2184A
326     (Dryden, John):  A defence of the papers. London.
                Henry Hills. 1686. 4to. FSL; O 4° Z
                Jur. 5 (2); N̲N̲ *KC p.v. 26; TU; OS
                #1739 (On authorship see Macdonald
                #133 and 83 PMLA - 1968 - p. 401
                n. 9). Wing D 2261
327     (Dryden, J. ):  The hind and the panther. London f.
                Jacob Tonson. 1687. 4to. T̲U̲; L Ashley
                3153; CN; Macdonald #24a; P̲F̲O̲R̲. Wing
                D 2281
328     (Dryden, J. ):  The hind and the panther. Holy Rood
                house, reprinted by James Watson.
                1687. 4to. F̲S̲L̲; Macdonald #24b. Wing
                D 2282
329     (Dryden, John):  The hind and the panther. Dublin,
                reprinted by Andrew Crook and Samuel
                Helsham. 1687. 4to. F̲S̲L̲; Macdonald
                24c. Wing D 2283
330     (Dryden, John):  The hind and the panther. Second
                ed. London f. Jacob Tonson. 1687. 4to.
                Macdonald 24d. L 11631 a 29; NU; F̲S̲L̲.

Wing D 2284

331    (Dryden, John): The hind and the panther. Third
        edition. London f. Jacob Tonson. 1687.
        4to. FSL Macdonald 24 e; L 11626 f. 5.
        Wing D 2285

Duns Scotus, John: Dialectica, see Moor (J.)

332    (Duns Scotus, John): Idiota's or Duns contemplations..
        by J. D. Paris. (vere London) 1662.
        12mo. L 527 (Preliminary matter signed
        W. B. i. e. Walter Blount? translator?)
        Wing D 2615A

333    DuPerron, Jacques Davy Cardinal: Luther's alcoran..
        By Cardinal.. Peron. Trans. N. N. P.
        n. p. 1642. 8vo. LSC + A 69. 4 P 42.
        Wing D 2638

334    Dymock, J.: An eye catechism. n. p. (London) Mr.
        Turner. 1688. brds. OC Arch. Inf.
        B. 1. 17; (Not in Hiscock)

335    (Dymock, James): The great sacrifice of the new
        law. n. p. 1676. 12mo. FSL 166791;
        O Mason AA 122; TU; Ware; L 698 b. 36;
        CN 3 A 1912. Wing D 2972

336    (Dymock, J.): The great sacrifice. Antwerp f. G. W.
        1685. 12mo. O 8° B 13 Linc.

337    (Dymock, James): The great sacrifice. By J. D.
        Fourth edition. Antwerp f. G. W. 1685.
        12mo. Hiscock D 2973+; OC Main a.
        2. 84; CS O. 15. 22; TU; L 4380 d. e.
        21. Wing D 2973

338    (Dymock, J.): The great sacrifice. The fifth edition.
        By J. D. Antwerp f. B. W. 1685. 12mo.
        CS Tt 10. 38

339    (Dymock, J.): The great sacrifice of the new law.
        By J. D. The fifth addition (sic). n. p.
        Printed f. B. W. 1686. 12mo. CN Case
        3 A 1914 (This is perhaps identical with
        the next item which I have not seen).
        2 Wing D 2973A

340    (Dymock, J.): The great sacrifice. n. p. 1686.
        12mo. Wing D 2974

341    Dymock, J.: The great sacrifice. 8th edition.
        London f. Matthew Turner. 1687.
        12mo. FSL 189214; L 3477 aa 51; O 8°
        L 610 BS; WGT; TU. Wing D 2975

E., A.: see Errington (A.)

342　E., F.J.: A clear looking-glas for all wandring
　　　　　　　　sinners. Roane. 1654. 12mo. CN Case
　　　　　　　　3 A 1915

343　E., J.: A soveraign counter-Poyson prepared by a
　　　　　　　　faithfull hand for speedy reviviscence
　　　　　　　　of Andrew Sall. Louain. 1674. 8vo. DT
　　　　　　　　F.o. 2/3. Wing E 16

E., J.: see Everard (J.)

344　Eason, Laurence: A guide to salvation. Bruges.
　　　　　　　　Luke Kerchove. 1673. 4to. BUTE; HP;
　　　　　　　　TU; C E. 14. 61; CN Case 3 A 1916.
　　　　　　　　2 Wing E 99A

345　Entry cancelled

346　The effects and virtues of the crosse or medal of
　　　　　　　　the great patriarch St. Benedict. (Trans.
　　　　　　　　from the german). n.p. 1669. 4to. 12
　　　　　　　　p. DE; O Wood 893 (3)

347　Eikon basilike deutera (Greek characters). The
　　　　　　　　portraicture of his sacred majesty
　　　　　　　　King Charles II. n.p. 1694. 8vo. NU
　　　　　　　　1694 E 34; TU. Wing E 312

348　Ellis, Philip Michael: (Six sermons). Henry Hills.
　　　　　　　　1686. 4to. OS #1783 (This consists in
　　　　　　　　the following sermons (E 595; E 597;
　　　　　　　　E 603; E 596; E 594; E 602) issued
　　　　　　　　together with an advertisement leaf.)

349　E(llis), P(hilip): The first sermon preached before
　　　　　　　　their majesties. London. Henry Hills.
　　　　　　　　1686. 4to. 31 p. O Mar 831 (12) & Z
　　　　　　　　Jur. 33 4º; NU 1686 E 47. Wing E 595

350　Ellis, Philip Michael: Second sermon preach'd.
　　　　　　　　London. Henry Hills. 1686. 4to. 32p.
　　　　　　　　O C.7.16. Lincs.; NU 1686 E 47. Wing
　　　　　　　　E 597

351　Ellis, Philip Michael: The third sermon. London.
　　　　　　　　Henry Hills. 1686. 4to. 29p. O Mar.
　　　　　　　　831 (13); CN; NU 1686 E 47. Wing E
　　　　　　　　603

352　Ellis, Philip Michael: The fourth sermon. London.
　　　　　　　　Henry Hills. 1686. 4to. 29p. O Mar.
　　　　　　　　831 (14); NU 1686 E 47. Wing E 596

353　Ellis, Philip Michael: The fifth sermon. London.
　　　　　　　　Henry Hills. 1686. 4to. 28p. O Mar
　　　　　　　　831 (15); NU 1686 E 47. Wing E 594

354 Ellis, Philip Michael: The sixth sermon. London.
    Henry Hills. 1686. 4to. 31p. <u>O</u> Mar
    831 (16); <u>NU</u> 1686 E 47. Wing E 602

355 Ellis, Philip Michael: A sermon preached before
    the King..Nov. 13, 1686. London.
    Henry Hills. 1686. 4to. 34p. <u>O</u> Mar
    831 (18). Wing E 598

356 Ellis, Philip Michael: A sermon preached before
    the King..Dec. 5, 1686. London. Henry
    Hills. 1686. 4to. 33p. <u>O</u> Mar 831 (19).
    Wing E 599

357 Ellis, Philip Michael: A sermon preached before
    the king and queen. London. Henry
    Hills. 1687. 4to. 35p. <u>O</u> Mar 831 (23);
    <u>NU</u> 1686 E 47. Wing E 600

358 Ellis, Philip Michael: A sermon preached before
    the Queen dowager. London. Henry
    Hills. 1687. 4to. 32p. <u>Y</u> Mhc 8. 1687
    E 1 59. Wing E 601

359 Ellis, Philip Michael: Two sermons. London. Henry
    Hills. 1686. 4to. 41p. <u>O</u> Mar 831 (22);
    CN; <u>NU</u> 1686 E 47; <u>TU</u>. Wing E 604

360 An encyclical epistle sent to their brethren. n. p. d.
    (London, 1660) 4to. 44p. <u>L</u> 3935 b. 33
    (1); CN. Wing E 725A

  An end to controversie, see Bayly (Thomas)

361 England's settlement upon the two solid foundations.
    London. 1659. 4to. 36p. <u>O</u>. Wing E
    3051

362 English loyalty vindicated. Trans. W. H. London.
    Nath. Thompson. 1681. 4to. 15p.
    <u>Ware.</u> Wing E 3096

  The English nunne, see Anderton (Lawrence)

363 An epistle of a catholique to his friend a protestant
    touching the doctrine of the reall
    presence. n. p. 1659. 4to. OS #1791

  Epistle to the author of Animadversions, see Canes
    (J. V. )

  Erastus Junior/Senior: see Lewgar (John)

364 E(rrington), A(nthony): Catechistical discourses.
    Paris. P. Targa. 1654. 8vo. <u>O</u> 1 b
    123; OS #163; CN (imp. ) Case 3 A
    1920; <u>TU</u>. Wing E 3246

  Errour non plust, see Sergeant (John)

365 E(verard), J(ohn): A winding sheet for the schism.
      Dublin. 1687. 8vo. 96p. <u>FSL</u> E 3534. 5;
      DMR; DE. <u>Ware</u>

366 Everard, Capt. Robert: An epistle to the several
      congregations. Paris. 1664. 4to. 40p.
      <u>O</u> Pamph. 121 D (38) & C. 13. 9. Linc.
      Wing E 3538

367 Everard, Capt. Robert: An epistle to the several
      congregations. Second edition. n. p.
      1664. 8vo. 92p. <u>TU</u>; <u>CN</u> Case 3 A 1924;
      L T 1829 (2); NU. Wing E 3539

Ewens, Maurice, see Newport (Maurice)
Exercise of the love of God, see S. , (J. )

368 An explanation of the holy ornaments & ceremonies.
      London. f. N. T. 1686. <u>O</u> 8º M 241 Th

369 (Eyston), Bernard: The christian duty. By B. Bernard
      Francis (name in religion) Aire.
      Claude Francois Tulliet. 1684. 4to. <u>O</u>
      100 g. 337; <u>WGT</u> (imp. ); Ware; CN
      Case 4 A 1845. 1 Wing B 1993

F. , M. W.: see P. (W. )

370 F. , R.: Epitaph upon... Sir Kenelm Digby. London.
      f. H. Herringman. 1665. brds. <u>O</u> Wood
      429 (22). Wing F 51

F. , R.: see Fuller (Robert)
Faith of the Catholick church, see Bruzeau
Faith vindicated, see Sergeant (John)

371 Felle, William: Juxta solam scripturam...a com-
      parison. London. 1688. 8vo. <u>HP</u>; NU.
      Wing F 645

372 Felle, Guillaume: La sage folie ou pensées extra-
      ordinaires. n. p. (London) 1679. 8vo.
      <u>CN</u> Y 762. F 32. Wing F 646

373 Felle, Wm.: Lapis Theologorum. Londini. 1688.
      8vo. <u>Ware</u>

374 Ferrier, Jean: Thesis theologica. n. p. d. (1660)
      12mo. <u>L</u> 702 c 41 (The 1st 8pp of this
      pamphlet are in Latin; the remaining
      8 in English)

I question: why are you a Catholique?, see Cressy
      (H. P. S. )

375 Fitzherbert, Thos.: A treatise concerning policy
      & religion. London f. Abel Roper.
      1652. 4to. <u>FSL</u>; <u>O</u> A 13. 7. Linc.; <u>TU.</u>
      Wing F 1102

376      Fitzherbert, Thos.: A treatise of policy and
religion. Part I. Third edition.
London (<u>vere</u> ECP St. Omer) Thomas
Hales. 1695. 8vo. <u>Ware</u>; <u>CN</u> Case J/D/
2994 & Case 3 A 2101. Wing F 1103

377      Fitzherbert, Thos.: A treatise on policy. Part II.
London. (<u>vere</u> ECP St. Omer) Thomas
Farmer. 1696. 8vo. <u>L</u> C 64 dd 11.
Wing F 1104

378      Fitzherbert, Thomas: A treatise of policy and
religion. Part II. Third edition. Lon-
don. (<u>vere</u> St. Omer. ECP) Thomas
Hales. 1695. 8vo. <u>CN</u> Case 3 A 1926

379      Fitzherbert, Thos.: A treatise of policy and religion.
Part II. Third edition. London (<u>vere</u>
ECP St. Omer) Thomas Hales. 1697.
8vo. <u>LFS.</u> Wing F 1104A

Five short treatises, see Walker (Obadiah)

380      Five treatises. n.p. 1651. 12mo. <u>HP</u>; (This consists in the following items bound with
a new tp: V 456; S 781; S 779; A 4213;
A 4205. All of them seem to have been
issued separately also.) Wing V 455

381      The following collections or pious little treatises.
4 parts. Douay. Michael Mairesse.
1684. 8vo. (The four treatises were:
Mary Gough, Pious Collection; S.
Bonaventure, Short Treatise; S. Clare,
Rule; St. Collette, Declarations. Of
these only the third seems to have been
issued separately.) BUTE; <u>CN</u> Case
3 A 1874 (imp.)

Fontaines, Louys, see Zacharie de Lisieux

382      A form or order of thanksgiving and prayer. London.
By Charles Bill, Henry Hills & Thomas
Newcomb. 1687. 4to. 6p. <u>O</u> Firth e
17 (8). 2 Wing C 4183

Fortescue, Geo.: see Soules Pilgrimage

Fouquet: Counsels of Wisdom, see Boutauld (M.)

383      (Francis of Assisi, St.): Riaghuil threas uird S.
Froinsias da ngoirthear ord na naithrighe
Louvain. 1641. 12mo. (Rule of St.
Francis ed. by Bernard Conny). Walsh
#137

384    Francis de Sales, (St. ): Conduite de la confession
                    Londres. Chez Henry Hills. 1686. L
                    1472 a. 9. Wing F 2068

385    Francis de Sales, (St. ): A new edition of the intro-
                    duction to a devout life. Paris. Giles
                    Blaizot. 1648. 32° in eights. L 4402
                    a 3; Ware. Wing F 2072

386    Francis de Sales, (St. ): An introduction to a devout
                    life. Paris. 1662. 12mo. Y mgv 55 F
                    847 In 8 g 6; DE; DMR; FSL; Ware
                    ( - tp. )

387    Francis de Sales, (St. ): A new edition of the intro-
                    duction to a devout life. n. p. (London)
                    1669. 12mo. Wing F 2072A

388    Francis de Sales, (St. ): Introduction to a devout life.
                    Dublin. Joseph Wilde. 1673. 12mo.
                    Wing F 2069

389    Francis de Sales, (St. ): An introduction to a devout
                    life. n. p. (London) By T. D. 1675.
                    12mo. Ware; OS #342; O Vet A 3 f.
                    483; TU; CN Case 3 A 1927. Wing F
                    2070

390    Francis de Sales, (St. ): Introduction to a devout
                    life. n. d. p. (c. 1675) 12s. O Vet A
                    3 f. 837

391    Francis de Sales, (St. ): Introduction to a devout life.
                    London. Henry Hills f. Mat. Turner.
                    1686. 12mo. Ware; OS #343; FSL
                    156047; TU; CN Case 3 A 1928. Wing
                    F 2071

Francis de Sales: Vive Jesus, see Augustine, St.
Francis, Bernard: see Mason (Richard) and Eyston
                    (Bernard)

392    (French, Nich. ): The bleeding Iphigenia. n. p. d.
                    (London. 1675) 8vo. cap. title. L G
                    5705; Walsh #250; CN Case F 423. 314.
                    Wing F 2177

393    (French, Nicholas): The dolefal fall of Andrew Sall.
                    Preface signed N. N. n. p. 1674. 8vo.
                    L G 5505; NU. Wing F 2178

394    (French, Nicholas): A narrative of the earl of
                    Clarendon's settlement and sale of
                    Ireland. By N. F. Louain. 1668. 4to.
                    38p. O 4° Sigma 55; L 809 c 46. Wing

F 2179
395    (French, Nich. ): A narrative of the settlement and
                sale of Ireland. Lovain. 1668. 4to.
                28p. FSL 154235. Wing F 2180
396    (French, Nicholas): The polititians catechism. By
                N. N. Antworp. 1658. 8vo. L C 37 b. 2.
                Wing F 2181
397    (French, Nich. ): Querees propounded. Paris. John
                Belier. 1644. 4to. 24p. L 601 d. 60;
                Walsh #242. Wing F 2182
398    (French, Nich. ): The unkinde deserter of loyall
                men. n. p. (Paris). 1676. 8vo. O
                Mason AA 185; FSL 181149. Wing F
                2183

A full and clear exposition, see Pulton (Andrew)
A full answer and confutation, See Castlemain.
399    A full answer to Dr. Tenisons conference. London.
                Henry Hills. 1687. s. sh. LW P. P. 7:
                48:4 (17); L 1865 c. 10. Wing F 2341
A full answer to the second defence, See Johnston
                (H. J. )
400    F(uller), R(obt. ): Missale romanum vindicatum or
                the mass vindicated. n. p. 1674. 4to.
                HP; TU (imp. ); CN Case 3 A 1929.
                Wing F 2395
401    Fundamental positions and queries thereupon.
                n. d. p. (London, c. 1690) fol. s. sh.
                OS #1868. Wing F 2529A
G., A. C. E.: see Warner (John)
402    G., E.: Pax Vobis or ghospell & libertie. n. p. 1679.
                12mo. Wing G 1990
403    G., E.: Pax vobis, or ghospel and liberty. n. p. 1685.
                12mo. in sixes. 90p. Ware; FSL; NU
                1685 G 10. Wing G 1991
404    G., E.: Pax vobis, or gospel and liberty. n. p. 1685.
                8s. 206p. NU 1685 G 10
405    G., E.: Pax vobis or gospel and liberty. Second
                edition. n. p. 1687. Sixes. 90p. Ware;
                OME. Wing G 1992
406    G., E.: Pax vobis or gospel and liberty. Second
                edition. n. p. (London) f. William
                Grantham. 1687. 8vo. OS #2001
407    G., E.: Pax vobis or gospel and liberty. Fourth
                edition. n. p. 1687. 12mo. 90 (i. e. 94)
                p. TU; CN Case 3 A 1944. Wing G 1993

408      (G., E.): Pax vobis or gospel and liberty. Fifth
                 edition. n.p. 1687. 12mo. OS. Wing G
                 1994

409      G., H.: A prudent and secure choyce. Written by
                 H. G. Gent. n.p. 1650. 8vo. 50p. CN
                 3 A 1930

410      G., J.: A sermon of the passion. London f. Matthew
                 Turner. 1686. 4to. 34p. FSL; NU 1686
                 E 47 (16); TU. Wing G 40

411      G., T.: A brief explanation of the several mysteries
                 of the holy mass. London. Nat. Thomp-
                 son f. the brother of the said T. G. 1686.
                 ON. (Also attributed to Thomas Gawen).

412      G., T.: A letter in answer to two main objections.
                 London f. M. T. 1687. 4to. 26p. NU
                 1687 + L 651; Ware. Wing G 64

      G., T.: See Godden (Thos.)

413      (Gage, John): The christian sodality. First tome.
                 Collected by F. P. n.p. 1652. 12mo.
                 3 parts. (Often found in 3 vols.) OS
                 #357; L 3205 aaaa 46; O 8° Z 506 Th
                 (Vol. I only); LFS (Vols. I & II only);
                 CN Case 3 A 1931 (imp.); TU. Wing G
                 107

414      (Gallonio, Antonio): The holy life of Philip Nerius.
                 Paris. 1659. 8vo. L E 1727. Wing G
                 181

415      Gernon, Ant.: Parrthas an anma. Louvain (press
                 of Irish Franciscans). 1645. 18mo.
                 Walsh #255

416      Giffard, Bonaventure: A sermon of the nativity.
                 London. Henry Hills. 1688. 4to. 33p.
                 O Mar. 831 (24); CN Case 3 A 2086.
                 Wing G 689

417      (Giffard, Bonaventure): A sermon preached before
                 the King and Queen. n.p.d. (1687).
                 4to. 23p. Ware; OS #1919

418      Gobinet, Charles: Instruction concerning pennance..
                 Second part of the Instruction of youth.
                 London. Printed by H. B. (f.) Matthew
                 Turner and John Tootel. 1689. 8vo.
                 FSL G 904. 5; L 1120 d 24; CN Case 3
                 A 1933; Fry and Davies G 904+

419      Gobinet, Charles: The instruction of youth. London.
                 Henry Hills. 1687. 8vo. L 1120 d. 23

O Antiq. e E 1687. 2; DAI. Fry and
Davies G 904++

420     (Godden, Thomas): Catholicks no idolaters. (Dedication signed "T. G.") n. p. 1672. 8vo. ND Div. S. 282 G 578 C; OS #898. Wing G 918

421     (Godden, Thomas): A just discharge to Dr. Stillingfleet's unjust charge. Paris. Rene Guignard. 1677. 8vo. 3 parts. O 8º B 111 Linc.; Mason E 30; OS #899. Wing G 919

422     Godden, Thomas: A sermon of St. Peter. London. Henry Hills. 1686. 4to. 40p. L T 1841 (1); NU 1686 E 47. Wing G 920

423     Godden, Thomas: A sermon of St. Peter. London. Henry Hills. 1688. 4to. 29p. Ware; NN CI p. v. 47

424     Godden, Thomas: A sermon of the nativity. London. Henry Hills. 1686. 4to. 33p. L 1021 D 23 (3); NU 1686 E 47. Wing G 921

425     Godden, Thomas: A sermon of the transfiguration. London. Henry Hills. 1688. 4to. 30p. L 1021 d 23 (9); O Mar 831 (25); TU. Wing G 922

426     (Godeau, Antoine): The life of the apostle St. Paul. London. James Young f. Henry Twyford. 1653. 12mo. FSL 158227; L E 1546 (Dedication signed "F. D." who says Edward Lord Vaux was trans.). Wing G 923

Good advice to the pulpits, see Gother (John)

427     The good catholick no bad subject. London. 1660. 4to. 6p. L E 1027 (13); NU. Wing G 1038

428     The good catholic no bad subject. London f. John Dakins. 1660. 4to. 6p. NU 1660 G 65. Wing G 1039

429     The good old test reviv'd. London. Randall Taylor. 1687. 4to. Cap. title. Ware. Wing G 1080

430     (Gooden, Peter): The sum of a conference. London. Henry Hills f. him and Matthew Turner. 1687. 4to. 40p. FSL 159283; L T 1883 (2); Y Mhc 8.9; NN CI p. v. 10; CN. Wing G 1099

431     (Gother, John): Afternoon instructions for the whole
                 year. n. p. 1699. 12mo. 2 vols. OS
                 #1946 TU; CN Case 3 A 1940

432     (Gother, John): An agreement between the Church
                 of England and the church of Rome.
                 London. Henry Hills. 1687. 4to. 88p.
                 O Ashm. 1018 (2); FSL 142622; NU 1686
                 S 41 (4); LFS; HP; TU (imp. ); NN CI
                 p. v. 47. Wing G 1324

433     (Gother, John): An amicable accomodation of the
                 difference. London. Henry Hills. 1686.
                 4to. O Pamph. 171 (17) C; CN; FSL
                 128833 (These copies have as the 1st
                 words on p. 34 "or as she...") . Wing
                 G 1325

434     (Gother, John): An amicable accomodation. London.
                 Henry Hills. 1686. 4to. O G pamph
                 1784 (14); 4° Z 3 (9) Jur. Firth e 16 (5);
                 Ware Tracts B; NN C. I. p. v. 7 (This
                 edition has as the 1st words on p. 34
                 "of England...")

435     (Gother, John): An answer to a discourse against
                 transubstantiation. London. Henry
                 Hills. 1687. 4to. 80p. FSL bd. w. H
                 3257; O Vet A 3 E 473 (5); Ware; Y Mhc
                 8 14/24. Wing G 1326

436     (Gother, John): The catholic representer: or, the
                 papist misrepresented and represented.
                 London. Henry Hills. 1687. 4to. 88p.
                 FSL 147412; O 4° A 23 (6) Art; Ware.
                 Wing G 1327

437     (Gother, J. ): A discourse of the use of images.
                 London. Henry Hills. 1687. 4to. 39p.
                 FSL 13307. 8; O 1373 d. 57 (1); TU.
                 Wing G 1328

438     (Gother, J. ): Good advice to the pulpits. London.
                 Henry Hills. 1687. 4to. 70p. FSL
                 133307. 9; O Ashm. 1024 (14) & Z Jur.
                 18. 4° & C. 11. 6 Linc (6); NN ZMY
                 p. v. 11. Wing G 1329

439     (Gother, J. ): Good advice to the pulpits. London.
                 Henry Hills. 1687. 4to. 48p. O Firth
                 e. 17; TU

440     (Gother, J. ): Instructions and devotions for hearing
                 mass. n. p. 1699 12mo. FSL G 1329. 5

441 (Gother, J.): Instructions for children. n.p. 1698. 12mo. 38p. O Don. f. 466

442 (Gother, J.): Instructions for masters, traders, laborers &c. n.p. 1699. 8vo. 57p. O Don f. 468. Wing I 245

443 (Gother, J.): Instructions for particular states. n.p. 1689. 12mo. L 1121 c. 55; TU. Wing G 1329A

444 (Gother, J.): Instructions for the whole year. Part I. n.p. 1695. 12mo. (This ed. has no emblem on tp. Text begins at sigl. A9 and runs to p. 343) TU B 1901

445 (Gother, John): Instructions for the whole year. Part I. n.p. 1695. 12mo. (In this copy there is a sunburst emblem on tp. The text begins at B 1 and runs to p. 336). CN 3 A 1942

446 (Gother, J.): Instructions for the whole year. Part II. n.p. 1695. 12mo. OS #1960; DAI; TU

447 (Gother, J.): Instructions for the whole year. Part II. n.p. 1698. 12mo. 2 vols. OS #1962; TU

448 (Gother, J.): Instructions for the whole year. Part III. For festivals. n.p. 1696. 8vo. OS #1961

449 (Gother, J.): Instructions for the whole year. Part III. Tom. 1. For festivals, n.p. 1699. 12mo. TU

449A (Gother, J.): Instructions for the whole year. Part IV for Sundays. n.p. 1698. 12mo. LGL

450 (Gother, J.): Instructions for youth. n.p. 1698. 12s. 53p. O Don f. 469. Wing I 249

451 (Gother, J.): A letter from a dissenter to the divines. n.p. (London) Randal Taylor. 1687. 4to. Cap. title. 4p. Y Mhc 8.14.21. Wing G 1330

452 (Gother, J.): A letter from a dissenter. Reprinted at Holy Rood house. 1687. 4to. Wing G 1331

453 (Gother, J.): Nubes testium; or a collection of the primitive fathers. London. Henry Hills. 1686. 4to. FSL bd. w. H 3257; O Z Jur. 4° 11 (1); TU. Wing G 1332

454    (Gother, J.): A papist misrepresented and represented.
By J. L. London. 1665. (i. e. 1685). 4to.
O G. Pamph. 1054 (5). Wing G 1333

455    (Gother, J.): A papist misrepresented and represented.
n. p. 1685. 4to. (8) + 79 + 8 p. O 4º A
23 (5) Art.; Ware; TU; CN Case 3 A
1939 & Case J 5454. 264. Wing G 1334
(one of which is an important variant. )

456    (Gother, J.): A papist misrepresented. By J. L.
London. 1685. 4to (8) + 80 + 8 p. O Z
Jur. 3. 4º

457    (Gother, J.): A papist misrepresented. n. p. 1685.
4to. (6) + 63 + 8 p. O Vet A 3 e 1376;
TU. Wing G 1335

458    (Gother, J.): A papist misrepresented. n. p. 1685.
4to. (11) + 127 p. FSL 133307. 1; O G.
Pamph. 1055 (2); ND Div. S. 282 G
684 P; NN C. I. p. v. 7; CN Case J 5454.
338 & Case 3 A 1938 (one of which is
an important variant. However the
latter copy is missing everything
before B and hence it is not listed
separately. ) Wing G 1335A

459    (Gother, John): A papist misrepresented and represented.. J. L. n. p. 1685. 4to. 120 + 8
p. CS Ee 12. 4; NU Auburn KJ 95. 3
G68 1685; TU; NC; CN Case C 64. 75

460    (Gother, J.): The papist misrepresented and represented. Second part. coloph. London.
Henry Hills. 1686. 4to. 64 p. O Z Jur.
4. 4º; FSL 1333072. 2; TU. Wing G 1337

461    (Gother, John): The papist misrepresented. Part II.
London. Henry Hills. 1687. 4to. 88 p.
O 4º A 23 (5) Art. Wing G 1338

462    (Gother, J.): The papist misrepresented. Third
part. London. Henry Hills. 1687. 4to.
61p. FSL 133307. 3; O G Pamph. 1055
& 4º Z Jur. 7 (3); Ware. Wing G 1339

463    (Gother, J.): Papists protesting against protestant-
popery. London. Henry Hills. 1686.
4to. 39p. FSL. Wing G 1340

464    (Gother, J.): Papists protesting. London. Henry
Hills. 1687. 38p. O Pamph. 178 (7) &
Pamph. 172C (10); NN CI p. v. 17; NC;
NU Auburn KJ 95. 3 G 68. 1685; TU;

CN Case C 64.75. Wing G 1341

465     (Gother, J. ): Papists protesting. London. Henry Hills. 1687. 4to. 36p. FSL. Wing G 1342

466     (Gother, J. ): Pius IV his profession of faith. London. Henry Hills. 1687. 4to. 40p. FSL bd. w. H 3257; O C. 11. 7 (4) Linc.; L 3935 dd 4 (11); TU. Wing G 1343/P 2324

467     (Gother, J. ): The pope's supremacy asserted. London. Henry Hills. 1688. 4to. 52p. L 222 a 8 (6); TU; CN; NU 1688 + G684. Wing G 1344

468     (Gother, J. ): The primitive fathers no protestants. London. Henry Hills. 1687. 4to. 48p. L 222 e 8 (4); FSL 133307. 7; TU. Wing G 1345

469     (Gother, J. ): Principles and rules of the gospel. n. p. 1700. 12mo. O Vet A 3 f. 1363; TU. Wing G 1346

470     (Gother, J. ): Pulpit-sayings or the characters of the pulpit-papist. London. Henry Hills. 1688. 4to. 58p. OC Pamph. 9 C 83 (12); FSL; O Z Jur 18 4°; NN CI p. v. 17; TU. Wing G 1347

471     (Gother, J. ): Reflections upon the answer. n. d. p. (London. 1686) 4to. 19p. cap. title. FSL 128363; O 4° Z Jur. 3 (3) & 4° A 23 (4) Art.; (Both imp. ); OS # 1979; NN CI p. v. 7; TU; NC; CN. Wing G 1348

472     (Gother, J. ): A reply to the answer of the...Accomodation. London. Henry Hills. 1686. 4to. 46p. FSL; O Pamph. C 171 (15); TU; NN CI p. v. 17. Wing G 1349

473     (Gother, John): Transubstantiation defended. London. Henry Hills. 1687. 4to. 64p. FSL bd. w. H 3257; O Vet A 3 e 473 (4); Y Mhc 8. 14. 24. Wing C 1350

Gough, Mary: Pious collection, see Following collection

The great sacrifice of the new law: see Dymock (J. )

The Greeks' opinion touching the Eucharist: see Woodhead (Abraham)

474     (Grene, Martin): An account of the jesuites life and doctrine. By M. G. n. p. (London)

1661. 8vo. O 8° O 79 Th. ; OS # 380,
TU, CN Case 3 A 1943. Wing G 1825

475    (Grene, Martin): The voyce of truth... composed in
latin by M. G. and translated.. by F. G.
(i. e. Francis Grene? ? ). Gant. Robert
Walker. 1676. 12s. L 698 a 46

476    (Gualdo Priorato, Galeazzo): The history of the
sacred and royal majesty of Christina..
Queen of Swedland. Trans. John Burbery. For T. W. 1658. 12mo. O Douce
C 92; DAI. Wing G 2171

477    (Gualdo Priorato, Galeazzo): The history of...
Christina. Trans. John Burbery.
London. Printed f. A. W. 1660. 8vo.
OB 695 G 14; FSL G 2171. 2; Ware.
Wing G 2172

Guide in controversies, see Woodhead (Abraham)
Guide to salvation, see Eason
H., G.: see Holland, Guy
H., H.: See Humberston (Henry)
H., J.: See Hoddeson (John) & Hughes (John)
H., R.: See Walker (Obadaiah)

478    H., T.: Articles proposed to the catholiques of
England. Paris. 1648. cap. L E 458
(9) (Incomplete copy with only pp. 9-
16. Thomason's MS note states "..
There was a sheet printed before this
in Lattine the very same. ")

479    H., W.: A letter concerning the test and persecution.
London. Matthew Turner. 1687. 4to.
6p. FSL 144193; O G 1055 (12) & Ashm.
741 (24b). Wing H 156

480    Hales,   : A speech spoken by Mr. Hayles.
(coloph. ) London f. A. M. 1687. s.
sh. FSL bd. w. J 189. Wing H 1209

Hall, Francis: see Line (Francis)

481    Hall, William: A sermon preached before her
majesty the Queen dowager. London.
Henry Hills. f. William Grantham.
1686. 4to. 38p. O Pamph. C 171 (2)
& Mar 831 (17); NU 1686 E 47; TU.
Wing H 447

Hattecliffe, Vincent: see Spenser (John)
Hawley, Susan: see Brief Relation

482    (Heath, Henry Paul): Soliloquies or the documents
of christian perfection... (By) Father
Paul of St. Magdalen (Name in religion).
Doway. 1674. 12mo. <u>Ware</u>; DAI; <u>CN</u>
Case 2 A 121

483    Heath, Nicholas: The speech of. London. Printed
f. the author. 1688. 8vo. (Only the
first tenth of this volume is taken up
with Heath's speech, which is an in-
sert in a longer pro-Catholic argument).
<u>TU.</u> Wing H 1337

484    (Heigham, John): The touchstone of the reformed
gospel. (Coloph.) St. Omer. 1652.
12mo. <u>L</u> 3935 a 4; (This work is usually
attributed to Matthew Kellison. On
Heigham's authorship see Allison in 4
<u>RH,</u> 226 ff.). Wing K 240

485    (Heigham, John): The touchstone of the reformed
gospel. n. d. p. (c. 1674) 12mo. 141p.
<u>Ware</u>

486    (Heigham, J.): The touchstone of the reformed gospel. n. d. p. (c. 1674) 12mo. 140p.
<u>Ware</u>

487    (Heigham, J.): The touchstone of the reformed gospel. n. p. (England) 1675. 12mo. 141
p. <u>L</u> 698 a 39; <u>Ware</u>; <u>NN</u> * KC 1675;
NU; <u>CN</u> Case 3 A 1949. Wing K 241

488    (Heigham, John): The touchstone of the reformed
gospel. n. p. 1676. 12mo. DE

489    (Heigham, John): The touchstone of the reformed
gospel. n. p. 1677. 12mo. 141 p. <u>O</u>
Vet E 3 f. 96

490    (Heigham, J.): The touchstone of the reformed gospel. n. p. 1678. 12mo. 141p. <u>O</u> Vet L
3 f. 14

491    (Heigham, J.): The touchstone of the reformed gospel. n. p. (St. Omer) 1683. 12mo.
141p. <u>Y</u> Mhc5 K 288 T 6. Wing K 242

492    (Heigham, J.): The touchstone of the reformed
gospel. n. p. (St. Omer) 1685. Sixes.
129p. <u>L</u> T 1835 (1); 3936 a 28. Wing
K 243

493    (Heigham, J.): The touchstone of the reformed
gospel. n. p. d. (c. 1685) 12mo. 141
p. <u>L</u> 3935 a 3 & 3936 aaa 15. Wing K

494    (Heigham, J.): The touchstone of the reformed gos-
            pel. London. Henry Hills. 1687. 12mo.
            98p. L 692 a 43; <u>LFS.</u> Wing K 245

495    (Heigham, J.): The touchstone of the reformed gos-
            pel. Bordeaux. Simon Boë. 1691. 8vo.
            130p. <u>L</u> 3936 aaa 26. Wing K 246

496    Henry VIII: Assertio septem sacramentorum or an
            assertion. Trans. T. W. London. Nath.
            Thompson. 1687. 4to. <u>O</u> 4° Z 12 Jur.
            Wing H 1468

497    Henry VIII: Assertio septem sacramentorum or an
            assertion. Trans. T. W. Second edition.
            London f. Nath. Thompson. 1688. 12mo.
            in 6s. <u>O</u> 8° W 52 Th BS; <u>TU</u>; <u>CN</u> Case 3
            A 1950. Wing H 1469

498    Hilton, Walter: The scale (or ladder) of perfection.
            London. Printed by T. R. 1659. 8vo.
            OS #420; <u>L</u> E 1791; <u>TU</u>; CN 3 A 1952.
            Wing H 2042

       Historical collection: see Touchet (G.)
       Historical epistle of the great amitie: see Smith (R.)
       Historical narration of the life: see Woodhead (A.)
       History of the iconoclasts: see Anderton (T.)

499    The history of the life and death of that antient father...
            Dr. Joh. Thauler. n.p. (London) Printed
            f. Lodowick Lloyd. 1663. 8vo. <u>CN</u> Case
            3 A 1953

500    The history of the reformation of the church of
            England. n.p. 1685. Sixes. <u>LFS</u>

501    (Hoddeson, Jo.): The history of the life and death
            of S. Thomas More.. by J.H. London f.
            George Eversden & Henry Eversden.
            1662. 12mo. FSL 131271; TU; R. W.
            Gibson #105. Wing H 2293

502    H(oddeson), J(ohn): Tho. Mori vita et exitus or the
            history. London. E.Cotes f. Geo.Evers-
            den. 1652. 8vo. <u>O</u> Crynes 563; OS #595;
            R. W. Gibson #104. (R. W. Gibson notes
            that some tpp. have "by J. H. Gent";
            others have "by Jo. Hoddeson"; still
            others have both tpp.) Wing H 2296

503    Holden, Henry: The Analysis of divine faith. Trans.
            W. G. Paris. 1658. 4to. <u>O</u> Antiq. e F
            1658/1; <u>TU</u>; OS #411. Wing H 2375

504    (Holden, Henry):  A check; or enquiry. London. 1662.
             4to. 20p. O B 6. 11 Linc. (4); Ware.
             Wing H 2376

505    Holden, Henry:  Divinae fidei analysis. Editio altera.
             Coloniae Agrippinae apud C ab E &
             socios. (Blind, vere England). 12mo.
             1655. WGT; CN Case 3 A 1954

506    Holden, Henry:  Dr. Holden's letter. n. p. 1657. 4to.
             cap. 4p. L 701 h 4 (6); TU. Wing H 2377

507    Holden, Henry:  A letter written by. Paris. 1661. 4to
             22p. L 698 f 3 (4). Wing H 2379

508    Holden, Henry:  A letter written by... touching the
             prohibition. n. p. 1657. 4to. cap. 16p.
             L C 38 a 41 (4). Wing H 2378

509    (Holland, Guy):  The grand prerogative of human
             nature.. By G. H. London. Roger Daniel
             to be sold by Antony Williamson. 1653.
             8vo. FSL; L E 1438 (2); OS #413. Wing
             H 2417

The holy desires of death, See Lallemant
The holy life of Gregory Lopez, See Losa (Francisco
             de)
Holy life of Philip Nerius, see Gallonio (Antonio)
Howard, William: see Stafford

510    (Huddleston, John):  The law of laws. London. Mary
             Thompson. 1688

511    (Huddleston, John):  A new plot of the papists. Lon-
             don. 1679. 4to. 16p. L 100 g. 83. Wing
             D 1924

512    (Huddleston, John):  The pharisees' council.. By J. D.
             London. Mary Thompson f. the author.
             1688. 4to. 32p. O Mar 831 (21). Wing D
             1926

513    (Huddleston, John):  The phoenix, sepulchre & cradle.
             By J. D. London. 1691. 4to. 22p. HP;
             L 113 f 21. Wing D 39

514    (Huddleston, John):  Rebellion arraigned, a sermon.
             London. Mary Thompson. 1688; L

515    (Huddleston, John):  A sermon of judgment. London.
             Nat. Thompson. 1687. 4to. 32p. O Ser-
             mons 6 (8); L 1021 d. 23 (7); NU 1647
             E 47. Wing D 1927

516    (Huddleston, John):  A sermon preached before their
             majesties. By J. D. London. Nat.
             Thompson. 1687. 4to. 30p. O Pamphlet

C 171 (1); <u>TU.</u> Wing D 1928

517     (Huddleston, John): Usury explained. By Philopenes.
London by D. E. 1695/6. 8vo. <u>FSL</u>
171365; <u>Ware</u>; <u>LFS</u> (All these copies
have 116 p. ). 2 Wing D 1928A

518     (Huddleston, John): Usury explained. By Philopenes.
London by D. E. 1695/6. 121 p. <u>O</u> 8° F
121 Linc.

519     (Huddleston, John): The why's and the how's or a
good enquiry: A sermon. London. Nat.
Thompson. 1687. 4to. 34p. <u>O</u> Mar. 831
(20); <u>NU</u> 1686 E 47. Wing D 1929

520     Hudleston, Richard: A short and plain way. London.
Henry Hills. 1688. 4to. 38p. <u>Ware</u>; <u>OC</u>
I B 55; <u>O</u> Vet A 3 e 473 (8) & 4° Z Jur.
5 & D. 12. 4. Linc. ; <u>Y</u> Mhc 8. 14. 24; <u>TU</u>
(ed. John Hudleston O. S. B. ) Wing H
3257

521     Hudleston, Richard: A short and plain way. London.
Henry Hills. 18mo. 2 parts 91 + 34p.
Hiscock H 3257 +; <u>OC</u> O I 6. 17; <u>HP</u>;
<u>Ware</u> (2 copies); <u>TU</u>; <u>CN</u> Case 3 A 1956
(ed. John Hudleston O. S. B. )

522     Hudleston, Richard: A short and plain way. Holy
Rood House by P. B. 1688. 12mo.
Wing H 3258

523     Hudleston, Richard: A short and plain way. Dublin
reprinted f. William Weston. 1688.
Wing H 3259

524     Hugh of St. Victor: The rule of the great S. Augustin
expounded. Bridges (i. e. Bruges) John
de Cock. n. d. (1697?) 3 parts. <u>TU</u>; CN
Case 3 A 1957

525     H(ughes), J(ohn): Allwydd neu agoriad paradwys i'r
cymry. Luyck (<u>vere</u> London) 1670.
12mo. <u>FSL</u> H 3311. 5; <u>L</u> C 37 c 37 (Title
in English: The key or opening of heaven
to the Welsh)

526     Hugo, Herman: Pia desideria. Editio postrema.
Londinii. Excudit J. C. sumptibus
Roberti Pawlet. 1677. 24° in 8s. <u>TU</u>;
<u>CN</u> Case 3 A 1958. Wing H 3349

527     H(umberston), H(enry): A sermon preached at
Worcester. London. f. Matthew Turner.
1686. 4to. 22p. <u>NU</u> 1686 t H 92; <u>TU</u>.

Wing H 3365

528    An humble adoration of our blessed lord Jesus. n. d. p.
        (1664) 28p. <u>O</u>

The humble apologie of the English catholicks, see
        Castlemaine

529    Humble petition of the brownists. n. p. 1641. 4to. 9p.
        <u>L</u> E 178 (10). (Anr. ed. of Wing N 698)
        Wing H 3487

530    (Hutchinson, Wm.): A rational discourse concerning
        transubstantiation. n. p. 1676. 4to. 46p.
        <u>HP</u>; <u>Yale</u> Mhc 8 1676 H 97. Wing H 3838

531    I., P.: A letter written by a minister. London. Henry
        Hills. 1686. 4to. 38p. <u>LW</u> PP 7.48.4
        (3). 2 Wing B 185

532    I., P.: A letter written by a minister. London. Henry
        Hills. 1688. 4to. 38p. <u>O</u> G. Pamph. 1055
        (5); <u>Y</u> Brit. Tracts 1688 L 565. Wing B
        185A

Idaea of a perfect princesse, see Leslie (Wm.)
Idiota or duns contemplation, see Duns

533    Indulgences and priviledges granted to the sodality.
        n. p. 1670. 8vo. 30p. <u>O</u> 8° C 437 (3)
        Linc. (imp. copy lacking tp. and pp. 13-
        14)

534    Indulgence to tender consciences. London. Henry
        Hills. 1687. 4to. 6p. <u>O</u> Ashm. 1018
        (6). Wing I 157

Infallibility, see Canes (J. B. V.)
The infallibility of the Roman Catholick Church: see
        Worsley (E.)
Infidelity unmasked: see Wilson (Matthew)
Innocency acknowledged: see Ceriziers

535    An instance of the church of England's loyalty. Lon-
        don. Henry Hills. 1687. 4to. 12p. <u>FSL</u>
        bd. w. H 3257. Wing I 231

536    The institutions of the congregation of the Oratory
        at... Vallicella. Oxford. 1687. 8° in
        4s. Hiscock V 49+; Madan 1687.19
        (attributes to O. Walker); O 8° I 34 (2)
        Linc.

537    An instruction to performe with fruit the devotion of
        ten Fridays in honour of S. Francis
        Xaverius. n. p. d. (St. Omer. c. 1670)
        12mo. 124p. (Preliminaries signed N. N.
        i. e. editor/trans. ?) <u>L</u> 1018 b. 31; <u>TU</u>;

CN Case 3 A 1959; HP. Wing I 235

Instructions and devotions for hearing mass: see
    Gother (J.)

538    Instructions and devotions for the afflicted and sick.
    n.p. (London) 1697. 12mo. L 4412 e 16;
    LFS; CN Case 3 A 1941

Instructions for children: see Gother (J.)

539    Instructions for confession and communion. n.p. 1700.
    DE

Instructions for masters: see Gother (J.)

Instructions for particular states: see Gother (J.)

Instructions for the whole year: see Gother (J.)

Instructions for youth, see Gother (J.)

An invitation of a seeker: see S. (I.)

Ireland's case briefly stated: see Reilly (H.)

540    J., C. and McC., J.: A net for the fishers of men.
    n.p. 1687. Sixes. 100 p. LFS

541    (Jenks, Sylvester): The blind obedience of an humble
    pentitent. n.p. 1698. 12mo. O 1.c. 318
    (2); Ware. Wing J 629

542    (Jenks, Sylv.): The blind obedience. Second edition.
    n.p. 1699. 12mo. OS #2138; DAI; L 1471
    e 22; TU; CN 3 A 1963

543    (Jenks, S.): A contrite and humble heart. Paris. 1692.
    12mo. Ware; CN Case 3 A 1963

544    (Jenks, S.): A contrite and humble heart. Second
    edition. n.p. 1693. 12mo. O 1.c. c.
    215; Ware; FSL 181152; TU (imp.) Wing
    J 630

545    (Jenks, S.): A contrite and humble heart. Fourth
    edition. 12mo. n.p. 1698. Ware; CN
    Case 3 A 1964;

546    (Jenks, Sylv.): A letter concerning the council of
    Trent. n.p. 1686. Signed N.N. (This
    appears to have been designed as part of
    N 60 but to have been issued separately.
    The three copies at Oscott - OS #886 -
    all run p. 147-264); TU

547    (Jenks, S.): Practical discourses upon the morality
    of the gospel. n.p. 1699. 12mo. Ware.
    Wing P 3153

548    (Jenks, S.): Practical discourses upon the morality
    of the gospel. Part II. n.p. 1700. 24$^o$
    in 12s. Ware; WGT

549        (Jenks, S.): Three sermons upon the sacrament. London. 1688. 12s. Signed N.N. (Jenks claims this work in the introduction to J 629. There are actually four sermons of which one was preached in 1687 and three in 1688. Pp. 147-264 constitute #546 supra and are dated at the end 22 Sept. 1686. Following p. 264 there is another work, "Search the Scriptures" with new signatures and pagination - 1-23.) O 1. c. 318 (1); Ware. Wing N 60

Jerusalem and Babel, see Patteson

550        The jesuites plea in answer to a letter. London. 1679. 4to. 15p. Y Brit. Tracts 1679 J 49. Wing J 722

551        The jesuits reasons unreasonable. London. 1662. 4to. 21p. O B. 6. 11. Linc.; NU 1662 + J58; CN Case 3 A 2034. Wing J 725

552        (Jesus Psalter): Devout and godly petitions commonly called the Jesus psalter. n.p. 1673. 18s. O 138 g 231

553        The Jesus psalter. n. d. p. (c. 1675?) 12mo. 31p. L 3455 df. 10

554        The Jesus psalter. London. 1687. 24p. DAI

555        (John Evangelist of Balduke): The kingdom of God in the soule. Editor, B. P. S. (i. e. Brother Peter Salvin). Paris. Lewis de la Fosse. 1657. 12mo. L 4401 n. 31; OS #439; TU; CN Case 3 A 1965. Wing J 744A

John of the holy Cross: see Moor (John)

556        Johnson, William: Novelty represt. Paris f. E. C. 1661. 8vo. HP; OS #442; TU; CN Case 3 A 1966. Wing J 861

557        (Johnston, Henry Jos.): A full answer to the second defence. (coloph.) London. Henry Hills. 1687. 4to. 12p. Cap. title. FSL 142433; OS #2149. Wing J 868

558        (Johnston, H. J.): A letter from the vindicator. (coloph.) London. Henry Hills. 1687. 4to. 4p. Cap. title. OS #2150. Wing J 869

559        (Johnston, H. J.): A reply to the defence of the exposition. London. Henry Hills. 1686. 4to. O 4° Z Jur. 7 (1)

560      (Johnston, H.J.): A reply to the defence of the doc-
               trine. London. Henry Hills. 1687. 4to.
               L 222 d.9 (2); OS #2151. Wing 870

561      (Johnston, H.J.): A vindication of the bishop of Con-
               dom's exposition. London. Henry Hills.
               1686. 4to. O Pamph. C 171 (10); HP;
               TU; NN CI p.v. 25. Wing J 871

562      (Joyner, Wm.): Some observations upon the life of
               Reginaldus Polus.. by G. L. (i.e. Wm.
               Joyner whose alias was Lyde). London
               f. Matthew Turner. 1686. 8vo. FSL; OS
               #693; L 295 g.28 (Based on biog. of Pole
               by L. Beccatelli) Wing J 1160

563      Juliana of Norwich: XVI revelations of divine love.
               (Dedication signed "H. Cressy" who was
               editor) n.p. 1670. 8vo. FSL. Wing J
               1188

564      Jupiter: Doctor Stillingfleet's true god. n.p.d. (c.
               1674). O C 8° 31 (5)

        K., J.: see Kemeys
        Kalendarium Catholicum: see Blount
        Ka mee and I'le ka thee: see Abbot (John)

565      (Keepe, Henry): A true and perfect narrative...by
               Charles Taylor (pseud.) London. By
               J.B. and are to be sold by Randall Tay-
               lor. 1688. 4to. 34p. FSL 149199; TU.
               Wing K 128

566      Kellison, Matthew: A devout paraphrase on the 50th
               psalme. Paris. 1655. 8vo. L E 1662
               (1); Ware; L E 1662 (1). Wing K 239

        Kellison, M.: Touchstone, see Heigham (John)

567      (Kemeys, T.): Veritas evangelica or the gospel-truth.
               Written by T.K. and now published by
               R.C. London. Nat. Thompson. 1687.
               4to. Ware; O Ashm. 1014 (12); TU; CN;
               Y Mhc 8.14.24. Wing K 256

568      Key of paradise. Paris. 1662. 12mo. LFS ( - tp;
               date, place and title taken from adver-
               tisement)

569      Key of paradise...newly reviewed and augmented with
               three offices of Our Lady by T.F.S.
               priest (i.e. Thomas Fitzsimon). (Rouen)
               Printed by David Maurry. n.d. (c. 1674)
               12mo in 6s. DMR

570      The key of paradise. n.p. (St. Omer. ECP) 1674.

Sixes. ST
571 The key of paradise. St. Omers. 1675. 18°. O 138
g. 231; TU (imp.) Wing K 384
572 The key of paradise. Paris. 1681. 18°. Ware; C G
16.71
The key of paradise (in Welsh): see Hughes (John)
573 K(eynes), J(ohn): A rational compendious way to con-
vince. n.p. 1674. 12mo. O Wood 869 (5)
& Mason E. 2; OS #454. Wing K 393
574 (Keynes, George): The roman martyrologe. Trans.
G. K. Second edition. S. Omers. Thomas
Geubels. 1667. 8vo. (Preface signed
W. B., i.e., Wm. Blount?) OS #563;
TU; Ware; CN 3 A 1967; HP. Wing K
392/R 1892
575 (L., A.): A letter to a friend touching Dr. Jeremy
Taylor's Disswasive. n.p. 1665. 4to.
43p. FSL; Hiscock L 4⁺; OC 0.5.9
Allestree & 0.5.5 Allestree; O Pamph.
D 122 (11); FSL. Wing L 1655A
L., E.: see Lydeott, E. & Lutton, E.
L., G.: see Leyburne (George)
L., I.: See Lewgar (John)
576 (Lallemant, Jacques Philippe): The holy desires of
death. Trans. T. V. Sadler. n.p. 1678.
12mo. L 4410 b.34; Ware
577 Langhorne, Richard: Considerations touching the great
question of the kings right. London.
Printed f. H.H. for the assigns of R.
Langhorne & sould by N. Thompson.
1687. fol. FSL 148848. Wing L 396
578 Langhorne, Richard: Mr. Langhorne's memoires.
n.p. (London) 1679. F'scap fol. 22p.
O Wood 425 (5) FSL 130660. Wing L 397
579 Langhorne, Richard: The speech of. n.p. (London)
1679. F'scap fol. 4p. FSL 127650; TU;
CN f K 645.836. Wing L 399
580 A large summary of the doctrines contained in the
catechism.... Trent. n.p. Printed f.
A. L. 1675. 8vo. 2 parts. NU 1675 L 32.
Wing 439
581 Lassells, Richard: An excellent way of hearing mass
with profit and devotion. The fifth edi-
tion. n.p. (London) 1686. 12mo. 2 parts
(41)⁺ 58 + 52 pp. Ware

55

582    (Lassells, R.): A most excellent way of hearing mass
with profit and devotion. n.p. (London)
Printed by T. G. 1687. 12mo. (This edition is much longer than the preceding
item) O 8° Th M 241; DAI

The layman's opinion: see Darrell (William)

The layman's ritual: see Tootel (C.)

583    Le Camus, Etienne: A pastoral letter of the lord
cardinal. London. Nath. Thompson.
1687. 4to. LFS; Y Mhc 8.14.24. Wing L
806

Legacie left to protestants: see Bayly (Thomas)

584    (Leigh, Philip): A sermon preached before the right
worshipful the mayor of... Newcastle..
By Phil. Metcalfe (alias of Leigh). London. Henry Hills. 1688. 4to. 40p. WGT;
L 1021 d.23 (8)

Leo de Vennes: see Parlor (John)

585    (Leslie, Wm. Lewis): Idaea of a perfect princesse.
Paris. 1661. 8vo. 101p. Dedication
signed J.R. L G 5452; 288 a 23; FSL;
BUTE; TU; CN Case E 5 M 33093. Wing
L 1173

586    (Lessius, Leonard): A consultation about religion, or
what religion is best to be chosen. Lon-
don (vere St. Omer??) 1693. 8vo. in
4s. NU 1693 S 893; TU; CN Case 3 A
1972. Wing S 5928A

587    Lessius, Leonard: Sir Walter Rawleigh's ghost.
London. By Thomas Newcomb f. John
Holden. 1651. 12mo. L E 1275. WGT.
Wing L 1180

A letter concerning the council of Trent: see Jenks
(S.)

588    A letter concerning the jesuits. n.p. 1661. 4to. 14p.
O Pamph. 114 C (1). Wing L 1352

A letter concerning the test: see H. (W.)

A letter desiring a just and merciful regard: see
Walsh (Peter)

A letter desiring information: see Meredith (E.)

A letter from a dissenter: see Gother (John)

A letter from a gentleman: see R. (T.)

A letter from Amsterdam: see Morgan (Wm.)

A letter from the author of Sure-Footing: see
Sergeant (John)

A letter from the vindicator: see Johnston (H. J.)
A letter in answer to the late dispensers: see White
   (Thomas)
A letter in answer to two main objections: see G. (T.)
A letter to a friend: see L. (A.)
A letter to a lady: see Darrell (Wm.)
A letter to a peer: see Sabran (Lewis)
A letter to both houses of Parliament: see P. (E.)
A letter to the D. of P.: see Sergeant (John)
A letter to the honourable Collonel Okey: see B. (A.)
A letter written by a minister: see I. (P.)

589 (Lewgar, John): Erastus junior or a fatal blow. Lon-
     don. Livewell Chapman. 1660. 4to. 24p.
     FSL 138659 (Signed Joshua Web, i.e.,
     pseud.). Wing L 1831

590 (Lewgar, John): Erastus senior, scholastically
     demonstrating. n.p. (London) 1662.
     8vo. FSL 129622; HP. Wing L 1832

591 L(ewgar), J(ohn): The only way to rest of soule.
     n.p. printed f. the author. 1657. 12mo.
     WGT; HP. Wing L 36

592 (Lewgar, John): The second part of Erastus junior.
     London. 1660. 4to. 23p. CS Gg 3.426;
     FSL

Lewis of Granada: see Luis de Granada

593 Leyburn, George: Dr. Leyburn's encyclicall answere.
     Doway. L. Kellam. 1661. 4to. 96p. L
     3935 bb (3). Wing L 1936

594 (Leyburn, G.): An epistle declaratorie, or manifest,
     written by G. L. n.p. (Douai) Widdowe
     of Marke Wyon. 1657. 4to. 51 p. L C
     38 a 41 (1). Wing L 1937

595 Leyburn, G.: Holy characters. Doway. Baltazar
     Bellier. 1662. 8vo. 2 parts. FSL 181138;
     O Bliss B 351; OS #486; TU; CN Case 3
     A 1975. Wing L 1938

596 Leyburn, G.: A letter written by G. L. n.p.d. (Douai,
     1657). 12mo. cap. title. 5 p. L C 38 a
     41 (2). Wing L 1890

597 Leyburn, G.: The summe of Dr. Leybourne's answere.
     Douay. Widowe of Mark Wyon. 1657.
     4to. 42 p. L C 38 a 41 (3). Wing L 1939/
     S 6169

598 Leyburn, G.: To her most excellent maiestie Henri-
     etta Maria. n.d.p. (c. 1660) 4to. cap.

title. 16p. L 3935 b 33/2. Wing L 1940

Leyburn, John: Pastoral letter, see title

599 (Leyburn, J.): A reply to the answer made upon 3
royal papers. London f. Matthew Tur-
ner. 1686. 4to. 56 p. FSL; O 4º Z Jur.
5 (3); NU 1686 S 41; NN *KC p.v. 26.
Wing L 1941

The life and death of S. Thomas More; see More (C.)

The life and doctrine of our saviour: see More (H.)

600 The life of Boetius recommended to the author of the
life of Julian. London. W. Davis. 1683.
8vo. FSL; LFS. Wing L 2024

The life of lady Warner: see Scarisbrick

601 The life of St. Anthony of Padua with the miracles.
Trans. J. Burbury (who signs dedica-
tion). Paris. 1660. 12mo. L G 14361

The life of the apostle St. Paul: see Godeau (A.)

602 Line, Francis: An explication of the diall.. By Father
Francis Hall, otherwise Line. Liege.
Guillaume Henry Streel. 1673. 4to. 59 p.
FSL; NC P 529.78 A. Phoenix collection.
Wing H 332

Liturgical discourse: see Mason (R.)

603 (Lobb, Emmanuel): An answer to Dr. Pierce's sermon.. By J.S. (i.e. Jos. Symonds,
alias) n.p. 1663. 8vo. O 8º A 15 Linc.;
FSL; TU; CN Case 3 A 2041. Wing S
3805

Lominus: see Talbot (P.)

604 (Losa, Francisco de): The holy life of Gregory Lopez.
Second edition. n.p. 1675. 8vo. O 8º I
34 (1) Linc.; Y Mexico Ct. K188/613
1gb; NN *KC 1675. Wing L 3080

605 (Losa, Francisco de): The holy life of Gregory Lopez.
Second edition. London. Printed f. W.
C. 1686. 8vo. CN Case 3 A 1776

606 Lucilla and Elizabeth or donatist and protestant
schism parallel'd. (Coloph.) London.
Henry Hills. 1686. 4to. Cap. title. 4
p. L T 1846 (5); FSL 144545; OS #2317;
NN C.I. p.v. 22 (6). Wing L 3441

607 Luis de Granada: A memorial of the christian life.
The first part. London f. Matthew Tur-
ner. 1688. 8vo. OS #499; Ware; TU.
Wing L 3471 C

58

608     Luis de Granada: A memorial of the christian life..
              The three last treatises. Trans. C.J.S.
              The second volume. n.p. 1699. 8vo.
              Ware

609     L(utton), E(dward): The funerall sermon of Mr. Miles
              Pinckney. Paris. Vincent du Moutier.
              1675. 4to. 22p. L 1417 f. 45. Wing L 14

610     L(ydeott), (E.): The prodigal returned home. n.p.
              (London. Nat. Thompson) 1684. 8vo.
              FSL; O 8° C 271 Linc.; Ware; (On pub-
              lisher see Rostenburg in 10 Library -
              1955 - p. 201.) Wing L 3525

     M., C.: see Soules Pilgrimage
     M., G.: see Martin (Gregory)
     M., J.: see Mumford (James)

611     M., P.: A letter to the answerer of the apology. n.p.
              (London) 1667. 4to. Cap. 8p. Ware. Wing
              M 65A

612     M., P.: Some queries...concerning the English re-
              formation. n.p. f. the author. 1688.
              4to. 8p. OC Pamph. 9. C. 83; Hiscock M
              66[+]

     M., P.D.: see Patteson
     M., W.: see Marsh (W.)
     McC., J.: see J. (C.)

613     Macedo, Francisco: Lituus lusitanus. Londinii excu-
              debat R. Norton. 1654. 4to. Y Me65.27.
              M 151. L 5. Wing M 123

614     Macedo, Francisco: Mens divinitus inspirata. 2 parts.
              Londini. R. Norton. 1653. 4to. L E 218.
              Wing M 124

615     (Macedo, Francisco): Scrinium divi Augustini. Lon-
              dini. T. Roycroft. 1654. 4to. TU. Wing
              M 125

616     Macedo, Francisco: Tessera romana authoritatis
              pontificiae. Londini. R. Norton. 1654.
              4to. O 130 e 45. Wing M 126

617     (Maimbourg, Louis): A discourse concerning the
              foundation and prerogative. London f.
              Jos. Hindmarsh. 1688. 8vo. Trans. A.
              Lovell. FSL M 289.2 (This is 2nd ed. of
              Wing M 289)

618     Maimbourg, L.: An historical treatise of the founda-
              tion and prerogatives of the church of
              Rome. Trans. A. Lovell. London. f.

Jos. Hindmarsh. 1685. 8vo. O Vet A
3 e 472; OS #516; TU; CN Case 3 A 1862;
THC. Wing M 289

619 Maimbourg, Lewis: A peaceable method for the re-
uniting protestants and catholicks. Trans.
T. W. Paris (vere London) 1671. 8vo. O
8° C 58 Linc. Wing M 293

620 Maimbourg, Lewis: A peaceable method for the re-
uniting n. p. Printed f. G. W. 1686. 4to.
87p. Translator's preface signed "W. G."
O 4° Z Jur. 11 (7). Wing M 294

621 Manby, Peter: The considerations which obliged.
Dublin. Christopher Ians. 1687. 4to.
19p. L T 1846 (3); FSL. Wing M 383

622 Manby, Peter: The considerations which oblig'd
Peter Manby...to embrace the roman
catholic religion. London. Reprinted f.
Nath. Thompson. 1687. 4to. 15p. O Vet
A 3 e 473 (7) Wing M 384

623 Manby, Peter: The considerations which obliged Peter
Manby...to embrace the catholique reli-
gion. London. Printed f. Nathaniel
Thompson. 1687. 4to. Ware (This ed. is
distinguished from the preceding by the
tp and by the fact that this ed. has 19 p. )

624 Manby, Peter: A letter from a protestant in London.
Dublin. 1690. brds. Wing M 385

625 Manby, Peter: A letter to a friend. Dublin. 1688.
4to. Wing M 386

626 Manby, Peter: A reformed catechism. Dublin. Jos.
Ray. 1687. 4to. Wing M 387

627 Manby, Peter: A reformed catechism. n. p. (London)
N. Thompson. 1687. 4to. O Vet. A 3 e
473 (1). Wing M 388

628 A manifest publisht to their brethren by the general
chapter. n. p. (London). 1661. 4to. Cap.
title. 6 p. L 701 h. 4 (8); CN Case 3 A
1919

629 The manner of performing the novena or nine days
devotion to St. Francis Xavierus. n. d. p.
(c. 1700) 12mo. 2 parts 24 + 92 p. OS
#1418; WGT; TU; Ware

630 A manuall of devotions. n. p. 1644. 8vo. L 345 c 22
631 A manual of devout prayers. Paris. 1671. 12mo.
Wing M 542

632      A manuall of devout prayers. Paris. 1675. 12mo. L
          3455 df. 10

633      A Manual of devout prayers. 1686. DMR; O Vet A 3
          g. 25

634      A manuall of devout prayers and devotions. (London)
          Printed by N. T. 1687. 24°. DAI; O 8°
          Th M 241

635      A manual of devout prayers and devotions. (London)
          Printed by N. Thompson. 1687. Ware
          (Very similar to preceding item but this
          one is longer).

635A     A manual of devout prayers. (London). Mary Thompson.
          1688. 12mo. LGL

636      A manual of devout prayers. London. Henry Hills.
          1688. 18mo. L C 25 a 8 (This ed. has
          298p) Wing M 543

637      A manual of devout prayers. Holy Rood House.
          Printed by Mr. P. B. 1688. 12s. FSL
          141708; L 1486 a 20. Wing M 544

638      A manual (of) devout prayers and other christian de-
          votions. n. p. (England) 1696

639      Manual of godly praiers and litanies. To Antworpe.
          Widow of John Cnobbaert f. James
          Thompson. 1650. O Tanner 7 (imp. );
          Ware (imp. ); DE

639A     A manuall of godly prayers & litanies. S. Omer. 1652.
          12s. LGL (= Wing Ghosts O M 544 B)

640      Manual of godly prayers and litanies. Antwerpe by
          Michael Cnobbaert. 1671. 12mo. O
          Mason AA 202; TU (imp. )

640A     A manuall of prayers and litanies. Paris. 1670. 12s.
          LGL

641      Manual of prayers and litanies distributed according
          to the dayes of the week. Paris. 1674.
          12mo. NN *KC 1674 (imp. lacking all
          after p. 526)

642      A Manual of prayers and litanies distributed according
          to the days of the week. n. p. 1688. 12mo.
          Ware; EC; CN Case 3 A 1983 (imp. )

642A     A manual of prayers and other christian devotions.
          London. Henry Hills. 1686. Sixes.
          LGL

643      A manual of prayers and other christian devotions
          n. p. 1698. Ware

644    Manzini, John Baptists: The loving husband & prudent
                    wife. Trans. J. Burbery. London. f. J.
                    Martin and J. Allestrye. 1657. 12mo.
                    HP. Wing M 556
645    (Marsh, W. ): A sermon preach'd before the king and
                    queen. . by the Rev. Dom W. M. monk of
                    the holy order of S. Benedict. London.
                    Nat. Thompson. 1687. 4to. 48p. L 1021
                    d. 23(6); FSL 128472; NU 1686 E 47.
                    Wing M 108/769/2424
646    M(artin), G(regory): The love of the soule. (coloph. )
                    S. Omers. 1652. 92p. L 3935 a 4 (2)
647    (Mason, Richard): Liturgical discourse of the... Mass.
                    The first part. n. p. 1670. 8vo. O 8°
                    C 482 Linc. Ware; TU. Wing M 936
648    (Mason, Richard): Liturgical discourse. Second part
                    n. p. 1669. 8vo. O 8° C 482 Linc. ; Ware;
                    TU. Wing M 937
649    (Mason, Richard): Liturgical discourse. By A. F.
                    (i. e. Angelus Francis, name in reli-
                    gion). n. p. 1675. 12mo. L 3477 aa 52;
                    Ware. Wing M 938
650    (Mason, Richard): A manuell of the arch-confrater-
                    nity. By Brother Angelus Francis (name
                    in religion) Second edition. Doway.
                    Baltazar Bellers. 1654. 12mo. NU 1654
                    M 41 Wing M 939
651    (Mason, Richard): A manuell of the arch-confrater-
                    nity. By Brother Angelus Francis (name
                    in religion). Second edition. 2 parts.
                    Doway. Baltazar Bellere. 1654. 12mo.
                    O 138 g. 291. Ware; Y; NN *KC 1654;
                    CN 3 A 1988
652    (Mason, Richard): A manuall of the third order of..
                    St. Francis. By Br. A. F. Doway.
                    Widow of Marke Wyon. 1643. 12mo. O
                    Antiq. f. F 1643. 1
653    (Mason, Richard): The rule of pennance of. . St. Francis.
                    The first part. By Br. Angelus Francis
                    (name in religion). Doway. Widdow of
                    Marke Wyon. 1644. 12mo. L C 118 a 3;
                    Ware; CN Case 3 A 1989
654    (Mason, Richard): The rule of pennance. The second
                    part. By Br. Angelus Francis
                    (name in religion) Doway. Widowe of

Mark Wyon. 1644. 12mo. <u>L</u> C 38 a 52;
<u>Ware</u>

655   (Matthew, Tobie): A missive of consolation. Louain.
1647. 8vo. <u>FSL</u>; Ware; <u>TU</u>; CN Case 3
A 2102. Wing M 1322

656   (Matthew, Tobie): An epistle of consolation. n. p.
1663. 8vo. <u>TU</u>

657   (Matthieu de Saint-Quentin): The true portraiture of
the church of Jesus Christ. Translated
by Theolulus Philadelphus. Boulogne.
Peter Battut. 1670. 12mo. <u>O</u> 8° A 58
Linc.; <u>HP</u>; <u>TU</u>; CN Case 3 A 2053. Wing
T 2857

Meditations collected: see Daniel (E. )

658   Mercurius catholicus. (No. 1) n. d. p. (London. 15
Sept. 1648) 4to. 12p. <u>L</u> E 464 (2)

659   Mercurius catholicus. No. 2. n. d. p. (London. 11
Dec. 1648) 4to. 8p. <u>L</u> E 475 (35). Wing
M 1760

660   (Meredith, Edward): A letter desiring information.
London. Henry Hills. 1687. 4to. cap.
4p. <u>FSL</u> 142416; <u>O</u> Firth e. 16(13) &
Ashm. 1018; <u>TU</u>. Wing M 1781

661   (Meredith, Edward): A letter to Dr. E. S. London.
Henry Hills. 1687. 4to. 36p. <u>O</u> Pamph.
174; <u>LW</u> P. P. 7. 48. 4; <u>L</u> T 1883 (5); <u>TU</u>;
<u>NN</u> CI p. v. 20. Wing M 1782

662   (Meredith, Edward): Some farther remarks on the
late account. London. Henry Hills.
1688. 4to. <u>FSL</u> 149724; <u>O</u> G. Pamph.
141; <u>Y</u> Mhc8. 9 & Mhc 8. 14. 13; <u>TU</u>.
Wing M 1783

663   (Meredith, Edward): Some remarques upon a late
popular piece. London. f. T. Davies.
1682. fol. 35p. <u>FSL</u> 132637; <u>O</u> C. 11. 15.
Wing M 1784

664   A messenger from the dead. (London) f. Tho. Vere
& W. Gilbertson. 1658. 4to. 20p. <u>FSL</u>;
L E 936 (4) (Poem at end signed R. P.
This work is often attributed to R. Per-
rinchief). Wing P 1597

Metcalfe, Philip: see Leigh (P. )

665   A method how to offer up mass according to the four
ends. London. T. H. 1694. 29p. <u>Ware</u>;
<u>LFS</u>

A method of conversing with God: see Boutauld (M.)

666    Method of gaining the whole christian world. London.
Henry Hills. 1687. brds. FSL 155322;
TU; CN Case F 4554.65. Wing M 1945

667    Method of saying the rosary. n.p. 1669. DE

668    Method of saying the rosary. 1684. 12mo. Wing M
1947

669    Method of saying the rosary... in the English Benedic-
tine college of St. Gregories at Douay.
Duaci apud B. Bellerum. 1684. 24°. L

670    Method of saying the Rosary. 17th edition. n.p. 1686.
12mo. 24p. Hiscock M 1947 +; L 843 a.
21 (imp.)

671    Method of saying the rosary of our blessed lady in
latine and English. 17th edition. Lon-
don. Printed by N. T. 1687. DAI

Method to arrive at satisfaction in religion: see
Sergeant (John)

672    (Milton, Christopher): The state of church-affairs in
this island. London. By Nat. Thomp-
son f. author. 1687. 4to. foolscap. O
Ashm. F.1 (86); CN Case 5 A 42. Wing
M 2085

Miraculous origin: see Termano (Pietro)

673    A mirrour of truth of the highest concern. Signed on
last page: B.P.S. (i.e. Salvin, Bro.
Peter?) London. Mary Thompson. 1688.
4to. 19p. LFS. Wing M 2224

A missive of consolation: see Matthew (Tobie)

Mister Whitebread's contemplations: see White
(Thomas, Jesuit)

674    A moderate and safe expedient. n.p. 1646. 4to. 16p.
LIL Mendham Collection, Tracts 193.
Wing M 2322

A modest and true account: see C. (N.)

675    Modus recitandi rosarium.. in sodalitate collegii
Anglo-Benedictini S. Gregorii M. Duac.
Duaci. J. F. Willverval. n. d. 2 parts.
(of which the 1st part is in latin and the
second part is in English with the cap.
title "Out of Blosius") 16°. 43 + 36 p.
CN Case 2 A 128

676    Montague, Walter: Miscellanea spiritualia, or devout
essaies. London f. William Lee, Daniel
Pakeman & Gabriell Bedell. 1648. 4to.

OS #591; <u>FSL</u>; <u>TU</u>; <u>CN</u> 4 A 1857 vol. 1
& Case B 692. 587 (One of which is a
variant ed. ) Wing M 2473

677     Montague, Walter: Miscellanea spiritualia.. Second
part. London f. John Crook, Gabriel
Bedell & partners. 1654. 4to. <u>OS</u> #592;
<u>TU</u>; <u>CN</u> 4 A 1857 Vol. II & Case B 692.
587. Wing M 2474

678     (Moor, John): An apology for the contemplations on
the life and glory of the holy mother. By
J. C. D. D. (i. e. John Cross, name in
religion). London. Nath. Thompson. 1687.
8vo. <u>Ware</u>; <u>CN</u> Case 3 A 1894. Wing C
7249

679     (Moor, John): Contemplations on the life and glory
of holy Mary. By J. C. D. D. Paris. 1685.
4to. OS #214. <u>O</u> 8$^{\circ}$ C 506 Linc. ; <u>Ware</u>;
<u>TU</u>; <u>CN</u> Case 3 A 1995. Wing C 7250

680     (Moor, John): Contemplations on the life and glory.
Third edition. By J. C. D. D. London.
Nath. Thompson. 1687. 8vo. 79p. <u>Ware</u>

681     (Moor, John): Dialectica ad mentem...Joannis Scoti..
Opera Joannis Sancrucii Nordoviciensis
(i. e. John of the holy cross of Norwich).
Londini. Impensis J. Martini. 1673. 8vo.
<u>FSL</u> C 7250. 5; <u>WGT</u>; <u>O</u> Art 8$^{\circ}$ I 52

682     (Moor, John): Philothea's pilgrimage. (By) Brother
John of the holy crosse (i. e. name in
religion). Bruges. Luke Kerchove. 1668.
8vo. <u>O</u> Antiq. f. B 1 (2);<u> L</u> 698 a. 38; <u>Ware</u>;
<u>CN</u> 3 A 1994. 2 Wing C 7250A

683     (Moor, John): A sermon preached before their sacred
majesties. (By) Fa. John Crosse (name
in religion). London. Nath. Thompson.
1687. 4to. 34p. <u>L</u> 1021 d. 23 (5); <u>NU</u>
1686 E 47. Wing C 7251

684     (More, Cresacre): The life and death of sr. Thomas
Moore. n. p. f. N. V. 1642. 4to. <u>O</u> 4$^{\circ}$ S
14 Th BS; TU. Wing M 2630

685     (More, Gertrude): The holy practices of a divine
lover. Paris. Lewis de la Fosse. 1657.
12mo. <u>O</u> Antiq. f. F. 1657/5; <u>TU</u>; <u>CN</u>
Case 3 A 1991 (Austin Baker edited this
work and it is sometimes attributed to
him. ) 1 Wing B 479

686    More, Gertrude: The spiritual exercises of. Paris.
Lewis de la Fosse. 1658. 12mo. 2 parts.
OS #596; LW 1094 T 22 (i.e. Vol. 2);
TU (This work was collected by Austin
Baker and translated by Francis Gas-
coigne.) Wing M 2632

687    (More, Henry): Life and doctrine of our saviour.
Gant. Maximilian Graet. 1656. 2 parts.
8vo. O Antiq. e B 1656/1; TU; CN Case
3 A 1993. Wing M 2665

688    Morgan, Edward: Edward Morgan, a priest his letter.
London f. T. E. 1642. 4to. 6p. L 8122
d 75; O Wood 616. Wing M 2730

689    Morgan, Edward: A prisoner's letter. London. 1641
(/2). 4to. 6p. L E 144 (17) (1st ed. of
preceding item.) Wing M 2731

690    (Morgan, Wm.): A letter from Amsterdam to a friend
in England. London f. G. H. 1678. 4to.
6p. FSL 128473. Wing L 1439

691    (Morgan, Wm.): A letter from Amsterdam to a friend
in Paris. n.p.d. (1679). 4to. 6p. L 101
c. 14

692    A most devout prayer unto the glorious virgin Mary.
n.p. 1686. Sixes. 21 p. L 843 a. 22

693    A most devout prayer unto the glorious virgin. n. p.
(London) Printed by N. T. 1687. DAI

A most excellent way of hearing mass: see Lassells
(R.)

Motives to holy living: see Woodhead (Abraham)

694    Mount Sion or a treatise shewing to a protestant.
Doway. 1658. ST

Mumford, James: Brief relation, see Brief relation

695    M(umford), J(ames): The catholick scripturist. Gant.
Maximilian Graet. 1662. 8vo. FSL
181137. Wing M 3063

696    Mumford, Joseph (i.e. James): The catholic scripturist. Second edition. London. f.
Matthew Turner. 1686. 12mo. Ware; OS
#611. Wing M 3064

697    Mumford, Joseph (i.e. James): The catholic scrip-
turist. Third edition. (Edinburgh) Holy
Rood House. James Watson. 8vo. 1687.
FSL 150439. Wing M 3065

698    (Mumford, James): The question of questions. By
Optatus Ductor (pseud.) Gant. Maxi-

milian Graet. 1658. 4to. <u>FSL</u>; CN Case
3 A 1997.Wing M 3066

699      (Mumford, James): The question of questions. By
Optatus Ductor (pseud.) n. p. 1686. 4to.
NU 1686 M 96; <u>TU.</u> Wing M 3067

700      Mumford, James: The question of questions. Second
edition. London. Henry Hills f. him and
Matt. Turner. 1686/7. 12mo. <u>Ware</u>; <u>TU</u>;
<u>CN</u> Case 3 A 1998. Wing M 3068

701      (Mumford, James): A remembrance of the living to
pray for the dead. n. p. (St. Omer) 1641.
12mo. <u>L</u> C 26 gg 7; <u>CN</u> Case 3 A 1836.
Wing M 3069

702      (Mumford, James): A remembrance for the living.
By J. M. Second edition. First and funda-
mentall part. Paris. 1660. 8vo. <u>FSL</u>;
<u>TU</u>; <u>Ware</u>; <u>LFS</u>; <u>CN</u> Case 3 A 1999. Wing
M 3070

703      M(umford), J(ames): A remembrance for the living.
The second part and second edition. n. p.
1661. 8vo. <u>LFS</u>; L 4409 b. 55; <u>TU</u>. Wing
M 3071

704      (Mumford, James): A vindication of St. Gregorie his
dialogues. London. Printed f. Jo. Crook.
1660. 4to. 19p. <u>O</u> Pamph. 119 C (34)

     N., M.: see Newport (M.)

705      N., N.: An answer to M. de Rodon's funerall of the
mass. Douay. 1681. 4to. <u>O</u> I c. 149 (2);
<u>Ware</u>; <u>L</u> 3936 aaa 5; <u>TU</u>; <u>CN</u> 3 A 200
(imp. ) Wing N 27

706      N., N.: The Catholick answer to the seeker's request.
London f. John & Thomas Lane. 1687.
4to. 8p. <u>FSL</u> 165111; NU; <u>O</u> Montague
350; <u>L</u> 222 d 14; <u>NN</u> CI p. v. 17 (4). Wing
N 30

707      N., N.: The catholick answer to the seeker's request.
(Edinburgh) Reprinted at Holy Rood House.
1687. 4to. EN Ry. 1. 2. 111 (18). Wing N
31

708      N., N.: The catholick letter to the seeker. n. p.
(London) John Lane. 1688. 4to. 34p.
<u>L</u> 222 d. 14 (11); <u>FSL</u>; <u>NN</u> CI p. v. 17
(15). Wing N 32

     N., N.: Daily exercises: see Nepveu (F.)

     N., N.: Garland of pious and godly songs, see Wadding

N., N.: Instruction to perform, see Instruction
N., N.: Letter concerning, see Jenks (S.)
N., N.: The manner of performing, see Manner
709 N., N.: Old popery as good as new. n.p. 1688. 4to.
19p. L T 763; O Ashm. 1018 (4); Y
Mhc 8. 1688. 01 14; CN Case C 6526.
1693. Wing N 47
710 N., N.: Old popery as good, or rather then new.
n.p. (London) 1688. 4to. 19p. DT
Crofton 107/13 (Anr. issue of preceding
item). Wing N 48
N., N.: Polititians catechism, see French (N.)
N., N.: Treatise of the nature, see Talbot (Peter)
Narrative of the Earl of Clarendon's settlement, see
French (Nich.)
Narrative of the settlement, see French (Nich.)
711 A necessary advice for profitably reading books of
controversie. n.p.d. (1690) 4to. 8p.
OS #2517 A. Wing N 364
Nephew; see Nepveu
712 (Nepveu, Francois): The daily exercises of a christian
life. Paris. (coloph.) Estienne Michallet.
1684. 8vo. This edition has 219 + 5 pp.
L 4409 de 14; Ware; FSL 147093; DAI;
TU; CN Case 3 A 2002. Wing N 33
713 (Nepveu, Francois): The daily exercises of a christian
life. Paris. 1684. 8vo. This ed. has
247 pp. with a separate pagination of 5
pp. between pp. 16 & 17. O Vet E 3 f.
104; TU (variant)
714 (Nepveu, Francois): Daily exercises of a christian
life. The 2. edition. Trans. I.W. of
the Society of Jesus (i.e. Sir John Warner, alias Clare) St. Omers. Ludovicus
Carlier. 1689. LFS
715 Nepveu, (Francois): The method of mental prayer.
Composed...by R.F. Francis Nephew
S.J. (trans. J. Warner, alias Clare)
London (vere St. Omer, ECP) Thomas
Hales. 1694. 12mo. 96p. LFS; Ware; L
843 c.24
Net for the fisher of men, see J. (C.)
New almanack, see Blount (Thomas)
New heresie of the jesuits, see Arnauld (Antoine)

716    New petition of the papists. n. p. (London) 1641. 4to.
           Cap. title 9p. O Pamph. C 42 (4);
           (Another edition of Wing H 3487). Wing
           N 698

717    A new test of the church of England's loyalty. London.
           1687. 4to. 8p. NU 1687 N 53. Wing N
           782

718    A new test of the church of England's loyalty. London
           f. N. T. 1687. 4to. 8p. O Ashm. 1018
           (12 & 15); FSL bd. w. J 180; NN CI p. v.
           4. Wing N 783

719    N(ewport), M(aurice): Ob pacem toti fere christiano
           orbi mediante. Typis Roberti Carnii.
           1679. 4to. (This is 4th edition of following
           item). FSL 180125; L 11408 e 35. Wing
           N 938A

720    N(ewport, M(aurice): Sereniss. principi Carolo
           secundo.. votum candidum. Typis
           Roberti Viti. 1665. 4to. L 11408 e 34.
           Wing N 939

721    Newport, Maurice: Sereniss. principi Carolo secundo..
           votum candidum. Authore Mauritio Neo-
           porto. Editio altera emendantior. Lon-
           dini. Typis Neucomianis. 1669. 4to. FSL
           144376; L C 69 b. 12; CN Y 682 N 475.
           Wing N 939A

722    Newport, Maurice: Sereniss. principi Carolo secundo..
           votum candidum. Authore Mauritio Neo-
           porto. Editio tertia. Londini. 1676. NU
           (Wing N 939B? )

723    Nicodemus his gospel. n. p. 1646. 8vo. 73p. O Vet E
           3 f 160 (Reissue of A &R 572 with the
           preliminaries revised and reset). Pre-
           face is signed J. W. (i. e. John Warrin,
           translator/editor)

724    Nieremberg, John: Of adoration in spirit & truth.
           Trans. R. S. S. I. (i. e. Richard Stange
           S. J. ) n. p. (St. Omers) 1673. 8vo.
           Ware; HP; O 8° P 364 Art. ; TU

725    Nieremberg, Juan: A treatise on the difference betwixt
           the temporal and eternal. (London)
           1672. 8vo. Trans. Sir Vivien Mullineaux.
           Preface signed J. W. (i. e. editor). O
           Vet A 3 e 1237; TU; CN Case 3 A 2003;
           WGT (variant). Wing N 1151

726    No papist nor presbyterian. n. p. 1649. 4to. 6p. C
              Syn. 7. 64. 124 (26) & 7. 64 110 (50).
              Wing N 1185

Non est inventus, see Cressy (H. P. S. )
Non ultra or a letter, see Sergeant (John)

727    (Nouet, Jacques & Annat, Francois): An answer to
              the provinciall letters. Paris. 1659.
              12mo  in 6s. FSL 145136; O Linc. 8°
              B 77 & 130 g. 20; TU; CN Case 3 A 2004.
              Wing N 1414

Nubes testium, see Gother (John)
Nullity of the prelatiqe clergy, see Talbot (Peter)

728    Nuntius a mortuis hoc est stupendum. Londini. Sump-
              tibus R. P. et vaeneunt Parisiis. 1657.
              4to. L E 912 (10). Wing P 1598

729    Nuntius a mortuis: or, a messenger from the dead.
              Trans. G. T. Paris. 1657. 4to. 32p.
              CN Case F 455. 853

730    Nuntius a mortuis hoc est stupendum. Londini. Sump-
              tibus Guil. Palinggenii Rolandi. 1659.
              8vo. 2 parts. 102 + 17 p. TU. Wing P
              1599

731    Entry cancelled

732    O my dear God (incipit) n. d. p. (London, 1679) s. sh.
              L 1850 c 5 (55)

O., N.: see Woodhead (A. )
Observations upon the oath: see Winter (J. )

733    O'Cleary, Michael: Focloir no sansan (Gaelic
              characters) Louvain. 1642. 8vo.
              Walsh #359

734    O'Cleary, Michael: Focloir no sanasan nua. (Gaelic
              characters). Louvain. 1643. 8vo. CN
              Bonaparte 7181; KNY. (See D-K #4056.
              This work is fully described in N&Q,
              3rd series, Vol. 7, p. 415. Issue of 27
              March 1865)

735    (O'Dowley, John): Suim bhunudhasach an teaguisg.
              (Gaelic characters) n. p. (Louvain) 1663.
              8vo in 4s. Walsh #381 (See A &R p. 53);
              L 1018 h. 10; CN Bonaparte 7206

Of devotion: see Sergeant (J. )
Of faith necessary to salvation: see Walker (O. )
Of the all-sufficient external proposer: see Smith (R. )
Of the distinction of fundamentall: see Smith (R. )

736     An office in time of affliction. n. p. 1681. 8vo. 95p.
          OS #2564
737     Office of the B. V. Mary. London. Henry Hills. 1687.
          16mo. L 3355 a. 27; OM. Wing O 149
738     The office of the holy week. Paris. Printed by the
          widow Chrestien. 1670. Dedication
          signed W. K. B. (Walter Kirkham Blount? ?)
          8vo. FSL; L 3356 b. 28; TU; CN Case 3
          A 2098. (This is the first ed. of Wing C
          5648). Wing O 150
739     Office of the holy week. n. p. 1687. 8vo. Wing O 151
740     Office of the holy week. London. Henry Hills. 1688.
          24$^o$. (ed. B. L. ) L 3366 de 21; Ware;
          LGL
741     Officium B. Mariae virginis nuper reformatum. Lon-
          dini. Typis Henrici Hills. (1687).16$^o$.
          OS; L 1018 b. 7; CN Case 2 A 123. Wing
          O 154
        Old popery as good as new, see N. N.
742     O'Molloy, Francis: Grammatica latino-hibernica.
          (text in Latin and Gaelic) Roma. Ex
          typographia S. Cong. de Propag. 1677.
          12mo. Walsh #425; L 628 a 22 & G 971
743     O'Molloy, Francis: Lucerna fidelium seu fasciculus.
          Roma. Typis Sacrae cong. de propaganda
          fide. 1676. 8vo. (Latin & Gaelic text.
          2nd tp in Gaelic) Walsh 424; L G 4770;
          CN; NU TL 43 M 72; CN Case 4 A 1858
744     O'Molloy, Francis: Lucerna fidelium seu fasciculus.
          Romae. Typis sacrae congregationis de
          Propanda (sic) fide. 1686. 8vo. O 8$^o$
          delta 21 BS
745     Ordo baptizandi aliaque sacramenta administrandi...
          pro Anglia, Hibernia, & Scotia. Parisiis.
          Per Ludovicum de la Fosse. 1657. 24$^o$
          in 8s. O 8$^o$ Z 77 Art. BS & Douce S 319;
          L 1018 a 7; OS; TU; CN Case 2 A 125
746     Ordo baptizandi aliaque sacramenta administrandi.
          Londini. Hen. Hills. 1686. Sixes. Ware;
          OS #2579; FSL 157696; O Crynes 43 &
          Douce BB 36 & Vet A 3 f. 430; TU. Wing
          O 416
747     Ordo baptizandi aliaque sacramenta administrandi...
          pro Anglia, Hibernia & Scotia. Parisiis.
          Per Ludovicum de la Fosse. 1687. DAI

748    O'Sheill, James: An answer to the challenge. 2 parts.
n.p. 1699. 8vo. O Vet L 3 f. 4

Owen, Hugh: see Hughes (John)

749    P., B.: An answer to the most materiall parts of
Dr. Hammond's book. London. 1654.
4to. 28p. O Pamph. 99 C; L 108 d 36.
Wing P 5

750    P., E.: A letter to both houses of parliament. Paris.
1679. 4to. 14p. Y (incomplete); OS
#2592. Wing P 19

751    P., F., Philopater: The nurse of pious thoughts.
Douay. 1652. 24°. Ware; L 3936 a 11;
NU. Wing P 21

752    P., F., Philopater: Prayer to saints vindicated.
Paris. 1652. Twelves. Ware

P., F.: see Gage (John)

P., F.P.M.O.: i.e. Fr. P.M. Order of Preachers,
see Collins (Wm.)

P., I.W.: i.e. John Wilson, priest q.v.

753    P., J.: Truth manifested or a short discourse. Doway.
L.K. (Kellam??) 1655. 12mo. 61p. OS
#639

754    (P., L.): The right religion evinced. By L.B. Paris.
1652. 12mo. HP (The initials L.P. are
used since the 1658 ed. was signed thus.)

755    P., L.: The right religion, reviewed and enlarged.
Paris. 1658. 12mo. BUTE; CN Case 2 A
124

756    P., T.: Reason regulated or brief reflections. (London) 1675. 8vo. 74p. NU. Wing P 117

757    (P.), W.: A manifest touching Mr. M.W.F. (sic. F
is here an obvious mistake for P. See
9 RH 74. No. 12.) ed. H.P. brother of
author. n.p. 1650. 8vo. ST

Palmer, Roger: see Castlemaine

Papist misrepresented: see Gother (J.)

Papists protesting: see Gother (J.)

758    (Parlor, John): Pious instructions in meeter. Preface signed B. Leo of M. Magdalene
(name in religion). n.p. (Doway.
Michael Mairesse) 1693. 8vo in 4s. O
Vet E 3 f. 130; (See 24 CRS 279 for
author.) Wing L 1097

759    (Parlor, John): The second nativity of Jesus. Trans.
John Weldon of Ruffin. Antwerp by

T. N. f. the author. 1686. Ware; O
Antiq. e B 1686/1; LGL

Parsons, Robert: see Persons

760 A pastoral letter from the four Catholic bishops.
(Coloph.) London. Henry Hills. 1688.
Cap. title. 4to. 8p. Ware; THC; O Tan-
ner MS f. 143; NN C.I. p.v. 22 (19);
CN Case 4 A 1859; TU; NC; Y Mhc8.14.
24. Wing P 675

761 A pastoral letter from the four Catholic bishops. Holy
Rood house, reprinted by Mr. P.B.
1688. 4to. 8p. EN Ry 1.6.144. Wing L
1940A

A pastoral letter: see Bossuet

762 (Patteson): Jerusalem and Babel or the image of
both churches. Second edition. By P.
D.M. n.p. 1653. 12mo. L 874 d 19;
TU. Wing P 868

763 (Patteson): Jerusalem and Babel or the image.
Second edition reviewed and corrected.
London. 1653. NU; OS #630; O 8° C 251
Linc. (For authorship see A&R 599).
Wing P 869

Paul of St. Magdalen: see Heath (H.)
Paul of St. Ubald: see Brown (S.)
Pax vobis: see G. (E.)
The penitent bandito: see Biondo (G.)
Penn, Wm.: Reasons why, see title
Pensez-y bien: see Barry (P. de)
Perpetual crosse or passion: see Andries (J.)
Perrinchief, R.: see Messenger from the dead &
Nuntius a mortuis

764 Persall, John: A sermon preach'd before the king
and queen...Oct. 25, 1685. London.
Henry Hills. 1686. 4to. 25p. NU 1686
E 47; TU. Wing P 1652

765 Persall, John: A sermon preached before the king
and queen...May 30, 1686. London.
Henry Hills. 1686. 4to. 29p. TU; NU
1686 E 47. Wing P 1651

766 Persons, Robert: A christian directory. n.p. 1650.
8vo. OS #2652; THC; O Vet B 3 f. 294;
TU; CN Case 3 A 2008. Wing P 563

767 Persons, Robt.: A christian directory. n.p. 1660.
8vo. O G. 8. Linc. (Reissue of the 1650

ed. with a new tp.) Wing P 564

768    Persons, R.: A christian directory. n. p. 1673. 8vo.
       OS #665; <u>TU</u>; <u>CN</u> Case 3 A 2009; HP.
       Wing P 565

769    Persons, R.: A christian directory. London. Henry
       Hills f. him and Matt. Turner. 1687.
       8vo. OS #666; <u>TU</u>

770    Persons, R.: A christian directory. London. 1696.
       8vo. <u>LFS</u>; BN; <u>TU</u>; Y; LSC. Wing P 566

771    (Persons, R.): A treatise of three conversions of
       England. The first two parts. By N. D.
       London. Reprinted by Henry Hills. 1688.
       Fol. <u>L</u> 1487 K 16; FSL; <u>WGT</u>; OS #667;
       <u>TU</u>; <u>CN</u> 6 A 337. Wing P 575

772    Peter of Alcantara, (St.): Pax animo. A short treatise.
       Trans. T. W. Paris. 1665. CHEL. Wing
       P 1680

773    Petre, William: The declaration of Lord Petre. Lon-
       don. By T. B. f. R. Mead. 1684. s. sh.
       <u>FSL</u> 137015. Wing P 1877

       Philalethus: see Reply to the two answers
       Philo: see Abbot (J.)
       Philopater: see P. (F.)
       Philopenes: see Huddleston (J.)
       Philotheus: see Reflections

774    (Pinckney, Miles): Occasionall discourses by Thomas
       Carre (pseud.).. as also an answer to a
       libell... by Thomas Vane. Paris. 1646.
       8vo. 2 parts. OS #149 (1st part only);
       <u>O</u> 100 c. 90. Wing P 2272

775    (Pinckney, Miles): Pietas parisiensis or a short
       description. By Thomas Carre (pseud.)
       Paris. Vincent du Moutier. 1666. 12mo.
       <u>FSL</u> 141967; OS #150. Wing P 2273

       (Pinckney, Miles): Pietas romana, see Amydenus

776    (Pinckney, Miles): A proper looking glasse for the
       daughters of Sion. By Thomas Carre.
       Paris. 1665. 12mo. 288p. <u>FSL</u> 142521;
       <u>O</u> 1. g. 62. Wing P 2274

777    (Pinckney, Miles): A proper looking glasse. By
       Thomas Carre. Paris. 1665. 12mo.
       292 p. <u>Ware</u>; <u>CN</u> 3 A 2012

778    (Pinckney, Miles): Spiritual exercise according to
       the custom of Windesem.. Englished
       by Thomas Carre. Paris. 1657. 12mo.

95 p. <u>CN</u> Case 3 A 2104 ( - tp); SN
(Pinckney wrote a good deal of this book.)

779    (Pinckney, Miles): Sweete thoughts of Jesus and Marie. By Thomas Carre. Paris. 1658. 12mo. 3 parts. <u>CS</u> U. 7. 27; <u>Ware</u>; <u>TU</u>. Wing P 2275

780    (Pinckney, Miles): Sweet thoughts of Jesus and Marie. Paris. Vincent du Moutier. 1665. 8vo. 2 parts. <u>FSL</u> 145892; <u>O</u> l. b. 46; <u>Ware</u> (imp.). Wing P 2276

781    A pious collection of severall profitable directions. Douay. M. Mairesse. n. d. (1684) 18°. O Antiq. f. F. 1684/1 (Wm. Warren signs preface and was probably author or compiler. See 14 CRS 164 n.)

782    Pious exercise of devotion to the sacred passion. London. 1688. 12mo. DE

783    Pious exercise of devotion to the sacred passion. London. Henry Hills. n. d. (1686?) 12mo. 47p. <u>OS</u> #838

Pious instructions in meeter: see Parlor (J.)
Pius IV: His profession of faith, see Gother (J.)

784    The plain-man's answer to his country parson's admonition. London. Henry Hills. 1686. 12mo. 22p. <u>O</u> Ashm. 1330. Wing P 2263

785    Plessington, William: The speech of. n. p. d. (1679) s. sh. <u>O</u> Wood 425 (10); <u>TU</u>. Wing P 2567

786    (Plunket, Oliver): Jus primatiale: or, the ancient right. Asserted by O. A. T. H. P. (i. e. <u>O</u>liverus <u>A</u>rmachanus <u>t</u>otius <u>H</u>iberniae <u>p</u>rimatus) n. p. Printed in the year 1672. 8vo. 75p. DT MM. 00. 25; L G 5511. Wing P 2623

787    (Plunket, Oliver): The last speech of... written by his own hand. (coloph.) London. N. Thompson. 1681. fol. 4 p. cap. title. <u>CN</u> Case f J 5454. 2644; L T 1* (81). Wing D 2626

The polititians catechism: see French (N.)
Poor man's mite: see Batt
Pope Pius his profession of faith: see Gother (J.)

788    Popery anatomis' d in a letter to a friend, n. d. p. (c. 1686) 4to. Wing P 2920A

789      Popery anatomis'd in a letter to a friend. n.p. 1686.
           4to. 11p. <u>FSL</u> bd. w. S 5562

790      Popery anatomis'd, or, the papists clear'd. n.p.
           1686. 4to. 16p. OS #2715; <u>FSL</u> 154783;
           <u>Y</u> Mhc8. 14. 24; <u>CN</u> Case C 64. 711.
           Wing P 2921

        Pope's supremacy asserted: see Gother (J.)

791      Pora, Charles: A sovereign balsom to cure the
           languishing diseases of this corrupt age.
           n.p. (Brussels) 1678. 8vo. <u>L</u> 4405 d. 33.

792      Pora, C.: A sovereign balsom. n.p. (London) 1679.
           8vo. 3 parts. (Parts 2 & 3 have imprint,
           "London. 1677") <u>O</u> 1419 f. 2077

        Practical discourses: see Jenks (S.)
        Practice of devotion: see Woodhead (A.)

793      Prayers, &... Our help standeth in the name of the
           Lord. n.d.p. 4to-sized brds. (c. 1689);
           <u>TU</u>

        Presbyteries triall: see Walker (J.)

794      The primer more ample and in a new order (ed.
           Thomas Fitzsimon) Rouen. David
           Maurry. 1669. 12mo. in 6s. <u>O</u> Antiq.
           f. F. 1669. 1; <u>TU</u>; <u>Y</u> Mzd 45 H 6. 1673 B;
           <u>CN</u> Case 3 A 2014. Wing P 3461

795      The primer more ample. (ed. Thomas Fitzsimon)
           Rouen. Nicholas Le Tourneur. 1684.
           Sixes. Hoskins #284; <u>O</u> Vet E 3 f. 40.
           Wing P 3462

796      The primer more ample and in a new order. (Ed.
           Thomas Fitzsimon) Reviewed and cor-
           rected by P. R. Rouen. N. Le Turner.
           1700. 12mo. <u>L</u> 3306 a 50. Hoskins
           #288

797      The primer or office of the blessed virgin. Antworpe.
           Widow of John Cnobbaert f. Jas. Thomp-
           son. 1650. 12mo. Hoskins #280; <u>C</u> Rel.
           e 65. 8; <u>TU</u>; ST. Wing P 3464

798      Primer or office of the blessed virgin. St. Omers.
           1651. 12mo. <u>L</u> (Not catalogued Feb.
           1966)

799      The primer or office of the blessed virgin. Antwerpe
           Balthasar Moret. 1658. 12mo. in 6s.
           Hoskins #281; <u>C</u> G. 6. 52; <u>TU.</u> Wing P
           3465

800     Primer or office of the blessed virgin. S. Omers.
               1673. 12mo. O 8° R 138 Th; Hoskins
               #283. Wing P 2466

801     The primer, or office of the blessed virgin. S.
               Omers. 1685. 12mo. CN Case 3 A 2015

802     The primer or office of the blessed virgin. Antwerp
               f. T. D. 1685. 12mo. O Vet B. 3 f. 139;
               L 3355 aa 31; TU. Wing P 3467

803     The primer, or, office of the blessed virgin. n. p. 1699.
               12mo. Hoskins #288; Ware; TU; CN
               Case 3 A 2016

803A    The primer or three offices of the B. virgin Mari.
               Rouen. n. d. 8vo. LGL

804     Primitive christian discipline not to be slighted.
               n. p. 1658. 8vo. TU. Wing P 3469

The primitive fathers no protestants: see Gother (J. )

805     The primitive rule before the reformation. Antwerp.
               1663. 4to. 2 parts. 56 + 56 p. O 4° L
               69 Th. Wing P 3471

806     The primitive rule of reformation. London. Mary
               Thompson. 1688. 4to. 40p. L 3477
               c. 40; NU 1687 H 52; TU. Wing P 3472

Principles and rules of the Gospel:  see Gother (J. )

Protestancy condemned:  see Wilson (M. )

807     Protestancy destitute of scripture proofs. (Coloph. )
               London. Henry Hills. 1687. 4to. 11 p.
               Cap. title. FSL 13307; NN CI p. v. 22;
               CN Case 4 A 1861. Wing P 3817

808     Protestancy destitute of scripture proofs.  Edinburgh.
               Reprinted by James Watson. 1687. 4to.
               Wing P 3818

Protestancy without principles:  see Worsley (E. )

The protestant's plain confession:  see Smith (R. )

The protestant's plea for the socinian:  see Gother (J. )

809     The psalmes of David translated from the vulgat.
               n. p. (St. Germaine) 1700. 12mo. 347p.
               (Trans. E. or John Caryll) TU; CN
               Case 3 A 1833. Wing B 2621 = B 2628?

810     The psalmes of David translated from the vulgat.
               n. p. (St. Germaine) 1700. 12mo. 374
               p. (anr. issue of the preceding without
               the printer's device on the tp and with
               errata leaves placed after the text. )
               TU; CN Case 3 A 1861

811        Pugh, Robert: Blacklo's cabal. Second ed. n.p.
                  (Liege. Peter Danthez) 1680. 4to.
                  LFS. Wing P 4186

812        (Pugh, Robert): Elenchus elenchi, sive animadver-
                  siones. Autore R.P. Parisiis ('vere
                  London). 1664. 8vo. 61 p. CN Case 3
                  A 2018; L 599 c.17; NU

        Pugh, Robert: see Castlemaine
        Pulpit sayings: see Gother (J.)

813        (Pulton, Andrew): A full and clear exposition of the
                  protestant rule of faith. n.p.d. (London,
                  c. 1687) 4to. cap. title. 20 p. OC I B
                  55 (3); Y Mhc 8.9 & Mhc 8.14.24; NN.
                  Wing P 4205

814        (Pulton, Andrew): A full and clear exposition. Lon-
                  don. Mary Thompson. 1688. 4to. 20 p.
                  FSL 197181. Wing P 4206

815        Pulton, Andrew: Remarks of. London. Nathaniel
                  Thompson. 1687. 4to. 42p. L T 1878
                  (4); Y Mhc 8.9; LFS. Wing P 4207

816        Pulton, Andrew: Some reflections upon the author
                  and licenser. London. Mary Thompson..
                  to be sold by Matthew Turner & John
                  Lane. 1688. 4to. 14p. L T 1839 (3);
                  LFS; O Z Jur. 26 4°; Y Mhc 8. 1688
                  P 97; NN CI p.v.9; CN Case 4 A 1862.
                  Wing P 4208

817        Pulton, Andrew: A total defeat of the protestant
                  rule of faith. n.p.d. (c. 1681) 4to.
                  31p. OS #2766

818        (Pulton, Andrew): A true and full account of a con-
                  ference. London. Nathaniel Thompson.
                  1687. 4to. 18p. LFS; O Linc C.11.7(5);
                  TU; Y Mhc 8. 1687. P 97. Wing P 4209

        Purgatory survey'd: see Binet (E.)
        Questions propounded: see Spenser (J.)
        Querees propounded: see French (N.)
        Q. Why are you a Catholick?: see Cressy (S.)
        R., C.: see Smith (R.)
        R., F.J.: see Reed (F.J.)

819        R., T.: A letter from a gentleman to his friend.
                  n.p. 1660. Sixes. 50p. L C 38 a 41 (5).
                  Wing R 86

        R., W.: see Rowlands (W.)
        Rapin, René: The spirit of christianity, see title

A rational account of the doctrine: see Woodhead (A.)

820 A rational discourse concerning prayer. n.p. 1669.
8vo. TU. Wing R 302

A rational discourse concerning transubstantiation:
see Hutchinson (W.)

Reason against raillery: see Sergeant (J.)

Reason and authority: see Basset (J.)

Reason and religion: see Worsley (E.)

Reason for religion: see Tichbourne (H.)

821 Reasons why Roman-catholicks should not be per-
secuted. n.p.d. (London, c. 1661) 4to.
cap. title. 8 p. O Pamph. 166 C (42);
FSL. (Sometimes attributed to Wm.
Penn). Wing R 586

822 Reasons why the church of England as well as the
dissenters should make their address
of thanks. London. Henry Hills. 1687.
4to. 12 p. LFS. Wing R 587

The reclaimed papist: see Canes (J.)

823 Recusancy justified in a dialogue. Antwerp. Balthasar
Moret. 1658. 8vo. 71 p. OC N.7.12.
Allestree. (Hiscock R 655 + makes
this 1678, but the tp is clipped and the
better reading is 1658.)

824 (Reed, F.J.): Animadversions by way of answer to
a sermon..by Dr. Thomas Kenne.
London f. Nat. Thompson. 1687. 4to.
22 p. OS #2792; FSL 181688; L 1497
c 32 (10); Y Mhc 8.14.24. Wing R 665

825 (Reed, Thomas): An answer to a book. By R.T.
Paris. 1654. 12mo. OS #870; O Linc.
8° C 185. Wing T 42

825A Reflections upon bulls of the popes. Preface signed
Philotheus. n.p. 1686. 4to. 12 p. NU
1686 + R 32. Wing R 719

Reflections upon the answer: see Gother (J.)

826 Reflections upon the bulls of the popes. Preface
signed Philotheus. n.p. 1686. 4to.
12 p. FSL bd. w. S5562; CN Case 4
A 1863

Reflexions upon the oaths of supremacy and allegiance:
see Cressy (S.)

827 (Reilly, Hugh): Ireland's case briefly stated. n.p.
1695. 12mo. Walsh #458; L 601 d. 15
& G 4789; DT A.2.14. Wing R 767

The religion of Martin Luther:  see Deane (T. )

828  Remarks on the several sanguinary and penal laws.
London. Henry Hills. 1687. 4to. 24p.
<u>Ware.</u>  Wing R 936

Remembrance of the living: see Mumford (J. )

Reply to the answer of the amicable accomodation:
see Gother (J. )

Reply to the answer made upon three royal papers:
see Leyburn (J. )

A reply to the answer of the catholique apology: see
Castlemaine

A reply to the defence:  see Johnston (H. J. )

829  A reply to the two answers of the new test. London.
1687. 4to. 13p. OS #2658 B; <u>NN</u> CI
p. v. 4. (signed "Philalethus"). Wing
R 1083

830  A request to protestants to produce plain scriptures.
(Coloph. ) London. Henry Hills. 1686.
4to. 4 p. cap. title. <u>NN</u> CI p. v. 22 (3).
Wing R 1119

831  , Resolutions of a penitent soul. Holy Rood House.
By James Watson. 1687. 12mo. 34p.
<u>O</u> 138 g. 315. Wing R 1165

832  Ribadeneira, Peter:  The live of saints. Trans.
W. P. (i. e. Wm. Petre) S. Omers.
Ioachim Carlier. 1669. fol. <u>O</u> Douce
R subst. 12; <u>TU;</u> <u>CN</u> Case 6 A 338
(imp. ). Wing R 1545

833  Richelieu, Armand duPlessis Cardinal duc de:  The
instruction of a christian. Published
by... R. H. S. Kilkenny. 1647. 8vo.
ST RP 3. 49

834  Richelieu, Cardinal:  A christian instruction. The
30. edition. Trans. Thos. Carre
(i. e. Miles Pinckney). Paris. 1562
(i. e. 1662) 12mo. <u>O</u> Antiq. f. F 1662. 1;
<u>Ware;</u> <u>CN</u> Case 3 A 2023. Wing R 1417

The right religion evinced:  see P. (L. )

Rivers, J. A.:  see Abbot (J. )

Rochester, earl of:  see D. (B. )

835  Rodriguez, Alphonsus:  The practice of christian
perfection. First part. London (<u>vere</u>
ECP St. Omer) Thomas Hales. 1697.
4to. OS #754; FSL; <u>TU;</u> <u>CN</u> 4 A 1864.
Wing R 1772

836       Rodriguez, Alphonsus: The practice of christian
                    perfection. The second part. London
                    (vere ECP St. Omer) Thomas Hales.
                    1698. 4to. WGT; TU; CN Case 4 A 1864

837       Rodriguez, Alphonsus: The practice of christian and
                    religious perfection. Third part. London
                    (vere ECP St. Omer) Thomas Hales.
                    1699. 4to. WGT; TU; CN Case 4 A 1864

Roman catholick doctrine: see Cressy (S.)

The roman church's devotions: see Woodhead (A.)

838       The roman church vindicated and M S convicted.
                    London f. the author. 1674. 8vo. HP;
                    L 1352 a. 3

The roman doctrine of repentance: see Woodhead
            (A.)

The roman martyrologe: see Keynes (G.)

839       (Rowlands, William): The late act of convocation at
                    Oxford examined. By W. R. Rouen (vere
                    Oxford, H. Hall. See Madan II, #2188)
                    1652. 12mo. O Th 8° L 108. Wing R
                    2075

The royall apologie: see Digby (K.)

840       The rules of the schools at the Jesuits in Fenchurch
                    street. London f. F. W. n. d. (c. 1687)
                    Brds. O Ashm. F. 1 (4)

841       The rules of the schools at the Savoy. London. Henry
                    Hills. 1687. London. brds. Wing R
                    2259A

842       The rules of the schools of the royal colledge. Holy
                    Rood house by Mr. P. B. 1688. brds.
                    Wing R 2260

843       The rules of the society of Jesus. S. Omers. Joachim
                    Carlier. 1670. 12mo. LFS; ST

844       Rushworth, William: The dialogues of. Paris. John
                    Mestais. 1648. Sixes. L 3936 a 10; TU.
                    Wing R 2338A = W 1819

845       Rushworth, Wm.: Rushworth's dialogues. Or the
                    judgement of common sence in the choyce
                    of religion. Last edition, corrected and
                    enlarg'd by Thomas White. Paris. Jean
                    Billaine. 1654. 8vo. OS #761; FSL; TU
                    (This ed. has 280 p. and is 14. 2 cm
                    high.) Wing R 2338B = W 1820

846       Rushworth, Wm.: Rushworth's dialogues. Or, the
                    judgement of common sence in the choice

of religion. The last edition, corrected and inlarg'd by Thomas White. Paris. Jean Billaine. 1654. Sixes. <u>LFS</u>; <u>Ware</u> (This ed. has 249 p. and is 12.6 cm. high.)

S., F.W.: see Walker (J.)

847    S., I.: An invitation of a seeker. London. 1670. 8vo. <u>Ware</u>; L 4403 b. 54; <u>NU</u> 1670 I 62; <u>CN</u> Case 3 A 2026. Wing S 40

848    Entry cancelled

S., J.: see Sergeant (J.)
        see Sharpe (J.)

S., J.: i.e. Symonds, Jos., see Lobb (E.)

S., J.: see Brown (Ignatius)

849    (S., J.): Exercise of the love of God. (Preface signed J.S. i.e. trans.?) 1667. (Newdigate)

S., R.: see Strange (R.)

850    (Sabran, Lewis): An answer to Dr. Sherlock's preservative against popery. London. Henry Hills. 1688. 4to. 8 p. OS #2826; <u>FSL</u> 159279; <u>LFS</u>; <u>CN</u> Case 4 A 1865. Wing S 214

851    Sabran, Lewis: The challenge of. (Coloph.) London. Henry Hills. 1688. 4to. Cap. title. 8 p. OS #2827; <u>L</u> 222 e 8. Wing S 215

852    (Sabran, Lewis): Dr. Sherlock sifted from his bran and chaff. London. Henry Hills. 1687. 4to. 28 p. <u>OC</u> I B 55 (5); <u>FSL</u> bd. w. H 3257; <u>TU</u>; <u>Y</u> Mhc8.14.24. Wing S 216

853    (Sabran, Lewis): Dr. Sherlock's preservative. London. Henry Hills. 1688. 4to. 88p. OS #2828; <u>LFS.</u> Wing S 217

854    Sabran, Lewis: A letter to a peer of the church of England. London. Henry Hills. 1687. 4to. 10p. OS #2829; <u>L</u> T 1883 (4); <u>TU</u>; <u>NN</u> CI p.v. 17 (5). Wing S 218

855    Sabran, Lewis: A letter to Dr. Wm. Needham. London. Henry Hills. 1688. 4to. 23 p. <u>FSL</u> 160018; <u>L</u> T 1883 (14); <u>OC</u> Wb 6.12. Pamph.; OS #2830; <u>NN</u> CI p.v. 17 (10). Wing S 219

856    Sabran, Lewis: A reply of. (Coloph.) London. Henry Hills. 1687. 4to. 8 p. Cap. title. <u>L</u> T 1883 (10*); OS #2831. Wing S 220

Sabran, Lewis: Seasonable address, see Alanson (J.)

857     Sabran, Lewis: A sermon preached before the King.
(28 Aug. 1687). London. Henry Hills.
1687. 4to. 33p. Y Mhc 8.14.24; L 114 f.
61. Wing S 221

858     Sabran, Lewis: A sermon preach'd... December 4,
1687. London. Henry Hills. 1687. 4to.
Hiscock S 221 +; HP

Sad condition of a distracted kingdom: see Abbot
(John)

859     (Sadler, Thomas Vincent): The childes catechism.
Paris (vere London) 1678. Fours. 49p.
O Wood 813. Wing C 3875

Sadler, T.V.: The Holy desires of death, see Lallemant

Sadler, T.V.: see Crowther, Arthur Anselm

860     Saint Jure, John Baptist: The holy life of Monr De
Renty. Trans. E.S. London f. John
Crook. 1658. 8vo. O Wood 301; TU; CN
Case 3 A 2028. Wing S 334

861     S(aint) Jure, John Baptist: The holy life of Monsieur
De Renty. Trans. E.S. London f. Ben-
jamin Tooke. 1684. 8vo. FSL 144173;
TU. Wing S 335

St. Peter's supremacy: see Clenche (Wm.)

862     Savanorola, Hierome: The felicity of a christian life.
n.p. (London. R. Daniel) 1651. 12mo.
78p. CN Case 3 A 2031. Wing S 779

863     Savanorola, Hierome: The verity of christian faith.
London. R. Daniel. 1651. 12mo. HP;
CN 3 A 2032. Wing S 781

864     Scarisbrick, Edward: Catholick loyalty. London f.
R. Booker. 1688. 4to. 25p. Ware; O
Ms. Ashm. 745; NU. Wing S 824

865     (Scarisbrick, Edward): The life of lady Warner.
London (vere ECP, St. Omer) Thomas
Hales. 1691. 8vo. LFS; FSL 199222;
L 862 e.26. Wing C 574

866     (Scarisbrick, Edward): The life of Lady Warner.
Second edition. London (vere St. Omer,
ECP) Thomas Hales. 1692. 8vo. WGT
(imp.); OS #2851; TU; CN Case 3 A
1858. Wing C 575

867     (Scarisbrick, Edward): The life of lady Warner.
Third edition. London (vere St. Omer,

ECP) Thomas Hales. 1696. 8vo. <u>OS.</u>
Wing C 576

868    Scarisbrick, Edward: Sermon preached before...the
Queen dowager...13th Sunday after
Pentecost. London f. Matthew Turner.
1686. 4to. 37p. <u>NU</u> 1686 E 47 (14); <u>FSL</u>
128460. Wing 825

869    Schelstrate, Emmanuel à: A dissertation concerning
patriarchal and metropolitical authority.
London f. Matthew Turner. 1688. 4to.
OS #2854; <u>O</u> Z Jur. 33. 4; <u>TU</u>; <u>Y</u> Mhc
8. 14. 24. Wing S 859

Schism dis-arm'd: see Sergeant (John)
Schism dispach't: see Sergeant (John)
Schisme of the church of England: see Spencer (John)
Scisme unmask't: see Spenser (John)

870    Sclater, Ed.: Consensus veterum or the reasons of.
London. Henry Hills f. him and Matt.
Turner. 1686. 4to. <u>LW</u> P.P. 7. 48. 4
(1); <u>Ware</u>; OS #2856; <u>TU.</u> Wing S 910

Scolding no scholarship: see Con (Alexander)

871    Scot, Philip: A treatise of the schism of England.
Amsterdam (<u>vere</u> London) 1650. 12s.
<u>HP</u>; <u>O</u> Mason E 12 & Wood 772; OS #782;
<u>TU.</u> Wing S 942

872    (Scupoli, Lorenzo): The christian pilgrim in his conflict and conquest. Paris. 1652. 12mo.
2 parts (i. e. Scupoli's Spiritual Combat
+ Crowther-Sadler's Spiritual Conquest)
<u>O</u> Mason AA 200; <u>L</u> 699 a 29; OS #154;
<u>TU;</u> <u>CN</u> Case 3 A 1862 & 1863 ( - tp. ).
1 Wing C 1218

873    (Scupoli, L. ): The spiritual combat. Trans. R(obt.)
R(eade). 2 parts (2nd part = Letter of
Eucherius to Valerian). Paris. 1656.
16° in 8s. <u>L</u> 1121 d. 10; <u>Ware</u>; <u>TU;</u> <u>CN</u>
Case 2 A 118. 1 Wing C 1218A

874    (Scupoli, L. ): The spiritual conflict. Second edition.
Paris. 1652. 8vo. <u>LGL;</u> OS. 1 Wing C
1219

Seasonable address to the church of England: see
Alanson (John)
Seasonable discourse: see Gother (John)
Second Catholic letter: see Sergeant (John)

Second and third treatises of.. Church government:
see Woodhead (A.)

875 A second letter to a dissenter upon occasion of his
majesties late gracious declaration.
London f. John Harris. 1687. 4to. 18 p.
FSL bd. w. J 189. Wing H 321

The second nativity of Jesus: see Parlor, John

876 Seek and you shall find: or, a search. London. Henry
Hills. 1685. 4to. Wing S 2407

877 Seek and you shall find, or, a search. London. Henry
Hills. 1686. 4to. 26p. FSL 142633; Ware;
CN C 68. 405; Y Mhc 8. 14. 26. Wing S
2408

878 A seekers request to catholick priests. London. f.
J. F. 1687. 4to. 8p. FSL 128842; NN
CI p. v. 17 (12); HP. Wing S 2411

879 A seekers request to catholick priests. Reprinted at
Holy Rood house. 1687. 4to. 8p. EN
Ry 1. 2. 111 (18). Wing S 2412

880 (Sergeant, John): Errour non-plust. n. p. 1673. 4s.
FSL 140418; CS Gg 18. 33; L 4103 bb 4;
CN Case 3 A 2037. Wing S 2565

881 (Sergeant, John): Faith vindicated. Louain. 1667.
8vo. OS #792; O 8° A 66 Linc.; FSL
157120; TU; CN Case 3 A 2033. Wing
S 2566

882 Sergeant, John: The fifth catholick letter. London.
Matthew Turner. 1688. 4to. FSL 136607;
NU 1688 S 48 (5); NN CI p. v. 20. Wing
S 2567

883 Sergeant, John: Five catholick letters. London.
Mat. Turner. 1688. 4to. 5 parts. OS
#794; O 4° Z 34 Jur; TU; NU. Wing S
2568

884 Sergeant, John: The fourth catholick letter. London.
Matthew Turner. 1688. 4to. 35p. FSL
bd. w. S 5602; Y Mhc8. 1688 Se 66; NN
CI p. v. 20; NU. Wing S 2569

885 S(ergeant), J(ohn): Ideae cartesianae ad Lydium.
Londinii. Venum prostant apud Abelem
Roper & Thomam Leigh & Thomam
Metcalf. 1698. 8vo. L 1133 b. 8; OS
#2884. Wing S 2571

Sergeant, J.: Jesuits reasons, see title

886      (Sergeant, John): A letter from the author of Sure-
Footing. n. p. 1665. 8vo. 24p. Hiscock
S 2574⁺⁺ OS #2885; OC I. 1. 7. 9 Main

887      (Sergeant, John): A letter of thanks from the author
of Sure-Footing. Paris. 1666. 8vo. OS
#795; O 12 Theta 1827. Wing S 2575

888      (Sergeant, John): A letter to the continuator. (coloph.)
London. Matthew Turner. 1688. 4to.
Cap. title. 16 p. OC Pamph. Wb 6. 12.
(imp.); L 906 K 13. Wing S 2576

889      (Sergeant, John): A letter to the D. of P. London.
Henry Hills. 1687. 4to. 36p. FSL bd.
w. S 5602; L T 1886 (7); OS #2886; O
Ashm. 1015; NU. (This was later re-
issued as the first item in S 2568).
Wing S 2577

890      (Sergeant, John): The method to arrive at satisfaction
in religion. n. p. d. (London. 1671). 12mo.
in 6s. 37p. O Wood 869 (3); L 1471 a.
36; Yale Mhc9 Se 66 M 4; TU. Wing S
2578

891      (Sergeant, John): The method to science. By J. S.
London. Printed by W. Redmayne f.
the author & are to be sold by Thomas
Metcalf. 1696. 8vo. OS #796; FSL
135818; NU. Wing S 2579

892      S(ergeant), J(ohn): Non ultra, or, a letter. London
f. A. Roper. 1698. 12mo. FSL 147098;
OS #797; L 3935 aa 11; NU. Wing S 2585

893      S(ergeant), J(ohn): Of devotion. n. p. (London) 1678
12mo. L 4410 g. 47; Wing S 2585A

894      Sergeant, John: Raillery defeated by calm reason.
London f. D. Brown.. & A. Roper. 1699.
12mo. L 526 g. 21; Y Mhc9 Se 66 R 3.
Wing S 2586

895      (Sergeant, John): Reason against raillery. n. p.
(London) 1672. 8vo. L FSL 161373; O
8° N 87 Th; TU; CN 3 A 2035. Wing S
2587

896    (Sergeant, John): Schism dis-arm'd. By S. W. Paris.
          M. Blageart. 1655. 8vo. FSL; OS #800;
          TU; CN Case 3 A 2038. Wing S 2589
897    (Sergeant, John): Schism dispach't or a rejoynder.
          n. p. 1657. 8vo. FSL 142237; OS #801;
          L E 1555; TU. Wing S 2590
898    (Sergeant, John): The second catholick letter. London.
          Matthew Turner. 1687. 4to. 80p. FSL
          bd. w. S 5602. NN CI p. v. 20; NU. Wing
          S 2592
899    (Sergeant, John): The sixth catholick letter. n. p. d.
          (London. 1688) 4to. cap. title. 42p. L
          222 e 6; TU; NU. Wing S 2593
900    S(ergeant), J(ohn): Solid philosophy asserted. London
          f. Roger Clavil, Abel Roper, & Thos.
          Metcalf. 1697, 8vo. L 8464 c. 26; CS
          Aa 2. 27 (This copy has Locke's MS
          marginalia). Wing S 2594
901    S(ergeant), J(ohn): Statera appensa. Londini. 1660.
          12°. 52p. OC Allestree R. 6. 12; O Vet
          A. f. 365 (1). Wing W 1844
902    S(ergeant), J(ohn): Sure footing in christianity. Lon-
          don. 1665. 8vo. OS #803; FSL; LW 1003
          N. 13; TU. Wing S 2595
903    (Sergeant, John): Surefooting in Christianity. Second
          edition. London. 1665. Wing S 2596
904    (Sergeant, John): The third catholick letter. By J.
          S. London. Matthew Turner. 1687. FSL
          bd. w. 5602; NN CI p. v. 20; NU. Wing
          S 2597
905    Sergeant, John: To Sir Kenelme Digby. (London,
          1653) 4to. Cap. title. 9p. L E 723 (11)
906    Sergeant, John: Transnatural philosophy, or meta-
          physicks. London. By the Author. Sold
          by D. Brown, Abel Roper, & Tho. Met-
          calf. 1700. 8vo. FSL 162433; L 1134 d. 1;
          O Vet A 4 e 768. Wing S 2598
       A sermon of the passion: see G. (J.)
       A sermon preached before the King and Queen:  see
          Giffard (Bonaventure)
907    Serra reciprocata or the controversy about the papist
          misrepresented. London. 1687. 4to.
          LFS (A reissue of ten pamphlets with a
          new tp. )

908    S(harpe), J.: Trial of a protestant private spirit. By
           J. S. S. J. n. p. 1680. HP
909    A short instruction for the better understanding & per-
           forming of mental prayer. Paris. L.
           Sevestre. 1691. Sixes. 49p. L 1018 e 34;
           DE; CN Case 3 A 1801. (Dedication
           signed C.A. S.J. = Trans?)
910    (Smith, Richard): A brief survey of the Lord of Derry.
           By R. C. Paris. 1655. 12mo. O 8° Z
           180 Th.; TU. Wing S 4152
911    (Smith, Richard): An historical epistle of the great
           amitie. Third edition. n. p. 1652. 8vo.
           72p. DT Fag. II 4. 57/7. Wing S 4153
912    Smith, Richard: Monita quaedam utilia. Editio nova.
           Londini. 1695. 12mo. (ed. John Perrot)
           FSL; OS #824; TU; CN Case 3 A 2043.
           Wing S 4155
913    (Smith, Richard): Of the all-sufficient external
           proposer. By C. R. Paris. 1653. 8vo.
           LFS. Wing S 4156
914    (Smith, Richard): Of the distinction of fundamentall
           and not fundamental points of faith. By
           C. R. n. p. 1645. 8vo. OS #821; O 1. c.
           290 & 8° C 460 Linc. Wing S 4157
915    (Smith, Richard): The protestants plain confession.
           By R. C. n. p. 1645. 8vo. LFS; TU.
           Wing S 4158
916    Smith, Richard: A treatise of the best kind of confes-
           sors. n. p. (London) 1651. 12mo. L 699
           a 7. Wing S 4159
       Some general observations upon Dr. Stillingfleet's
           book: see Thimelby, R.
917    The soules pilgrimage to the heavenly Hierusalem.
           n. p. 1650. 4to. 88p. L 11626 e 42 (Two
           poems at the end signed "Geo. Fortescue"
           and "C. M. ")
       Southwell, Nath.: see Bacon (N. )
       A soveraign counter-poyson: see E. (J. )
918    (Spenser, John): Aut Deus, aut nihil. God or nothing.
           By Vincent Hattecliffe (i. e. alias).
           London. Ralph Wood f. the author and
           are to be sold by Nath. Brooke. 1659.
           8vo. OS #837; O 8° N 74 Th. Wing S
           4956

919        (Spenser, John): Questions propounded for resolution.
Paris. 1657. 8vo. 63p. (preface signed
"V. H. " i. e. Vincent Hattecliffe, pseud. )
OC N 7/12 Allestree; CN Case 3 A 2047.
Wing S 4957

920        (Spenser, John): The schism of the church of England.
Oxon by Henry Cruttenden. 1688. 4to.
10p. CN Case 3 A 2048; Ware; TU; L
1473 bb 29 (2) (These copies have 10 p.
LFS copy has a second part of 99p. )
Wing S 2591

921        (Spenser, John): Scisme unmask't or a late conference.
Paris. 1658. 12mo. L 3936 a. 21; TU;
CN Case 3 A 2007. Wing P 1464

922        Spenser, John: Scripture mistaken. Antwerpe. I.
Meursius. 1655. 8vo. O Linc. 8° a 91;
TU; CN Case 2046. Wing S 4958

923        The spirit of christianity. London. Henry Hills. 1686.
12mo. in 6s. (Preface signed by Walter
Kirkham Blount who is probably the
trans. René Rapin was most likely the
author of the original. ) FSL; Ware; TU;
CN Case 3 A 1837. Wing B 3352

The spiritual combat: see Scupoli (L. )

Spiritual Exercise: see Pinckney

A spiritual retreat: see Croiset (J. )

924        Stafford, William Howard, Viscount: William, late
viscount Stafford his last speech. (Colph.)
London f. Benjamin Harris. n. d. (1680)
s. sh. O Ashm. 1678 (10); L 1851 c 19(54).
Wing S 5153

925        Stafford, Viscount: The speech of... seventh of Dec.
1680. 1680. fol. Wing S 5155

926        Stafford, Viscount: The speech of... on the scaffold...
Decemb. 29. 1680. London f. W. Bailey.
1680. fol. 4 p. O Ashm. 1678; L 515 1.2
(42). Wing S 5156

927        Stafford, Viscount: The speech of.. upon the scaffold..
Dec. 29. 1680. n. d. p. (London, 1680)
cap. title. fol. 6 p. O Wood 427 (3); L
515 1.2 (41). Wing S 5157

928        Stafford, Viscount: Speech of. Edinburgh. Reprinted
in the year 1681. fol. 7p. L C 28 K 23
(7). Wing S 5158

929 Stafford, Viscount: The two last prayers of. London.
     1681. 8vo. 11p. O Wood 427 (5). Wing S
     5159

930 (Strange, Richard): The life and gests of S. Thomas
     Cantilupe. Gant. Robert Walker. 1674.
     8vo. O 8° C 35 Linc.

931 (Strange, Richard): The life and gests of S. Thomas
     Cantilupe. By R. S. S. J. Gant. Robert
     Walker. 1674. 8vo. (Anr. issue of the
     preceding item with cancel titlepage
     bearing author's initials.) O 8° B 27 Med.
     BS & Wood 67. Wing S 5810

The state of church affairs: see Milton (C.)
Statera appensa: see Sergeant (J.)
Stuart, Wm.: see Walker (J.)

932 The succession of the church cleared and stated.
     London f. N. T. 1686. 4to. 37 p. FSL
     bd. w. M 1567; TU. Wing S 6114

The sum of a conference: see Gooden (P.)

933 A summe of christian doctrine which every christian
     is bound to know. London. Henry Hills.
     1686. 24°. 22p. O Ashm. 1329. Wing S
     6167

T., C.: see Tootel (C.)
T., H.: see Tichbourne (H.) & Turberville (H.)
T., R.: see Reed (T.)

934 (Talbot, Peter): Blackloanae haersis olim in Pelagio
     et manichaeis damnatae..historia et
     confutatio. Auctore M. Lomino (pseud.)
     Gandavi. 1675. 4to. WGT (This latin
     work has extensive sections in English)

935 (Talbot, Peter): The duty and comfort of suffering
     subjects. Cap. title. Signed on p. 16
     by Peter Talbot and dated Paris, May 2,
     1674. 4to. 16p. O Goodwin Pamph. 1046
     (11) (imp.) Wing T 115

936 (Talbot, Peter): The friar disciplined. Animadversions
     on friar Peter Walsh. By Robert Wilson
     (pseud.) Gant. 1674. 8vo. C Hib. 8. 674. 7;
     Wing T 116

937 (Talbot, Peter): The nullity of the prelatique clergy
     and church of England. Antwerp. 1659.
     4to. HP; NU 1659 T 141; Y. Wing T 117

Talbot, Peter: The polititians catechism, see French
   (N.)

938       Talbot, Peter: A treatise of religion and government.
n. p. 1670. 4to. <u>Ware.</u> Wing T 118

939       (Talbot, Peter): A treatise of the nature of catholick
faith and heresie. By N. N. Rouen. 1657.
8vo. 89p. Walsh #538; OS #872; <u>HP.</u>
Wing T 119

940       (Teramano, Pietro): The miraculous origin and
translation of the church of...Loreto.
Bononiae. Typis Jacobi Montii. 1678.
s. sh. <u>O</u> (2 copies) (New ed. of A &R 809.
Robt. Corbington was the translator. )
Wing M 2216

941       Teresa (of Avila, St. ): The flaming hart or the life
of...S. Teresa. (Trans. Tobie Matthew
who signs the dedication, "M. T.") Antwerpe. Johannes Meursius. 1642. 8vo.
<u>FSL</u>; <u>TU.</u> Wing T 753

942       Teresa (of Avila, St. ): The life of. Vol. I. n. p. (London) 1671. 4to. FSL; (Trans. A. Wood-
head. Printed secretly in London by Fr.
Simon Stock i. e. Walter Travers. This
includes Wing M 481. On this and the
following three items see John Buchanan
Brown in 21 <u>Library</u> (1966) fifth series,
pp. 234 ff. ) Wing T 754

943       Teresa (of Avila, St. ): The second part of the life of.
n. p. d. (London. 1669) 4to. DAI; <u>CN</u>
Case 4 A 1868. Wing T 755

944       Teresa (of Avila, St. ): The second part of the works
of. n. p. (London) 1675. 4to. <u>FSL</u>; <u>TU.</u>
Wing T 752A

945       Teresa, (of Avila, St. ): The works of. n. p. (London)
1675. 4to. <u>TU.</u> Wing T 752

946       (Thimelby, Richard): Some generall observations..
with a vindication of St. Ignatius. n. p.
1672. 4to. 96 (i. e. 69) p. OS #3021;
<u>LFS</u>; <u>CN</u> Case 3 A 2050; <u>HP.</u> Wing A
3942

Third catholic letter: see Sergeant (J. )

947       Thomas a Kempis: Dilyniad Christ, a elwir yn
gyffredin Thomas a Kempis. Gwedi ei
gyfieithu'n Gymraec ers talm a amser
ynol Editiwn yr Awdur gan Hyw Owen
Gwenyoe ym Mon, Esq. Llundain. Gwedi
ei imprintio ar gost I. H. 1684. (Title in

English: The following of Christ commonly called Thomas a Kempis. Translated into Welsh. )

948    Thomas a Kempis: The following of Christ. Second ed. Paris. M. Blagaert. 1642. 8vo. Trans. M. C. (i. e. Miles Car, i. e. Pinckney) (Anr. ed. of A&R 822) <u>O</u> Vet E 3 g. 5

949    Thomas a Kempis: The following of Christ. Roan. Julian Courant. 1670. 8vo. <u>O</u> 138 g. 498. Wing T 951

950    (Thomas a Kempis): The following of Christ.. written by John Gersen... of the holy order of St. Benedict. London. 1673. 12mo. <u>LFS</u>; <u>TU</u>; <u>CN</u> Case 3 A 2051; OS. Wing T 952

951    (Thomas a Kempis): The following of Christ. Antwerp f. T. D. 1686. 24°. <u>L</u> ix Eng. 52. Wing T 953

952    Thomas a Kempis: The following of Christ. Holy Rood House. By James Watson. 1687. 12mo. O 14198 g. 15 (imp. ); <u>L</u> ix Eng. 53; <u>CN</u> Case 2 A 126 (imp. ) Wing T 954

953    Thomas a Kempis: Imitatio Christi. The following of Christ. London f. M. T. 1686. <u>O</u> Vet A 3 g. 53; TMTH

954    (Thomas a Kempis): The imitation or following of Christ. Rohan. 1657. 32° in 8s. <u>CS</u> Yule collection; BUTE; <u>NN</u> * KC 1657

955    (Thomas a Kempis): The imitation or following of Christ. Rohan. 1658. 8vo. <u>O</u> 1. g. 134. Wing T 957

956    Thomas a Kempis: A paraphrase in english of the following of Christ. n. p. 1694. 8vo. <u>FSL</u> 140699; L ix Eng. 313

957    Thomas a Kempis: His sermons on the incarnation. Trans. Thomas Carre (i. e. Miles Pinckney). Paris. Mrs. Blagaert. 1653. 12mo. <u>L</u> 4403 aaa 44

958    Thomas a Kempis: Meditations and prayers. Trans. Thomas Carre (i. e. Miles Pinckney) Paris. Vincent du Moutier. 1664. 8vo. <u>L</u> 3834 a 26; O 8° delta 68 BS

959    Thomas a Kempis: His soliloquies. Trans. Thomas Carre (i. e. Miles Pinckney). Paris. M. Blagaert. 1653. 12mo. OS #878;

960    Three and thirty most godly and devout prayers...
against the day of Pentecost. n. p. d.
(c. 1641) cap. title. 12mo. 48p. Ware

961    Three and thirty most godly and devout prayers...for
faithful soules departed. n. p. d. (1641)
12mo. 48p. L C 26 gg. 7; CN Case 3 A
1836 (Both these copies are catalogued
as part of M 3069 - see #701 supra. -
but the signatures and pagination are
separate. Compare this item with the
preceding one and with A&R 823 which
might be identical. )

Three sermons upon the sacrament:  see Jenks (Sylv. )

962    (Tichbourne, Henry):  Reason for religion. n. p. 1673.
4to. (Signed H. T. at end. ) Ware; DE

To Katholiko:  see Canes (J. B. V. )

963    To the honourable, the knights, citizens & burgesses
of the Commons house in parliament...
the humble petition of the lay-catholique
recusants. n. p. 1641. s. sh. L 669 f. 4
(23). Wing T 1472

964    To the honourable, the knights, citizens and burgesses
of Commons...the humble petition of
the lay-catholique recusants. n. p. f.
Geo. Bailey. 1642. s. sh. L 669 f. 4
(49) Wing T 1473

965    To the kings most excellent majesty:  the faithful protestation and humble remonstrance of
the Roman Catholic nobility and gentry
of Ireland. (London, 1660) Brds. LL
Brydall 8. fol. 190.  Wing T 1500

966    To the kings most excellent majesty:  the faithful
protestation and humble remonstrance
of the Roman catholic nobility and gentry
of Ireland. n. d. p. (1660) Fol. Cap. title
4p. L 8122 il (22)

To the king's most excellent majesty: the humble
remonstrance: see Walsh (Peter)

967    To the king's most sacred majesty and clemency.
(incipit) "Whether it be not more ex-
pedient" O Carte MSS 71, 461. n. p. d.
(1661) brds.

968    Le tombeau des controverses: a grave for controversies. Trans. M. M. London. T. Mil-

bourne f. Dorman Newman. 1673. 4to.
44p. Y Mhc8.9. Wing T 1793

969    T(ootell), C(hristopher): The layman's ritual. n. p.
(London) 1698. 12mo. Ware; TU. Wing
T 1905

970    (Touchet, George Anselm): Historical collections.
n. p. 1674. 8vo. OS #884; L 852 e. 8.
Wing T 1954

971    (Touchet, George A. ): Historical collections. London.
Henry Hill f. him and Matt. Turner. 1686.
8vo. OS #3062; Ware (John Dryden's copy
with MS notes); NN * KC 1686; TU. Wing
T 1955

Transubstantiation defended: see Gother (John)
Trial of a protestant private spirit: see Sharpe (J. )

972    Trinder, Charles: The speech of. London. Randall
Taylor. 1687/8. fol. 16p. FSL 159991.
Wing T 2283

True and perfect narrative: see Keepe (Henry)

973    The true interest of the legal English protestants.
London. Nathaniel Thompson. 1687.
fol. 6p. Y Brit. Tracts 1687 + T 76.
Wing T 2714

True portraiture of the church: see Matthieu de Saint
Quentin

Truth will out: see Worsley (Ed. )

974    (Turberville, Henry): An abridgment of christian
doctrine. Doway. 1648. 12mo. CN Case
3 A 2054

975    (Turberville, Henry): An abridgment of christian
doctrine. Doway. 1661. 12mo. C Kkk
431; Ware. Wing T 3253

976    (Turberville, Henry): An abridgment of christian
doctrine. Fourteenth edition. n. p. f.
A. L. 1676. 12mo. Wing T 3254

977    T(urberville), H(enry): An bridgment of christian
doctrine. The last edition. Basileae.
1680. 12mo. O 130 g. 191

978    (Turberville, Henry): An abridgment of christian
doctrine. The last edition. Basileae.
1680. 12mo. CS A. 3. 85; Ware; CN 3 A
2055

979    (Turberville, Henry): An abridgment of christian
doctrine. Fifteenth edition. n. p. (Douai)
1684. 12mo. Wing T 3255

980 (Turberville, Henry): An abridgment of christian
   doctrine. Last edition. n.p. 1687. NU
   1687 T 93. Wing T 3256

981 T(urberville), H(enry): An abridgment of christian
   doctrine. The last edition. Doway. n.d.
   (1689?). FSL T 3256a

982 (Turberville, Henry): An abridgment of christian
   doctrine. London. 1698. Sixes. OS #889

983 T(urberville), H(enry): A manual of controversies.
   Doway. Lawrence Kellam. 1654. 8vo.
   OS #890 FSL 131333; TU; CN Case 3 A
   2056. Wing T 3257

984 T(urberville), H(enry): A manuel of controversies.
   Doway. Christopher Serrurier. 1671.
   12mo. in Sixes. 310 p. OS #891; TU.
   Wing T 3258

985 T(urberville), H(enry): A manuel of controversies.
   Doway. Christopher Serrurier. 1671.
   12mo. in gatherings of 8s & 4s. This
   edition has 265 p. FSL 181368; CN Case
   3 A 2057

986 (Turberville, Henry): A manuel of controversies.
   By H. T. Doway. Christopher Serrurier.
   1671. 12mo. in 6s. 297p. TU

987 Tubervil, Henry: A manual of controversie. Fourth
   edition... collected by J. D. London.
   Matthew Turner. 1686. 12mo. in 6s.
   OS #892; Ware; TU; CN Case 3 A 2057.
   Wing T 3259

988 Twenty one conclusions further demonstrating the
   Schism. Oxon. H. Cruttenden. 1688.
   4to. 15p. FSL Bd. w. H 3257; NN CI
   p. v. 22; TU. Wing T 3413

Two discourses: see Woodhead (Abraham)

989 Two hymnes for the nativity of Christ. Music by R. M.
   13p. followed by engravings by Samuel
   Ward. London. 1650. L C 110 b. 16

Tylden, Thomas: see Godden

Unkinde deserter of loyall men: see French (Nich.)

Unerrable church: see Brown (Ignatius)

990 The use and great moment of the notes of the church
   as deliver'd by C. Bellarmine. London.
   Nath. Thompson. 1687. 4to. 46p. LW
   P. P. 7:48:4 (19) (This is a rebuttal of
   1 Wing B 1823 and not written by Bellar-

mine.) Wing B 1824

Valesius ad Haroldum:  see Walsh (Peter)

991      Vane, Thomas:  An answer to a libell. Paris. 1646.
98p. 8vo. O 8° K 48 Linc. (2) (This is a
reissue of the sheets issued with Pinckney's
Occasional Discourses. See No. 774
supra.) Wing V 81

992      Vane, Thomas:  A lost sheepe returned home. Paris.
1645. 4to. O Antiq. f. F. 1645. 1; TU.
Wing V 82

993      Vane, Thomas:  A lost sheep. Second edition. Paris.
1648. 12mo. O 8° B 176 Linc.; L 3935
aa 10. Wing V 83

994      Vane, Thomas:  A lost sheep returned home. Third
edition. Paris. 1648. 12mo. O l. g. 74;
TU. Wing V 84

995      Vane, Thomas:  A lost sheep. Third edition. Paris.
1649. 12mo. TU (A reissue of the sheets
of the preceding item with a cancel tp.)
Wing V 85

996      Vane, Thomas:  A lost sheep. Fourth edition. Paris.
1649. 12mo. Ware; CN Case 2 A 127.
Wing V 86

997      Vane, Thomas:  A lost sheep. Fifth edition. Paris.
1666. 12mo. in 6s. L 1481 a 10; CN 3
A 2059. Wing V 87

998      Vane, Thomas:  Wisdom and Innocence or prudence
and simplicity in the examples of the
serpent and the dove. London. f. J.
Crook & J. Baker. 1652. 12mo. L E
1406 (1). Wing V 89

999      Vane, Thomas:  Wisdom & Innocence. Paris. 1652.
12mo. (anr. issue of preceding) Ware

1000      (Varet, A. L.):  The christian education of children.
Paris. John Baptist Coignard. 1678.
8vo. OS #3086; FSL. Wing V 108

Veritas evangelica:  see Kemeys (T.)

1001      Veron, Francois:  The rule of catholick faith.
Trans. E. S. (i. e. Ed. Sheldon) Paris
by John Billaine. 1660. 12mo. (34) +
214p. (last page mistakenly numbered
114) FSL 170703; O 8° B 192 (2) Linc.
TU; CN Case 3 A 2060. Wing V 256

1002      Veron, Francois:  The rule of catholick faith. Trans.
E. S. Paris by John Billaine. 1660. 12mo.

(34) + 219 p. (last page mistakenly numbered 119) This edition contains a postscript of 5 extra pages. TU

1003 Veron, Francois: The rule of catholick faith. Trans. E. S. Paris f. John Billain. 1660 (vere London 1672). 12mo. (24) + 144 p. O Wood 812 (In this copy Wood notes that Ralph Sheldon, nephew of the translator, published this ed. surreptitiously in London in 1672); TU. Wing V 255

1004 A very profitable exercise for offering the mass according to the four ends. n.p. 1670. 16s. 47p. L 1018 a 27; DE (imp.)

1005 Vespers or even-songs for all sundays and holy-days in the year. London f. Matthew Turner. 1688. 12mo. 96 p. CN 3 A 1913

1006 Vincent of Lerins: The golden treatise of. Trans. A. P. n.p. (London. R. Daniel) 1651. 12mo. CN Case 3 A 2062. Wing V 456

A vindication of St. Gregory: see Mumford (J.)

A vindication of the bishop of Condom's exposition: see Johnston (H.J.)

A vindication of the english catholics: see Warner (J.)

A vindication of the roman catholicks: see Caron (R.)

Vive Jesus, the rule of St. Austin: see Augustine

1007 W., E.: A brief explication of the office. Douay. Laurence Kellam. 1652. 8vo. OS #3105; O 138 g. 216; DAI; TU. Wing W 14

W., E.: see Worsley (Ed.)
see Warner (John)

W., H.: see Wilkinson (Henry)

W., L.: see Warner (John)

W., P.: see Walsh (Peter)

1008 W., S.: A vindication of the doctrine. Paris. 1659. 12mo. FSL 145401; O 1.g. 70; TU; CN Case 3 A 2039. Wing S 2599

W., T.: see Ward (Thomas)

1009 Wadding, Luke: A small garland of pious and godly songs. Ghent. 1684. 8vo. Walsh #616; BUTE

1010 (Walker, John): Presbyteries triall. Preface signed F. W. S. (pseud.). Paris. 1657. 8vo. WGT; O Mason AA 326; NN * KC 1675. Wing S 6028

1011     (Walker, O.): Five short treatises. Oxford. 1688.
                4to. n. d. p. on tp but 1st item has tp.
                with "Oxford. 1688". 5 parts. OS #3119;
                Ware. Wing W 396A

1012     Walker, Obadaiah: Of faith necessary to salvation.
                Oxford. 1688. 4to. 5 parts. FSL 179745
                Anr. issue of preceding. Wing W 404B

1013     (Walsh, Peter): The advocate of conscience liberty.
                n. p. 1673. 8vo. OS #938; Ware; TU; Y
                Zd 337; NU. Wing W 627

1014     (Walsh, Peter): An answer to three treatises. London,
                by J. B. for Henry Brome. 1678. 3 pts.
                4to. FSL 188230; O C. 8. 28. Linc.; OS
                #3122; TU. Wing W 628

1015     Walsh, Peter: Causa valesiana. Londini apud Joannam
                Brome. 1684. 8vo. L G 5713. Wing W
                629

1016     (Walsh, Peter): The controversial letters... The first
                two letters. London f. Henry Brome &
                Benj. Tooke. 4to. 1673. 46p. LFS; OS
                #3133; O KK 6 Th (6) & Pamph. 131 C
                (19). Wing W 630

1017     (Walsh, Peter): The controversial letters. Second
                edition. 1673. 4to. Y. Wing W 631

1018     (Walsh, Peter): The third and fourth controversial
                letters. London f. Henry Brome & Benj.
                Tooke. 1673. 4to. 37p. LFS; OS #3134;
                O KK 6 Th. (8); CN

1019     (Walsh, Peter): The fifth and sixth of the controversial
                letters. London f. Henry Brome & Benj.
                Tooke. 1673. 4to. 37p. LFS; O KK 6 Th.
                (9); CN; OS #3135

1020     (Walsh, Peter): The seventh & eighth of the contro-
                versial letters. London f. Henry Brome
                & Benj. Tooke. 1673. 4to. 54p. LFS;
                OS #3136; CN; O KK 6 Th (10) & Pamph.
                131 C (18)

1021     (Walsh, Peter): The ninth and tenth of the contro-
                versial letters. London f. Henry Brome
                & Benj. Tooke. 1674. 4to. 46p. O KK
                6 Th (11); LFS; CN; OS #3137

1022     (Walsh, Peter): The eleventh & twelfth of the contro-
                versial letters. London f. H. Brome &
                Benj. Tooke. 1674. 4to. 46p. OS #3138;
                CN; O KK 6 Th (12)

1023    (Walsh, Peter): The thirteenth & fourteenth of the controversial letters. London f. Henry Brome & Benj. Tooke. 1675. 4to. 70p. O KK 6 Th (13) & Pamph. 135 C (26); FSL 142800

1024    (Walsh, Peter): The fifteenth & sixteenth of the controversial letters. London f. Henry Brome & Benj. Tooke. 1679. 4to. 69p. OS #3139; O Pamph. 144 C (15)

1025    Walsh, Peter: Four letters on several subjects. n.p. 1686. 8vo. OS #939; WGT; FSL 179761; L G 19561; Ware; TU. Wing W 633

1026    Walsh, Peter: The history & vindication of the loyal formulary. Two parts. n.p. 1674. Folio. O L. 6. 3. Th.; FSL 146799. Wing W 634

1027    (Walsh, Peter): The Irish colours folded. London. 1662. 4to. 32p. L 806 d. 29(1). Wing W 635

1028    W(alsh), P(eter): A letter desiring a just & merciful regard of the roman catholicks. 1662. s. sh. O Carte MS 71 No. 430; L C 33 B 32. Wing W 636

1029    Walsh, Peter: A letter to the catholicks of England, Ireland and Scotland. n.p. (London) 1674. 8vo. L G 5712; FSL 130680; TU. Wing W 638

1030    Walsh, Peter: A more ample accompt. London. Thomas Mabb. 1662. 8vo. FSL 156057; L G 5711. Wing W 639

1031    W(alsh), P(eter): P. W.'s reply to the person of quality's answer. Paris. 1664. 4to. L G 5750; Hiscock W 639+

1032    (Walsh, Peter): A prospect of the state of Ireland. n. p. (London) f. Joanna Brome. 1682. 8vo. FSL 156058; L G 4548; Y Bz65. 21 e. Wing W 640

1033    (Walsh, Peter): Some few questions concerning the oath of allegiance. n.p. 1661; 4to. 35p. O Art. 4° D 15 BS; FSL 180854. Wing W 641

1034    (Walsh, Peter): Some few questions concerning the oath. London f. Hen. Brome & Benj. Tooke. 1674. 4to. 33p. L G 5752. Wing W 642

1035     (Walsh, Peter): Some few questions concerning the oath. (London) f. Henry Brome. 1677. 4to. O 4° A 30 Th. Wing W 643

1036     W(alsh), P(eter): To the king's most excellent majestie. The humble remonstrance acknowledgement protestation and petition of the roman-catholic clergy of Ireland. 1661(/2). Brds. O Carte Ms. 59, 406

1037     Walsh, Peter: Valesius ad Haroldum. n. p. (London) 1672. fol. 30p. L G 5801; CN D 242. 95. Wing W 626

1038     (Walton, John): A brief answer to the many calumnies of Dr. Henry More. n. p. (London) 1672. 8vo. HP; TU; CN Case 3 A 2067

1039     Ward, Thomas: The errata to the protestant bible. London. Printed by W. Downing. 1688. fol. 100p. NU 1688 f. W 26. Wing W 833

1040     W(ard), T(homas): The errata to the protestant bible. London f. the author. 1688. fol. 100p. O 4° Rawl. 377

1041     W(ard), T(homas): Monomachia or a duel between Dr. Tho. Tenison...and a roman catholick souldier. London f. the author. 1687. 4to. 48p. (This was printed by Nath. Thompson. See L. Rostenburg in 10 Library, 5th series, (1955) p. 202) O 4° P 23 Jur. (10); FSL 136171; OS #3148. Wing W 834

1042     W(ard), T(homas): The roman catholick souldier's letter to Dr. Tho. Tenison. n. p. d. (London, 1688) brds. Y Brit. Tracts 1688 + W 22; OS #3149. Wing W 835

1043     W(ard), T(homas): Some queries to the protestants. London. Nathaniel Thompson. 1687. 4to. 8p. O Vet A 3 e 473 (2) & C. 11. 7 Linc. (12); FSL bd. w. STC 14390 copy 2; OS #3150; CN Case C 6526. 9544. Wing W 836

1044     (Ward, Thomas): Some queries to the protestants. By J. W. gent. London. Nathaniel Thompson. 1687. 4to. 8p. CN 3 A 2088

1045     W(ard), T(homas): Speculum ecclesiasticum. London. Nathaniel Thompson. 1687. brds. L 1865c. 10 (28). Wing W 838

1046      W(ard), T(homas): Speculum ecclesiasticum. n. p. d.
                (London, 1688? ? ) brds. O Pamph. 181

1047      (Warner, John): Anti-Fimbria or an answer to the
                animadversions. By A. C. E. G. n. p. 1679.
                4to. 28p. L 860 1. 12 (5); HP; Birrell #12;
                CN 4 A 1872 (imp. )

1048      (Warner, John): Anti-Goliath or an epistle to Mr.
                Brevint. By E. W. n. p. 1678. 8vo. 60p.
                HP; C; DE; Birrell #7

1049      (Warner, John): Anti-Haman or an answer. By W. E.
                n. p. 1678. 8vo. LFS; WGT; C; O; L; DE;
                TU; CN 3 A 2069; Birrell #6

1050      (Warner, John): Anti-Haman or an answer. By W. E.
                n. p. 1679. 8vo. Anr. issue of preceding.
                OS #944; LFS. Wing W 905

1051      (Warner, John): Concerning the congregation of Jesuits.
                n. p. d. (1678-9) 4to. 8p. Birrell #10; L
                860 i. 12 (2)

1052      Warner, J(ohn): A defence of the doctrin. Second
                edition. London.f. Henry Hills. 1688.
                8vo. LFS; OS #945; TU; CN Case 3 A
                2070; Birrell #19. Wing W 907

1053      W(arner), J(ohn): A defence of the doctrin. Second
                edition. London. f. Henry Hills. 1688.
                8vo. O Vet A 3 f. 396; LFS; Ware (same
                as the preceding except that only the
                initials of the author appear on tp. )
                Wing W 908

1054      (Warner, John): A defence of the innocency of the
                lives. n. p. 1680. 4to. 32 pp. L 860 i
                12 (6); HP; LFS; Birrell #13

1055      (Warner, John): Doctor Stillingfleet against Doctor
                Stillingfleet. n. p. 1671. 8vo. 22p. By
                John Williams (Pseud. ) L 697 c 33 (1);
                Birrell #3. Wing W 909

1056      (Warner, John): Dr. Stillingfleet still against Dr.
                Stillingfleet. By J. W. n. p. 1675. 8vo.
                OS #946; LFS; CN; TU; CN 3 A 2068;
                Birrell #5. Wing W 910

1057      (Warner, John): Dr. Stillingfleet's principles. By
                J. W. n. p. 1673. 4to. 34p. L 3936 bb
                14; Birrell #4; TU. Wing W 911

1058      (Warner, John): A revision of Doctor George Morlei's
                judgment. By L. W. n. p. 1683. 4to. OS
                #947; LFS; Ware; TU; CN Case 4 A 1874;

Birrell #17. Wing W 912

1059    (Warner, John): A vindication of the Inglish Catho-
licks. Antwerp. 1680. 4to. 60p. <u>O</u>
C. 10. 3. Linc.; <u>TU</u>; Birrell #14a. Wing
V 504

1060    (Warner, John): A vindication of the Inglish catholicks. n. p. 1680. 4to. 62p. ST; Birrell
#14b

1061    (Warner, John): A vindication of the English Catholiks. The 2. edition. n. p. 1681. 4to.
94p. <u>L</u> 860 i 12 (8); LFS; Birrell #14c

The wayes of the crosse: see Boudon

1062    Weldon, John: The divine pedagogue or the assured
way to heaven. London. 1692. 8vo.
<u>Ware.</u> Wing W 1278

1063    White, Thomas (Blacklo): Apologia pro doctrina sua.
Londini. 1661. 12mo. 37p. <u>O</u> Vet A f.
365 (3); <u>OC</u> Allestree R. 6. 12. Wing W
1808

1064    White, Thomas: An apology for Rushworth's dialogues.
Paris. Jean Billain. 1654. 8vo. <u>FSL</u>;
OS #957; NCD; <u>TU</u>. Wing W 1809

1065    White, Thomas: Appendix theologica de origine
mundi. Londini. 1647. 12mo. 60p.
<u>Ware.</u> Wing W 1810

1066    White, Thomas: A catechism of christian doctrin.
Second edition. Paris. 1659. 12mo. <u>O</u>
138 g. 476; <u>FSL</u>; <u>TU</u>; <u>CN</u> Case 3 A 2073.
Wing W 1811

1067    (White, Thomas): A contemplation of heaven. Paris.
1654. 12mo. 189p. <u>O</u> 8° C 21 Th BS;
NU 1657 W 588 (2). Wing W 1814

1068    (White, Thomas): A contemplation of heaven. Paris.
1654. 12mo. 182p. Rubricated tp. <u>O</u>
Vet E 3 f. 140; <u>Ware</u>

1069    White, Thomas: Controversy-Logicke, or the method
to come to truth. n. p. 1659. 12mo.
<u>FSL</u> 144730; <u>O</u> 8° C 318 Linc.; <u>TU</u>; <u>CN</u>
Case 3 A 2074. Wing W 1816

1070    White, Thomas: Controversy-Logicke. Second edition. Roan. 1674. 12mo. <u>O</u> Wood 798;
<u>Ware.</u> Wing W 1817

1071    White, Thomas: Devotion and reason. Paris. 1661.
8vo. <u>FSL</u> 165046; <u>O</u> Vet E 3 f. 48; Case
3 A 2075; <u>TU</u>; <u>CN</u> Case 3 A 2075. Wing

1072 White, Thomas: Euclides metaphysicus. Londini.
    Typis J. M. impensis J. Martin, Ja.
    Allestry & Tho. Dicas. 8vo. 1658. OS
    #960; O Savile Cc20; NC Smith 513.
    1658. W 58; FSL 185001. Wing W 1821

1073 White, Thomas: Exceptiones duorum theologorum.
    n. p. (London) 1662. 12mo. 2 parts.
    OC a. 2. 249; O 8° X 58 Th; OS #966; TU.
    Wing W 1823

1074 White, Thomas: Exceptiones duorum theologorum.
    (anr. ed.) n. p. 1663. Wing W 1823A

1075 White, Thomas: An exclusion of scepticks. London.
    f. John Williams. 1665. 4to. 80p. L
    701 h 4 (10) OC. Wing W 1824

1076 (White, Thomas): Exemplar epistolae a D. Thoma
    Albio ad S. D. N. Alexandrum VII. (with
    an English trans.) Amsterdam. 1662.
    4to. 4 leaves. OS #3185

1077 White, Thomas: Exetasis scientiae. n. p. (London)
    1662. 12mo. O 972 f. 14; FSL 178903;
    OS #967; TU. Wing W 1826

1078 White, Thomas: The grounds of obedience & govern-
    ment. London by J. Flesher f. Laurence
    Chapman. 1655. 12mo. 183pp. O 8° S
    31 Jur.; FSL 143990; CN Case 3 A 2076.
    Wing W 1827

1079 White, Thomas: The grounds of obedience and govern-
    ment. Second edition. London. by J.
    Flesher f. Laurence Chapman. 1655.
    12mo. 183p. LW 1035 G 30; TU. Wing
    W 1827A

1080 White, Thomas: Institutionum ethicarum sive statera
    morum. Londini. 1660. 12mo. O 8° B
    274 Linc.; TU. Wing W 1830

1081 White, Thomas: Institutionum peripateticarum...ad
    mentem K. Digby. Editio secunda. Lon-
    dini. Ex officina R. Whittakeri. 1647.
    12mo. O 8° T 26 Art. Seld.; FSL 157085.
    Wing W 1831

1082 (White, Thomas): A letter in answer to the late dis-
    pensers of Pope Benedict XII. Paris.
    Printed by E. A. 1659. 42p. 12mo.
    42p. OC R 5/21 Allestree

1083    White, Thomas: A letter to a person of honor. n. p.
                1659. 12mo. 21p. unpaginated. OC R. 5.
                21. Allestree; $\underline{O}$ 8° C 412 Linc.; $\underline{CN}$
                Case 3 A 2077; $\underline{TU}$. Wing W 1832

1084    White, Thomas: A manuall of divine considerations.
                Trans. W. C. n. p. 1655. 12mo. $\underline{O}$ Vet
                A 3 f. 1245. Wing W 1833

1085    White, Thomas: The middle state of souls. n. p. 1659.
                12mo. $\underline{O}$ 141 m 515 & 8° C 516 Linc. &
                Vet L 3 f. 10; $\underline{TU}$; $\underline{CN}$ Case 3 A 2077.
                Wing W 1836

1086    White, Thomas: Mr. Blacklow's reply to Dr. Ley-
                burn's pamphlet. n. p. d. (1657) 4to.
                Cap. title. 32p. $\underline{O}$ 4° D 15 Art BS

1087    White, Thomas: Muscarium ad immissos. Londini.
                1661. 12mo. OS #965; $\underline{L}$ 1020 K 15 (3);
                $\underline{TU}$. Wing W 1837

1088    White, Thomas: Notes of Mr. F. D.'s result of a
                dialogue concerning the middle state
                of souls. Paris. 1660. 8vo. 80p. OS
                #963; $\underline{O}$ 8° $\underline{L}$ 559 B 8; $\underline{CN}$ Case 3 A
                2075; $\underline{TU}$. Wing W 1838

1089    White, Thomas: Peripatelicall institutions in the way
                of...K. Digby. The theoricall part.
                London. R. D. and are to be sold by John
                Williams. 1656. 8vo. OS #959; $\underline{O}$ 8° H
                20 Th BS; $\underline{L}$ E 1692. Wing W 1839

1090    White, Thomas: Religion and reason mutually cor-
                responding. Paris. 1660. 8vo. OS #964;
                FSL 137989; $\underline{O}$ 8° B 192 Linc.; $\underline{OC}$ All.
                P. 4. 25; $\underline{TU}$; $\underline{CN}$ 3 A 2075 (imp. ). Wing
                W 1840

1091    White, Thomas: Sciri, sive sceptices & scepticorum
                a jure disputationis exclusio. Londini.
                1663. 12mo. 2 parts. OS #968; $\underline{O}$ Vet A
                3 f. 387; $\underline{NU}$ 1663 W 588; $\underline{TU}$. Wing W
                1841

1092    White, Thomas: The state of the future life. n. p.
                (London) By T. W. f. John Ridley. 1654.
                12mo. L 847 a. 23; LW. Wing W 1842

1093    White, Thomas: The state of the future life. n. p.
                1657. 12mo. 68p. $\underline{NU}$ 1657 W 588. Wing
                W 1843

1094    White, Thomas: Staterae aequilibrium. Londini.
                1661. 12mo. 75p. L 857 a 9 (2); $\underline{OC}$

Allestree R. 6. 12. Wing W 1845

1095    White, Thomas: Tabulae suffragiales. Londini. 1655.
8vo. L E 1643 (1); OC Allestree 0. 7. 15;
O 8° C 555 Linc.; TU; CN Case 3 A 2079.
Wing W 1846

1096    (White, Thomas, Jesuit): Mr. Whitebread's contemplations. London. 1679. brds. O Good-
win Pamp. 2228 (73). Wing W 1815

1097    The whole duty of a christian as to faith & piety.
Antwerp. 1684. sixes. Ware; CN Case
3 A 2087. Wing Y 196

1098    (Wigmore, W. ): The catholick doctrine of transub-
stantiation. Paris. 1657. 8vo. 2 parts.
HP; Ware; CN Case 3 A 2081. 1 Wing
C 410

1099    W(ilkinson), H(enry): Meditations upon the marks of
the true church. Paris. 1655. 8vo. OS
#973 & 3192; L E 1666 (1); O 110 K 168;
HP; TU; CN Case 3 A 2064. Wing W 2223

Williams, John: see Warner (John)

Wilmot, Earl John: see D. (B. )

1100    (Wilson, John): The English martyrologe. The third
edition. n. p. (St. Omer) 1672. 8vo. O
Vet E 3 f. 115; DAI.Wing W 1080

1101    (Wilson, Matthew): Infidelity unmasked. Gant. Maximilian Graet. 1652. 4to. FSL; OS #196;
TU; CN Case 4 A 1875. Wing W 2929

1102    (Wilson, Matthew): Protestancy condemned. Doway.
1654. 4to. (Author admits in preface
that this is an adaptation of Brerely's
Protestant apology STC 3604=A&R 132-3)
HP; TU; O 4° K 64 Th BS; CN Case 3 A
2083. Wing W 2930

Wilson, Robert: see Talbot (Peter)

A winding sheet for the schism: see Everard (John)

1103    (Winter, John): Observations upon the oath. n. p. d.
(London, c. 1662) 4to. 17p. FSL 142583;
L 700 f. 12 (13). Wing W 3081

1104    (Woodhead, Abraham): A brief account of the ancient
church government. London. J. Cadwell
f. J. Crooke. 1662. 4to. O B. 10. 4. Linc.
Wing W 3436

1105    (Woodhead, Abraham): A brief account of ancient
church government. The second edition.
London f. Benj. Tooke. 1685. 4to. FSL

133998; O Vet A 3 e 415; TU. Wing W
3437

1106    (Woodhead, Abraham):  Catholick theses on several
chief heads. n.p. d. (Oxford, 1689) 4to.
FSL; TU. Wing W 3438

1107    (Woodhead, Abraham):  Church-government. Part V.
Oxford, 1687. 4to. OS #3223; FSL
159626; CN; TU; Y 2d 054. Wing W 3440

1108    (Woodhead, Abraham):  A compendious discourse on
the Eucharist. Oxford. 1688. 4to. NU
1686 S 41(2); FSL bd. w. H 3257; OS
#3224; TU; CN Case 4 A 1877. Wing W
3440A/3461

1109    (Woodhead, Abraham):  Concerning images and
idolatry. Oxford. 1689. 4to. 83p. FSL
131043; TU. Wing W 3441

1110    (Woodhead, Abraham):  Considerations on the council
of Trent. By R. H. n.p. 1671. 4to. OS
#981; FSL 160402; Ware; TU; Y Mhc
9. 57. C 65; CN Case 4 A 1830. Wing W
3442

1111    (Woodhead, Abraham);  Considerations on the council
of Trent. n.p. 1675. 4to. Wing W 3443

1112    (Woodhead, Abraham):  Considerations on the council
of Trent. By R. H. London. Printed f.
Wm. Cadman. 1687. 4to. OS #987 &
3225; TU; CN Case 5 A 419. Wing W
3444

1113    (Woodhead, Abraham):  A discourse on the necessity
of church guides. By R.H. n.p. 1675.
4to. OS #985; LFS; FSL 181394; TU;
CN Case 4 A 1880; NU 1673 W 18. Wing
W 3446

1114    (Woodhead, Abraham):  Dr. Stillingfleet's principles.
By N.O. Paris. Widow of Antonie
Christian & Charles Guillery. 1671. 8vo.
HP; O 8° N 43 Th  These copies have
100p. TU copy has 96p. (This also was
issued as Part IV of C 6891). Wing C
6892

1115    (Woodhead, Abraham):  The Greeks opinion touching
the Eucharist. n.p. 1686. 4to. 34p. OS
#3226; FSL 138418. Wing W 3447

1116    (Woodhead, Abraham):  The guide in controversies
or a rational account of the doctrine.

By R.H. n.p. 1667. 4to. 1st edition of
W 3452. This runs p. 139 to 366. CS
Rr 9. 31; O 8° F 261 BS; OS #980; WGT;
CN 4 A 1871 & Case 4 A 1878 (slight
variant)

1117    (Woodhead, Abraham): The guide in controversies.
n.p. 1673. Wing W 398

1118    (Woodhead, Abraham): An historical narration of
the life and death of Jesus Christ.
Printed at the theatre in Oxford. 1685.
4to. OS #3227; FSL 159244. Wing W
3448

1119    (Woodhead, Abraham): Motives to holy living. Oxford. 1688 4to. FSL 137978; OS #988;
TU; CN Case 4 A 1879. Wing W 3449

1120    (Woodhead, A.): The practice of devotion. By O.N.
n.p. 1672. 8vo. 114p. Ware. Anr. ed.
of W 3454

1121    (Woodhead, A.): The protestants plea for the
socinian. London. Henry Hills. 1686.
4to. 45p. FSL 142630; OS #3229; O 4°
Z Jur. 5 (2). Wing W 3451

1122    (Woodhead, A.): A rational account of the doctrine.
n.p. (London) 1673. (Probably identical
w. W 398). Wing W 3452

1123    (Woodhead, A.): A rational account of the doctrine.
By R.H. Second edition. n.p. 1673. 4to.
OS #984; FSL 158064; TU; CN 4 A 1880;
NU 1673 W 18. Wing W 3453

1124    (Woodhead, A.): The roman church's devotions. By
O.N. n.p. 1672. 8vo. OS #983. 114p.
4to. (This was issued as part II of C
6891 and may have never been issued
separately except in the form noted
supra No. 1120.) TU. Wing W 3454

1125    (Woodhead, A.): The roman doctrine of repentance
and of indulgences. n.p. 1672. 4to.
124p. OS #3230. (This was issued as
Part III of C 6891 and may have never
been issued separately.); TU. Wing W
3455

1126    (Woodhead, A.): The roman doctrine of repentance
and of indulgences. n.p. 1679. 4to.
53p. L 899 f. 15; OS #3231. Wing W
3456

1127    (Woodhead, A.): The second and third treatises of
            the first part of ancient church govern-
            ment. The second treatise. Oxford.
            1688. 4to. 99p. Ware. (This copy only
            contains the second treatise). Wing W
            3457-8?

1128    (Woodhead, A.): The second and third treatises of
            the first part of ancient church govern-
            ment. Oxford. 1688. 4to. <u>Ware</u> 2 T
            (This copy contains 2 parts, the 2nd
            and 3rd treatises 99 + 188 pp. with
            separate tpp. and signatures.); <u>TU</u>;
            <u>CN</u> Case 4 A 1881

1129    (Woodhead, A.): Two discourses concerning the
            adoration of our b. saviour in the H.
            Eucharist. Oxford. 1687. 2 parts. 4to.
            33 + 38pp. of which the second part =
            W 3439. OS #3223; FSL 138845; <u>TU</u>.
            Wing W 3459

1130    (Woodhead, Abraham): Two discourses concerning
            the adoration. Oxford. 1687. 4to. 32 +
            38p. NU; <u>Ware</u>; <u>CN</u> Case 4 A 1882

1131    (Woodhead, Abraham): Two discourses. The first,
            concerning the spirit of Martin Luther...
            The second, concerning the celibacy of
            the clergy. 2 parts with separate tpp.,
            pagination (104 + 39pp.), and signatures.
            (Second part = W 3445). Oxford. 1687.
            4to. OS #3233; <u>Ware</u>; <u>FSL</u>; DAI; <u>NU</u>
            1687 W 18 4 & 5; <u>TU</u>; <u>Y</u> Zd 104; <u>CN</u>
            Case 4 A 1882. Wing W 3460

1132    (Worsley, Edward): A discourse on miracles.. By
            E. W. Antwerp. Michael Cnobbaert.
            1676. 8vo. OS #992; <u>O</u> Antiq. e B 1761.1;
            <u>TU</u>; <u>CN</u> Case 4 A 1883. Wing W 3614

1133    (Worsley, Edward): The infallibility of the Roman
            catholick church. By E. W. Antwerp.
            Michael Cnobbaert. 1674. 8vo. 2 parts.
            260 + 88p. of which the 2nd is W 3613.
            OS #991; <u>TU</u>; <u>CN</u> Case 3 A 2085. Wing
            W 3615

1134    (Worsley, Ed.): Protestancy without principles. By
            E. W. Antwerp. Michael Cnobbaert.
            1688. 4to. 2 parts. OS #3234 A; DAI;
            <u>TU</u>; <u>CN</u> Case 4 A 1884. Wing W 3616

1135     (Worsley, Ed.): Reason and religion. By E.W. Ant-
               werpe. Michael Cnobbaert. 1672. 4to.
               OS #994; Ware; TU; CN Case 4 A 1885.
               Wing W 3617

1136     (Worsley, Ed.): Truth will out. By E.W. n.p. 1665.
               4to. LFS; OS #993; TU; CN 3 A 2086.
               Wing W 3618

1137     York, Anne Hyde, duchess of: A copy of a paper
               written by the late dutchess of York.
               n.d.p. s.sh. (c. 1686) CN Case f F
               4554.265 (In this copy pp. are numbered
               1,2 and there are no sigla. All other
               copies discovered seem to have been
               issued as part of C 2942 ff. See note on
               #215 supra.). Wing Y 46

1138     York, Anne Hyde, duchess of: Reasons of her leaving
               the communion. n.d.p. (c. 1686) cap.
               title. Wing Y 47

1139     (Zacharie de Lisieux): A relation of the country of
               Jansenia. By Louys Fontaines (pseud.)
               Trans. P.B. n.p. (London) f. the author
               and sold by A. Banks and C. Harper.
               1668. 8vo. L 873 f. 7. Wing F 1410

# APPENDIX I

This appendix is assembled in order to complement the main list. It includes six categories of books which fall outside the scope of the principal part of this work. It is numbered continuously with the main list but each serial number is followed by a letter in order to allow users to pick out rapidly the category of writings in which they are interested. The six categories are as follows:

1 Publications of the Catholic confederates in the Irish wars 1643-1648. Suffix: V
2 Ghosts which appear in standard sources, but which apparently do not exist today. Suffix: O
3 Religious books by British Catholic authors published under non-Catholic auspices. We have not included the many interesting non-British authors such as Hennepin, Las Casas, Molinos and Richard Simon. Nor have we listed pre-17th century authors except when these authors had previously been published by British catholics. Suffix: W
4 Works by 17th century English Catholic authors first published in Latin or languages other than the four languages of the British Isles. We have not included Latin translation of works written in English unless the Latin edition contains notable material not in the original English version. We have also included works by Irish authors if they are intimately connected with the English scene. Suffix: X
5 Books attributed to Catholic authors in standard sources, but written in fact by someone else. Suffix: Y
6 Books of doubtfully Catholic origin or which do not otherwise fall within the scope of the main list for some reason not immediately evident. We have also included books which we suspect are Catholic, but which we have not been able to inspect. Suffix: Z

Most of the books in the Appendix have been proposed for inclusion in the main list by helpful critics. It has also enabled us to give the complete bibliography during the years 1641-1700 of some important writers. It also contains a number of books not generally known to bibliographers which we have encountered in our researches.

| 1140Z | Albertus Magnus, St.: The secrets of. London. R. Cotes to be sold by Fulke Clifton. 1650. 16°. Not seen. 2 Wing A 8751 |
|---|---|
| 1141Z | Albertus Magnus, St.: The secrets of. n. d. (1691?) Not seen. 2 Wing A 875J |
| 1142W | Albertus Magnus, St.: Unum necessarium, or. London f. R. Baldwin. 1692. 2 Wing A 877 |
| 1143X | Alford, Michael: Britannia illustrata. Antwerpiae. 1641. L 1228 c. 6 |
| 1144X | Alford, Michael: Fides regia Britanica. Leodii. 1663. 4 vols. L 483 g 1-4; TU |
| 1145Z | Alvarez, Emmanuel: An introduction to the latin tongue... translated into English for young students of the same Society (of Jesus). London. Henry Hills... f. him and Matthew Turner. 1686. Sixes. MH. 2 Wing A 2942 |
| 1146Z | Alvarez, Emmanuel: An introduction to the latin tongue... translated into English for young students of the same Society (of Jesus). London. Henry Hills. 1689. Sixes. LGL |
| 1147X | (Anderton, T. ): Concordia Scientiae cum fide. Authore Thoma Bonarte (Anagram of Barton which was his alias). Col. Agrip. 1659 |
| 1148X | (Anderton, T. ): Concordia Scientiae cum fide. Authore Thoma Bonarte Nordtano. Coloniae. 1665. O B. 20. 17. Linc. ; BN 842 d 2; (Newdigate nn. ) |
| 1149Z | (Anderton, Thomas): A sovereign remedy against atheism. 1672. Not seen. 2 Wing A 3110A |
| 1150Z | An answer to a late pamphlet; entitled, A character of a popish successor. London. Nathaniel Thompson. 1681. TU (Tory pamphlet more political than relig.) |
| 1151Z | An answer to a letter to a dissenter. London. 1687. FSL bd. w. 189; (Tory and royalist, but not religious). 2 Wing A 3319 |
| 1152Z | An answer to the city conformists letter. London. Mary Thompson. 1688. 4to. Hiscock A 3399A+; FSL 144207. (Political) 2 Wing A 3399A |
| 1153Z | An answer to the protestation of the 19 Lords. London. Printed f. Cave Pulleyn. 1681. O |

Wood 427 (18); FSL 134687.9 (Called
popish in contemporary writings but
more Tory than religious). 2 Wing A
3437

1154Z   (Arnauld, A.): The sence of the french church concerning the pope's infallibility. n. p. d.
(London. 1663) O Pamphlet 119 C (30)
Probably published under non-Cath.
auspices. Wing S 2550

1155Z   The arts and pernicious designs of Rome... by a
person of their own communion. London.
f. Henry Brome. 1680. O C. 10.3 Linc.
2 Wing A 3895

1156W   Augustine, St.: St. Augustines confessions. London.
Printed by T.R. and E.M. f. Abel Roper.
1650. O Vet A 3 f. 350. (On tp. editors
promise to answer "the marginall notes
of a former Popish Translation"). 2
Wing A 4206

1157W   Augustine, St.: St. Augustines confessions. London.
1679. (Another ed. of previous item).
2 Wing A 4207

1158W   Augustine, St.: The judgement of the learned and
pious. London f. James Collins. 1670.
2 Wing A 4210

1159W   (Austin, John): Devotions in the ancient way of offices.
Reformed by a person of quality & pub-
lished by Geo. Hickes. London. J. Jones.
1700. CLC. 2 Wing A 4250C

1160Y   Austin, John: A Zealous sermon preached at Amsterdam by a Jew . Amsterdam (Vere Lon-
don) 1642. L E 149 (18) (Not our John
Austin). 2 Wing A 4252

1161X   Ayleworth, Guil.: Metaphysica scholastica. Leodii
apud J.W. Friessen. 1675. OS #32;
CN Case 6 A 329; (Ayleworth also known
as Harcourt. See Gillow III, 123, 1)

1162X   (Bacon, Nathaniel): Bibliotheca scriptorum societatis
Jesu. Romae. 1676. (Also known as
Nathaniel Southwell. He is not the author
of Wing B 348, 349, 350, 351, 355, 356,
357, 358, 359, 360, 361, 362, 363, 364,
365, 366)

1163W   Baltimore, George Calvert, Lord: An answer to Tom
Tell-Troth. London. 1642 (/3). FSL

(Basically political). 2 Wing B 611

1164W    Barnes, John:  Catholico-Romanus pacificus. Oxoniae
         e theatro Sheldoniano. 1680. L 3935 a
         14; Madan 3259. 2 Wing B 865

1165W    Bartoli, Daniel:  The learned man defended. London.
         R & W. Lewybourne...to be sold by
         Thomas Dring. 1660. O Wood 130 (5)
         (Author was a learned Italian Jesuit
         humanist and historian).  2 Wing B 988

         Barton, Thomas:  see Anderton (Thos. )

1166Z    Bayly, Thomas:  Certamen religiosum. 1649 etc.
         (this work written before Bayly became
         a Roman Catholic. The same is true
         for 2 following). 2 Wing B 1506-9

1167Z    Bayly, Thomas:  Herba parietis: or, the wall-flower.
         2 Wing B 1511 & B 1516

1168Z    Bayly, Thomas:  The royal charter. 1649 etc. 2
         Wing B 1514-5

1169Z    (Bayly, Thomas):  Witty apopthegms. 1658 etc.
         (These works are mostly drawn from
         the author's Certamen religiosum).
         Wing W 3236-8

1170W    Beccadelli, Lodovico:  Vita Reginaldi Poli. Londini.
         Impensis Jacobi Adamson. 1690. (This
         and the following were edited by the
         Church of England clergyman, Henry
         Wharton). 2 Wing B 1641

1171W    Beccadelli, Lodovico:  Vita Reginaldi Poli. Londini.
         Impensis Tho. Bennet. 1696. CS
         C. 13. 22; 2 Wing B 1641A

1172Y    (Bellarmine, Robert):  The notes of the Church.
         London f. Richard Chiswell. 1688.
         (This is not by Bellarmine but rather
         an answer to B 1824). Wing B 1823

1173X    (Bellings, Richard):  Annotationes in R. P. F. Poncii
         opus. Parisiis. 1654. Nicholas Pele.
         L 860e13/4; Walsh #55

1174X    Bellings, Richard:  Illustrissimi et reverendissimi
         DD. Archiepscopis praesulibus....vin-
         dicias. 1652

1175X    Bellings, Richard:  Lettre de...a Monsieur Callaghan.
         n. p. d. (Paris, 1652). Walsh #54

1176Z    Bernard, St.:  A looking glass for all new converts.
         1685. (See 1178 infra. ) 2 Wing B 1980A

1177Z    Bernard, St.: A mirror that flatters not. London f.
                Moses Pitt. 1677 (See 1178) 2 Wing B
                1981

1178Z    Bernard, St.: A mirror that flatters not. London.
                1677. FSL 187274. 2 Wing B 1982. (The
                original of this work as well as B 1980A
                & B 1981 and perhaps B 1982A - was
                probably St. Bernard's De conversione
                ad clericos. The editor deplores sectarian
                fights and pleads for the essence of
                Christian religious practice. Probably
                not Catholic)

1179Z    Bernard, St.: S. Bernard's pious meditations.
                London f. N. Boddington. 1700. 12mo.
                Not seen. 2 Wing B 1982A

1180Z    Bernard, St.: St. Bernard's vision. (London) f. J.
                Wright. brds. n.d. (1683?) Not seen.
                2 Wing B 1928B

1181Z    (Beverly, Thomas): Catholick catechism. London f.
                Thom. Parkhurst & Will. Miller. 1683.
                O G Pamph. 1565; (Not Roman Catholic).
                2 Wing B 2128

1182Z    Blosius, Ludovicus: Enchiridion parvulorum. 1655.
                Not seen. 2 Wing B 3202

1183W    Bona, Giovanni Cardinal: A guide to eternity. 1680
                etc. (This is Sir Roger L'Estrange's
                translation and is the protestant version
                of B 3549-50). 2 Wing B 3545-8

1184W    Bona, Giovanni Cardinal: Manuductio ad coelum.
                1672 & 1681. 2 Wing B 3551-2

1185W    Bona, Giovanni Cardinal: Precepts and practical
                rules. 1678. (Translator contributes a
                Protestant preface). 2 Wing B 3553

1186Z    Bossuet, Jacques: An exposition of the doctrine.
                f. Richard Chiswell. 1686. 12°. 2 Wing
                B 3784B. Not seen

1187W    Bossuet, Jacques: Maxims and reflections upon plays.
                London f. R. Sare. 1699. Y College
                Pamphlets v. 980. 2 Wing B 3786

1188W    Bossuet, Jacques: A relation of the famous conference.
                London by H. C. f. Thomas Malthus.
                1684. L 3902 i. 1; (This is the Prot.
                version of B 3780). 2 Wing B 3790

1189W    (Bouhours, Dominic): Christian thoughts. 1680 etc.
                (Probably non-Catholic). 2 Wing B

1190W   (Bouhours, Dominique): The life of the renowned
Peter D'Abusson. 1679. (Probably non-
Catholic). 2 Wing B 3827

1191W   (Boutauld, Michel): The councils of wisdom. Trans.
T. D. (i. e. Thomas Dare). Amsterdam
f. Stephen Swart. 1683. L 1159 b. 23;
(This trans. is different from that of
E. Sheldon #134.) 2 Wing B 3860B

1192W   (Boutauld, Michel): The councils of wisdom. London f. Sam Smith. 1683. FSL B 2634. 2
(Same translation as preceding number)
2 Wing B 3860C

1193Z   Bridget, St.: The prayers of. 1686. 8vo. Not seen.
2 Wing B 2959A

1194Z   Brief notes on the creed of St. Athanasius. n. d. p.
(c. 1694). Hiscock B 4614[+]; OC 1 F 53;
FSL B 4616. 5; (Appears to be a Socinian
or Unitarian work)

1195V   A brief relation of the most remarkable feates.
Waterford by Thomas Bourke. 1644.
2 Wing B 4626

1196V   C., P.: The inquisition of a sermon... by Robert
Daborne. Waterford by Thomas Bourke.
1644. 2 Wing C 94

Callaghan, John: see MacCallaghan (John)

1197W   (Camus, Jean-Pierre): Elise or Innocencie guilty.
London by T. Newcomb f. Humphrey
Moseley. 1655 L 1461 k 3; FSL 140484;
2 Wing C 413

1198W   (Camus, Jean-Pierre): A true tragicall history.
London f. Wm. Jacob. 1677. O 8° P
24 Art. (This book is licensed and hence
non-Catholic). 2 Wing C 419

1199Y   (Canes, J. B. V.): The pope's poesie. London f. John
Crook. 1663. O G. Pamph. 1525 (11);
(This was written as an answer to Canes
by J. D. D.) 2 Wing C 434

1200O   (Canes, J. V.): Fiat Lux. 1664. (I have never found
this work at L or elsewhere). 2 Wing
C 431

1201X   (Canfield, Benet): Regula perfectionis. Romae.
Typis Fabii de Falco. 1666. OS #140;

1202W   The canons and decrees of the council of Trent.
London f. f. T. Y. 1687. 2 Wing C 446

1203X    Carew, Thomas: Responsio veridica ad illotum libel-
lum. Sulzbach. Typis Abrahami Lichten-
thaleri sumptibus Michael & Johan Fred-
erici Enterorum. 1672. Walsh #104

1204X    Caron, Raymundus: Apostolicus evangelicus missionariorum. (Antwerp) Apud viduam Joan.
Cnobari. 1652. Walsh #109

1205X    Caron, Raymundus: Apostolatus missionariorum.
Parisiis. Symptibus Anthonii Bertier.
1659. O l. b. 86;

1206X    Caron, R.: Controversiae generales fidei contra
infideles omnes. Paris. Apud Frederi-
cum Leonard. 1660. Walsh 112-3

1207X    Caron, R.: Roma triumphans septicollis. Antwerp.
Apud viduam Joanni Cnobari. 1653.
(misprinted 1635) Walsh #110

1208Z    The case of divers roman Catholiques. London f.
Anna Seile. L 816 m 22 (68). Unseen.
2 Wing C 905

1209V    Castlehaven, James Touchet, Earl of: A remonstrance
of. Waterford by Thomas Bourke. 2
Wing C 1236

1210Z    Castlemaine, Roger Palmer, Earl of: An account of
the present war. London. 1666. (not a
religious book). 2 Wing C 1238

1211Z    Castlemaine, Roger Palmer, Earl of: The English
globe. London f. Joseph Moxon. 1679.
(Not a religious work). 2 Wing C 1242

1212Y    Castlemaine, Roger Palmer, Earl of: The late
apology. London f. M. N. 1667. (This
is an answer to Castlemaine-Pugh).
Wing C 1244

1213Z    Castlemaine, Roger Palmer, Earl of: Short and true
account. 1671 etc. (Not a religious work).
2 Wing C 1247-8

A Catholick catechism: see Beverly (Thomas)

1214Z    A catechisme of christian religion. Amsterdam. 1652.
Y Mzvh 428. 1652 G. (Not Catholic) 2
Wing C 1475

1215Z    A catholick and protestant almanack. London. Henry
Hills. 1688. Not seen. 2 Wing A 1389

1216Z    Catholick hymn, on the birth of the prince of Wales.
n. p. 1688. Not seen. 2 Wing C 1494

1216Z    A Catholick pill to purge popery. London f. J. Coles
& Will. Miller. 1677. Y Brit. Tracts

1677 c. 31; <u>FSL</u> 173338; (Not Catholic).
2 Wing C 1495

A catholicks resolution: see Swadlin (Thomas)

1217Z    (Caussin, Nich.): A voice from the dead. London.
1681. Not seen. 2 Wing C 1551C

1218W    (Ceriziers, Rene): The innocent lady. 1654, 1674.
(Protestant editions). 2 Wing C 1679-
1680

1219W    Ceriziers, Rene: The innocent lord. London by S. G.
f. Charles Adams. 1655. (Protestant
edition). 2 Wing C 1681

1220W    Charles II: Copies of two papers written by... To
which is added an answer. Dublin. Re-
printed by Jos. Ray f. Rob. Thornton.
1686. 4to. 2 parts 8 + 34p. <u>NU</u>. 2 Wing
C 2946

1221W    Chasteigner de la Roche-Pozay, Henri Louis: Cele-
briorum distinctionum philosophicarum
synopsis. Editio nova. Oxoniae Excudebat
Hen. Hall impensis Jos. Goodwin & Edw.
Forrest. 1667. <u>O</u> Crynes 75; Madan 2330;
(The latter third of this work was written
by Geo. Reeb, a Jesuit professor at
Dillengen. The principal author was the
bp. of Poitiers. This is purely philosophical). 2 Wing C 3729

1222Z    The christians guide: a treatise. London f. Henry
Rhodes. 1683 <u>FSL</u> 147946 (This is a
devotional manual not of Catholic prove-
nance). 2 Wing C 3955

1223X    Clarke, Robert: Christiado sive de passione Dni
libri 17. Brugis. Typis Kerchovianis.
1670. OS #184; <u>CN</u> Case 3 A 1875

1224X    Compton Carleton, Thomas: Cursus theologici
tomus prior. Leodii ex officina Jo.
Matthiae Hovii. 1659. <u>L</u>

1225X    Compton, Thomas: Cursus theologici Tomus posterior.
Leodii ex officina Jo. Matthiae Hovii.
1664. <u>L</u>

1226X    Compton, Thomas: Cursus theologici tomus prior.
Editio secunda. Antwerpiae apud Hiero-
nymum Verdussen. 1684. <u>L</u> 3559 g. 3;

1227X    Compton, Thomas: Cursus theologici tomus posterior.
Editio secunda. Antwerpiae. Apud viduam
et haeredes Hieronymi Verdussen. 1689.

L 3559 g. 3;

1228X   Compton, Thomas: Disputationes physicae. Sala-
manticae. Melchior Estevez. 1676. L
8460 d. 14;

1229X   Compton, Thomas: Philosophia universa. Antwerpiae.
apud Jacobum Meursium. 1649. L 8564
h. 8; O A. 8. 14. Th.;

1230X   Compton, Thomas: Philosophia universa. Antwerpiae
apud Jacobum Meursium. 1674

1231X   Compton, Thomas: Prometheus christianus seu
liber moralium. Secunda editio. Leodii,
Leonard Streel. 1653

Conclusiones theologicae: Disputations are listed
under name of president

1232X   Conroy, Florence: Peregrinus Jerichuntius, hoc est,
de natura humana. Paris. Apud Claudium
Calleville. 1641. Walsh #141

1223X   Conroy, Florence: Abregé de la doctrine de S.
Augustin. Paris. 1645. Walsh #142

1234X   Conroy, Florence: Tractatus de statu parvulorum.
Louvain apud Jacobum Zegers. 1641.
Walsh #140

1235X   Constitutiones collegii pontificii Anglorum duacensis.
Duaci. M. Mairesse. 1690. O Vet E 3
f. 85; TU

1236X   Constitutiones missionis benedictorum congregationis
anglicanae. Duaci. Typis I. Kellami.
1661. TU

1237X   (Corby, Ambrose): Certamen triplex. Antwerpiae
apud Joannem Meursium. 1645. O
Crynes 20; NU; CN Case 2 A 119

1238X   Corby, Ambrose: Certamen triplex. n. p. Luke
Straub f. John Wagner. 1646. O

1239X   Corby, Ambrose: Narratio gloriosae mortis...Hen-
ricus Mors. Gandavi (Graet) 1645. New-
digate nn

1240X   Courtney, Edward: R.P. Petri Writi...Mors. n. p. d.
(Antwerp 1651) HP Z; OS #202; (The
author is also known as Leedes)

1241Z   The court of Rome. London f. Henry Herringman.
1654. Ware; FSL 247943; (This is a
translation. Basically a travel book).
2 Wing C 6591

1242O   Cressy, Hugh Paul Serenus: Exomologesis. 1679.
(No such book. Wing reference is to a

bk. by Matthew Poole) Wing C 6897.
Not in 2 Wing

1243Y   (Cressy, Hugh Paulin Serenus): Why are you not a
Roman Catholic? London. H. Brome.
1679. (This is a reply to Cressy). Wing
C 6903. Cancelled in 2 Wing

1244Y   (Cressy, Hugh Paulin Serenus): Why are you not a
Roman Catholic? n. d. p. FSL C 6903.2
(Another edition of the preceding)

1245Y   Cross, Nicholas: A word to all the people. London
f. the author. 1661. (This is not our
author but a non-conformist). 2 Wing
C 7255

1246O   (Crowther, Arthur Anselm): The dayly exercise of
the devout christian. For S. Evans in
Worcester, sold by H. Sawbridge. 1684.
2 Wing C 7409C locates copies at FSL
and WGT but I have been unable to find
one there

1247O   (Crowther, Arthur Anselm): Jesu, Maria, Joseph.
Antwerp. William Cesteane. 1654. 2
Wing C 7409F locates copy at CN but
none is discoverable there

1248X   D. , C. Sc. S. J.: L'idée d'une reine parfaite en la
vie de S. Marguerite reine d'Ecosse.
Douay Chez Balthazar Bellere. 1660.
The dedication of this work which does
not bear any author's name is signed
C. D. Sc. S. I. which the L catalogue
deciphers as the initial letters of
Collegium Duacense Scoticarum Societatis Jesu. There is a copy in L 287 b. 8.
This was the French original of L 1173
which is in main list

1249O   D. , J.: A short justification. 1681
1250O   D. , J.: Seraphick offices. Paris. 1685. L. Not seen
1251O   D. , J.: Vindication of the practice of England. London. 1699.

       D. , J. D.: The Pope's posie. See #1199 supra

1252V   Darcy, Patrick: An argument delivered. Waterford.
Thos. Bourke O 226 f. 62. 2 Wing
D 246

1253Y   (Darrell, Wm. ): The layman's answer to the layman's opinion. London. 1687. (This is
an answer to D 266 and surely not by

Darrell). Wing D 265, but cancelled in
2 Wing

1254O    (Darrell, Wm.): A sermon preached by. 1688. 4to.
2 Wing D 269 gives MC location, but this
item is not findable there. Probably same
as 2 D 269A

1255X    Darrell, William: Theses theologicae. Liege. 1700.
HP (Newdigate). This was a theological
defense at which Darrell presided and
H. Turville defended

1256X    Davenport, Christopher: Manuale missionariorum
regularium. Duaci. Balthazar Belleri.
1658. O Gough Eccles. Top. 10; CN

1257X    Davenport, Christopher: Manuale missionariorum
regularium. Editio secunda. Duaci. O
Crynes 155; OS (imp.)

1258X    Davenport, Christopher: Operum omnium...tomus
primus. 1665, tomus secundus. 1667.
Duaci. Balthazar Beller. O Fol. Theta
177; CN

1259X    (Davenport, Christopher): Supplementum historiae
provinciae Angliae. Duaci. Typis Bal-
thazaris Belleri. 1671. L 489 i. 13 (a)

1260X    Davenport, Christopher: Systema Fidei sive tractatus. Leodii. Typis Joannis Tournay.
1648. O B. 2. 4. Linc.; CN

1261X    Declaratio Innocentiae suae ad fratres. n. p. 1662.
4to. 8p. OS, Old Brotherhood Archives
II, 125 (Latin version of Wing E 725A)

1262V    A declaration made by the major towne council...
Galway. Kilkenny. 1648. 2 Wing D 600B

1263V    A declaration of the supreme council of the Confederat Catholicks. Waterford. Thomas
Bourke. 1643, brds. 2 Wing D 769A

1264V    A declaration of the supreme councill of the confederate Catholicks...admonishing.
n. d. p. (Kilkenny, 1648). 2 Wing D
769B

1265X    Digby, Kenelm: Demonstratio immortalitatis animae
rationalis. Parisiis. 1651. (This trans.,
probably by John Leyburne, of Digby's
Two Treatises is included because of
the new matter Thomas White added in
the preface to this Latin version)

1266X    Digby, Kenelm: Demonstratio immortalitatis animae rationalis. Parisiis. Federicus Leonard. 1655

1267X    Digby, Kenelm: Demonstratio immortalis animae rationalis. Francofurti. 1664

1267O    The directory for the mass. (This work is mentioned by contemporaries as being printed in the late 1640's or early 1650's. See 9 RH 68 & appendix.)

1268Z    A discourse for taking off the tests and penal laws. London. Randal Taylor. 1687. 4to. 40p. FSL 137490. (More political than religious). 2 Wing D 1593

Dormer, John: see Huddleston (John)

1270W    Drexel(ius), Jeremy: All the works listed by Wing seem to have been published under Protestant auspices. 2 Wing D 2168-2186

1271W    (DuFour de Longuerue, Louis): An historical treatise written by an author of the communion romaine. London f. Richard Chiswell. 1687. OS #1744

1272W    (Du Four de Longuerue, Louis): Traité d'un auther de la Communion romaine. Londres. Chez B. Griffin pour Jean Cailloue. 1686. Hiscock T 2024 +. O 8° B 41 Linc.

Duns, John, Scotus: see Moor (John)

1273W    DuPerron, Jacques Davy Cardinal: A copy of a letter sent from. 1641. L E 163 (10). 2 Wing D 2637

1274Y    DuPerron, Jacques: A warning to the parliament of England. London f. R. W. 1647. (The author of this piece is not the Cardinal but Bishop DuPerron of Angouleme. Published under Protestant auspices). 2 Wing D 2634

1275X    Dymock, James: Le vice ridiculé et la vertu louée. Louvain. Pierre Sassenus. Louvain. 1671. L C 38 c 60;

1276Z    The English donatizing church: Or a parallel. n. p. d. 4to. 99p. LFS (Political but from the Catholic viewpoint).

1277V    Enos, Walter: Alexipharmacon or a soveraigne antidote. Waterford. Thomas Bourke. 1644. Wing 3129

1278V     Enos, Walter: The second part of the survey. Kilkenny. 1646. Wing E 3130

1279V     Enos, Walter: A survey of the articles of the late rejected peace. Kilkenny. 1646. L G 5594. Wing E 3131

1280X     Errington, Anthony: Missionarium; sive opusculum practicum. Romae. Typis sacrae congregationis de propaganda fide. 1672. NU McA. 1672 E 72;

1281W     Eustachius a Sancto Paulo: Ethica sive summa moralis desciplinae. Londini. Typis IR. impensis Joh. Williams. 1671. 8vo. CN Case 3 A 1922 (This scholastic author may have been English. He surely was Catholic. This & his other works, E 3429-33, were popular in 17th cent. Engl.)

Ewens, Maurice: see Newport

1282Z     An extraordinary express sent from pasquin at Rome. London f. Henry Hills. 1690. O G Pamph. 1691 (36); (Not a Catholic publication). Wing E 3931A

1283Z     A few short arguments proving that 'tis every Englishman's interest. London. Henry Hills. 1687. brds. Not seen. Wing F 837

1284O     Fitzherbert, Thomas: A treatise concerning policy and religion. Douay. 1646. (I have never seen a copy of this edition. No copy discovered at CE). Wing F 1101

1285W     Fleury, Claude: An historical account of the manner and behaviour of the Christians. f. Thomas Leigh. 1698. 8vo. L 4531 aa. 15. Wing F 1363

1286W     Francis de Sales: An introduction to a devout life... Fitted for the use of Protestants. n. d. p. (Dublin. 1679) CS O 15. 15;

1287Z     Francis de Sales, St.: An introduction to a devout life. London f. T. Bennett & J. Sprout. 1700. Not seen

1288X     French, Nicholas: Protesta y supplica de los catolicos. Sevilla por Juan Lorenco. 1659. O 4° A 44 Art. BS

1289X     French, Nicholas: Supplicatio Catholicorum magnae Britanniae et Hiberniae. Compostella. Ex typographia Josephi de Conto & Sierrae. 1659. Walsh 244

1290X    (French, Nicholas): Vera descriptio moderni status
Catholicorum in regno Hiberniae.
Coloniae. 1667. Walsh 245. L G 5761

1291O    The funeral sermon of the Queene of Great Britaine.
Paris. 1670. (This was an English
trans. of the sermon preached at the
funeral of Henrietta Maria. In the British
Museum Catalogue it is listed at 4423
a. 3, but it was destroyed during World
War II. Translation was by Miles Pinckney)

1292Z    G., J.: Satisfaction in religion. London. M. Turner.
1687. Not seen. Wing G 38

1293Y    G., J.: A seasonable discourse about religion. London f. Geo. Grefton. 1689. 4to. 74p.
CN Case F 4556. 65 (Sometimes attributed
to Gother, but definitely not his)

1294X    Gennings, Jo.: Institutio missionariorum. Duaci.
Typis Baltasaris Belleri. 1651. OS #363;
CN Case 3 A 120

1295X    (Gennings, Michael): Conclusiones theologicae de
sacramentis in genere. Duaci. Typis
Joannis de Fampoux. brds. OS (This
was a defense at which Gennings presided. The defendants were Henry Vere
and Thomas Downham.)

1296X    Goodwin, Ignatius: Lapis lydius controversiarum.
Leodii. Typis Jo. Matthiae Hovii. 1656.
HP; TU

1297X    Goodwin, Ignatius: Exercitatio divini amoris. Leodii.
1656. Newdigate nn

1298Y    (Gother, John): A papist misrepresented and repre-
sented. Dublin. Reprinted by A. C. &
S. H. for the Society of Stationers. 1686.
O Montague 201. (This is a work answering
John Gother's work of this name) Wing
G 1336

1299Y    Grene, Martin: Autokatakritoi (in greek characters)
or the Jesuits condemned. London f.
Chas. Harper. 1679. (This is an answer
to Grene's G 1825). Wing G 1826

Harcourt, Wm.: see Ayleworth

1300X    (Heath, Henry): Soliloquia seu documenta christiana
perfectionis Duaci. Typis Balthasaris
Belleri. 1651. OS #400; TU; (Signed

"Paulus a Sancta Magdalena" = name
in religion)

1301Z     Hoddeson, John: The holy lives of God's prophets.
London f. Wil. Hope. 1654. Not seen.
Wing H 2294

1302Z     Hoddeson, John: Sion and Parnassas. London.·R.
Daniel f. G. Eversden. 1650. FSL.
(Doubtfully Catholic). Wing H 2295

1303X     Holden, Henry: Divinae fidei analysis. Parisiis apud
Aegidium Blaizot. 1652. OS #412

1304X     Holden, Henry: Divinae fidei analysis. Parisiis.
J&M Villery. 1685. BN D 21361

1305X     Holden, Henry: Henrici Holdeni theologi parisensis
epistola brevis. n. p. d. (Paris. 1661)
BN D 8112 & D 10661

1306X     Holden, Henry: Novum Jesu Christi testamentum...
cum annotationibus brevissimis. Parisiis.
Apud Carolum Savreux. 1660. HP; OS

1307X     Holden, Henry: Typographus lectori.... Fragmentum
de gratia efficaci. n. p. d. (But some
years after Holden's death)

1308Z     (Huddleston, John): The new plot of the papists by
which they design'd to have laid the
guilt... London f. Robert Harford 1679.
(Put by Wing under Dormer, which was
Huddleston's alias, but this is definitely
not by him. He wrote his response to
this and its title corresponded in the
first six words with this title.) FSL
136916; CN Case F 4554.62. 2 Wing D
1923

1309Z     (Huddleston, John): A new plot of the papists. Dublin. 1679. Not seen. 2 Wing D 1923

1310O     (Hughes, John): He is said to have translated a
catechism into Welsh, but I have not
come across it

1311W     Hugo, Herman: Pia desideria or divine addresses.
1686 & 1690 (These two editions seem
to be published under Protestant
auspices.) Wing H 3350-1

1312Z     A humble hint to the king. n. p. (London) Nathaniel
Thompson. 1685. (This seems to be a
purely political work.) Wing H 3417

1313Y     Hutchinson, Wm.: A letter to the Jesuits in prison.
Coloph. London f. the author. 1679.

cap. follscep folio. 4p. <u>NC</u> Spec. Coll.
B 932. 5. H 975. Wing H 3837

1314Z      An impartial account of the doctrines of the Church
of Rome. London. Printed by H. L. 1679.
FSL 132620. Not Catholic. Wing I 69A

1315Z      An impartial account of the nature and tendencies of
the late addresses. London f. R. Bald-
win. 1681. <u>O</u> Ashm. 727 (26) (Though
called papist in contemporary publications this is rather a purely political
Tory pamphlet). Wing I 73-73A

IRELAND (under this head are grouped in chronological order
the publications of the Irish Catholics in the 1640's
which have titles awkward to index)

1316V      The Irish petition to this parliament. n. p. 1641.
Wing I 1043

1317V      By the supream councell of the confederate Catholicks.
Waterford. 1643. Wing I 354/394

1318V      By the supream councell of the confederat Catholicks.
Waterford Thomas Bourke. 1643. <u>O</u> Ms.
Carte 6 Fol. 511. Wing B 6371A/I 394

1319V      Admonition by the Supreame Councell of the Confederat Catholicks. Waterford. Thomas
Bourke. 1643. Wing A 593A

1320V      Admonitions by the Supreame Councell. Waterford.
Thomas Bourke. 1643. 2 Wing A 598

1321V      Declaration of the supreme council of the confederate
Catholicks. Waterford. Thomas Bourke.
brds. 1643. Wing D 769A

1322V      By the general assembly of the confederate catholics
of Ireland: "Whereas several declara-
tions..." 4 July 1645. Printed at Waterford 1645 and reprinted at Kilkenny in
the yeare 1646. <u>O</u> Carte MSS Vol. 18,
No. 8. Wing I 343/867

1323V      By the councell and congregation. "Whereas such of
the Roman.." 28 Sept. 1646. Kilkenny.
O Carte MSS XVII, 616. Wing I 342/885

1324V      By the general assembly of the Confederate Catholics.
Kilkenny. 1646 (2nd ed. of I 343). Wing
I 343A

1325V      By the supreme Councell of the Confederate Catholicks.
27 May 1648. Kilkenny. 1648. <u>O</u> Carte
XXII, 108. Wing I 355

125

1326V    By the supreme Councell of the Confederate Catholics. "The deepe sense we have of the sadd conditions..." 3 June 1648. Kilkenny. 1648. brds. O Carte MSS XXII, 122. Wing I 393

1327V    By the supreame Councell..."It cannot be expressed.." 7 July 1648. Kilkenny. 1648. O Carte MSS XXII, 145

1328V    By the supream councell..."Although we find our- selves..." 28 July 1648. Kilkenny. 1648. O Carte MSS XXII, 158

1329V    "Whereas by our late proclamation.." 13 August 1648. Kilkenny. (1648) O Carte MSS XXII, 167. Wing I 735

1330V    By the general assembly..."Whereas divers ill affected.." 14 Sept. 1648. Kilkenny. 1648. O Carte MSS XXII, 208. Wing I 767

1331V    By the general assembly. "Whereas Colonell Owen O'Neill.." 30 Sept. 1648. Kilkenny. 1648. O Carte MSS XXII, 261

1332V    By the general assemblie of the confederate..."This assembly taking seriously..." 30 Sept. 1648. Kilkenny. 1648. O MSS Carte XXII, 262

1333V    By the general assemblie..."The ensuing declaration..." (Kilkenny, 1648) O Carte MSS XXII, 185

1334V    Declaration of the supreme council of the confederate Catholics....admonishing. (Kilkenny. 1648) brds. Wing D 769B

1335V    Declaration of the supreme council...withdrawing. (Kilkenny. 1648) brds. Wing D 769C

1336V    Ireland's declaration being a remonstrance. 13 March 1649. Dublin. Wing I 1021

(resume alphabetical order)

1337Z    Ireland's tears..to the sacred memory of...King Charles II. London. Nath. Thompson. 1685. Not seen. Wing I 1026

1338Z    (Janson, Henry): Philanax anglicus or a christian caveat. London f. Theo. Sadler. 1663. (This work is sometimes attributed to Thomas Bellamy. Janson was a Catholic baronet and this work draws heavily on Patteson's IMAGE OF BOTH CHURCHES, first published 1633 (A&R 599) and re-

126

printed in 1653 (P 868) but the imprimatur shows that this edition is Protestant).
Wing J 482

1339Z   (Jarrige, Pierre): The works attributed to this author
by Wing are collections of Jansenistic
writings published in the Protestant
interest. Wing J 488-490

1340W   The jesuit reasons unreasonable. London f. Richard
Chiswell 1688. Wing J 726

1341O   Johnson, Wm.: Novelty represt. Paris f. E. C. 1664.
(The NU copy of this is simply the 1661
ed., J 861, with a 4 pencilled in on the
tp over the last digit of the date. N. B.
Wm. Johnson who wrote J 861 is not the
same man as the author of Wing J 858-
860, J 863.) Wing J 862

1342O   Key of paradise. (Crouch mentions a contemporary
edition of this work in his Man in the
Moon. No. 12 (27 June-4 July 1649) p.
100. See 9 RH 64 & n. 3)

1343X   (Keynes, John): Florus anglo-Bavaricus. Leodii
apud Henricum Streel. 1685. OS #557;
FSL DA 448 L 4 Cage; (This work is
traditionally attributed to Keynes, but
Birrel in 48 CRS 524 states that Thomas
Stapleton is the author)

1344W   Langhorne, Richard: Petition and declaration of...
in which he avowedly owneth several
popish principles. n. p. d. (London, 1679).
NU. Wing L 398

1345W   (La Peyrere, Isaac de): Men before Adam. London.
1656. (The second part of this two-part
work is L 428) O Crynes 348

1346W   (La Peyrere, Isaac de): Men before Adam. London.
1656. O Wood 889 (This is a variant of
the preceding item)

1347W   (La Peyrere, Isaac de): Praeadamitae sive exercitatio. n. p. (London? ?) 1655. O Crynes
848 (3); CN

1348O   Lascelles, Richard: A little way how to hear masse
with profit and devotion. Paris 1644
(According to Hugh Aveling in Northern
Catholics p. 252f. this work was dedicated to Lady Anne Brudenell. There
are other indications that Lascelles'

work has not survived in earlier edd. )

1349Z    Lazarus and his sisters discoursing of Paradise. n.
p. 1665. L 4371 d 2 (1). Not Catholic

Leedes, Edward: See Courtney

1350W    Le Grand, Antoine: This French franciscan spent
many years in England and most of his
books were published there, but those
listed by Wing L 945-959 are purely
philosophical and were probably not published under Catholic auspices. )

1351O    (Legrand, Antoine): Missae sacrificium neomystis
succincte expositum. Londini. 1695.
Not seen

1352X    Legrand, Antoine: Seydromedia, seu sermo quem
Alphonus de la Vida habuit.. Norimbergae.
1669. BN * E 2475 (1); L 522 a 25; Not
seen

1353W    Leicester's Commonwealth. 1641 etc. (None of the
edd. of this work after the first one
(A &R 261) were published under Catholic
auspices). Wing L 968-969A

1354W    Lessius, Leonard: The temperate man. London. J.
R. f. R. Starkey. 1678. Wing L 1181

1355Z    A letter from a gentleman of the Romish religion
1674, 1679 (This is not a Catholic work).
Wing L 1399-1400

1356Z    A letter from a Roman Catholick to one of his friends.
London f. R. Baldwin. 1689 (Not seen).
Wing L 1434

1357Z    A letter of a Jesuit of Liege concerning the methods.
n. p. d. (London, 1687) L 4091 bbb 14
(Definitely not a Catholic work)

1358W    A letter from the clergy of France...to Pope Innocent
XI. n. p. d. (London, 1682) cap. title.
4to. 26p. Wing L 1515

1359Z    A letter written by the grand vizier. Printed at London and reprinted at Holy Rood House.
1687. brds. Not seen. Wing L 1762

1360O    Levison, Richard: A sermon on untimely repentance.
Preached before Lord Petre. London.
Mary Thompson. 1688. Wing Ghosts O
L 1822 A

1361W    Line, Francis: Tractatus de corporum inseparabi-
litate. Londini. 1661. FSL (with same
publishers' names as given by Hiscock

H 334<sup>+</sup>) The author is also known as
Hall. (This is a purely scientific work).
Wing H 334

1362Y    Line, Francis: A sharp but short noise of war. 1650
(Does not appear to be our Line-Hall).
Wing H 332

1363O    (Lobb, Emmanuel): Diotrephes or the primitive rule.
Paris 1663. (There is a MS copy of a
book by this title in which Lobb, also
known as Symon, Simeon and Symonds,
answers Pierce's sermon at HP BT
450 PIE. For another answer by Lobb
to Pierce see S 3805)

1364X    (Lobb, Emmanuel): Zeno tragoedia. Romae. Typis
Corbelletti. 1648. L 11712 aa 12;

1365X    (Lobb, Emmanuel): Tragoediae quinque. Leodii.
1656. Typis Joannis Mathiae Hovii. 12s.
LGL;

1366X    (Lobb, Emmanuel): Josephi Simonis Angli...Tragoe-
diae quinque. Editio novissima. Coloniae
Agrippinae.. Typis viduae et haeredum
Pauli Metternich. 1680. L 636 b. 2;

1367X    Mac Callaghan, John: Letter de Monsieur Callaghan...
à un docteur de Sorbonne. n.p.d. (Paris,
1651) Walsh 300;

1368X    (Mac Callaghan, John): Vindiciarum Catholicorum
Hiberniae. 2 vols. Paris. 1650. 8vo.
O 8° C 557 Linc.; CN Case 3 A 1981;
Apud viduam J. Camusat et Petrum le
Petit

1369Z    (Macedo, Fran.): Illustrissimo domino dom. Israel
La Gherfelt. n.p. (London) 1653 (3). L
E 1069 (2) (A latin poem of no religious
significance). Wing M 122

1370Z    (Macedo, Fran.): Domus sadica. Regiis lineis fir-
mata. London. Typis Du Gard. 1653.
(Not seen. Description taken from
catalogue No. 60 of Charles Traylen)

1371X    (Mahoney, Cornelius): Disputatio apologetica et
manifestativa.. authore Constantino
Marullo.. Francofurti. Typis Bernardi
Govran (vere Lisbon). 1645. FSL BX
1504 M 3 1645 Cage. Walsh 420;

1372W    Maimbourg, L.: The history of the crusades. London. R.H. f. Thos. Dring. 1685. O U.

1373W    Maimbourg, L.: History of the Holy War. R.H. f.
Arthur Jones. 1683. Wing M 291

1374W    Maimbourg, L.: The history of the League. London.
M. Flesher f. Jacob Tonson. 1684. O
8° c 346 Linc.; OS 514; (Dryden's translation. In a special postscript he denounces
both papists and non-conformists.) Wing
M 292

1375Z    Manchester, Henry Montague, earl of: Manchester
al modo. 1642 etc. The first edition of
this (1631, STC 18024) is sometimes
attributed to Wat Montague. See e. g.
Dodd III, 94. Wing M 404-410

1376Z    Manual of devout prayers. Gant. R. Walker. 1670.
Not seen

1377Z    Manual of devout prayers. Paris. 1686. Not seen

1378Z    Manual of prayers and litanies. Antwerp. Michael
Cnobbaert. 1658. Copy said to be at EC.
Not seen

1379O    Manual of prayers and litanies. Paris. 1662

1380Z    (Martin, T.): Mary Magdalen's funeral tears wipt
off. 1659 etc. (Not a Catholic work).
Wing M 850-1

1381X    (Mason, Richard Angleus): Apologia pro Scoto anglo.
Duaci. Typis Balthasari Belleri. 1656

1382X    (Mason, Richard): Certamen seraphicum provinciae
Angliae. Duaci. Balt. Beller. 1649.
OS #20; CN Case 3 A 1986

1383Z    Miraculum signum coeleste: A discourse. n.p. 1658.
L 718 b.26; FSL (This is an astrological
work and not Catholic)

Missae sacrificum neomystis... see LeGrand

1384X    More, Henry S.J.: Historia missionis anglicanae
societatis Jesu. Audomari. Typis
Thomas Geubels. 1660. FSL; OS #599.
CN 6 A 336

1385X    More, Henry S.J.: Vita et doctrina Christi domini
in meditationes. Antwerpiae. Apud Jac.
Meursium. 1649. O; CN 3 A 1992 (Note
that the English version of this is put
among the works of Henry More the
Philosopher by Wing. See M 2665)

1386X    More, Wm.: Megalesia sacra in Assumptione magnae
Matris Dei. Duaci, Typis Balthazarii

Belleri. n. d. (1677). BN; <u>L</u> 836 g. 26

1378X      Mumford, James: De misericordia fidelibus defunctis exhibenda. Leodii. Leonard Streel. 1647. <u>HP</u>. LFS

1388X      Mumford, James: Tractatus de misericordia fidelibus defunctis. Coloniae. Typis Wilhelmi Friessenii. 1649. LFS; <u>HP</u>

1389Z      N. N.: The blatant beast muzzled or reflexions on a late libel. n. p. 1691. <u>O</u> Vet A 3 f. 584; <u>Ware</u> (Most of this consists in a letter from John Sergeant but it does not appear to be a Catholic publication)

1390O      (Newport, Maurice): A golden censer full of pretious incense. Paris. 1654. Wing <u>Ghosts</u> O N938*

1391W      (Nicole, Pierre): All the works listed by Wing seem to have been published under Protestant auspices

1392W      (Nicole, Pierre): Of the education of a prince. London. James Magnes & Richard Bentley. 1678. 12mo. <u>Y</u> Oc p. 78. 670 ng; CN (-tp. ) Not published by Catholics

1393W      Nieremberg, Juan: Contemplations of the state of man. London f. John Kidgell to be sold by Dormna Newman. 1684. Fry & Davies; Hiscock N 1151 + (Abridged by Jeremy Taylor)

1394W      Nieremberg, Juan: Contemplations of the state of man. London f. John Kidgell. 1684. anr. ed. Hiscock N 1141 ++.

1395W      Nieremberg, Juan: Flores solitudinis. London f. Humphrey Moseley. 1654. Wing N 1149A

1396W      Nieremberg, Juan: A meditation on life and death. Oxford by L. L. f. Thos. Fickus. 1682. <u>L</u> 4407 b. 12. Wing N 1150/E 3425

1397W      Nieremberg, Juan: Prudentiall reflections. 1674. Fry & Davies N 1150+

1398Z      O. , J. V. C.: Toleration, or no toleration; in a discourse. London. 1663. 8vo. 51p. Running title is "Amsterdam" and it is so listed in Fry & Davies. <u>FSL</u> O 9. 5. This is a toleration tract. John Vincent Canes (#158 ff supra. ) is one of the few 17th century authors to use the initials J. V. C. and this bears resemblances to his other works

13990     Ordo administrandi sacramenta et officia quaedam. Toulouse. 1678. This book is said to have been a ritual printed for Catholic priests in Ireland, but I have not seen a copy

O'Mahoney, Connor: see Mahoney (Cornelius)

1400X     O'Mollony, Cornelius: Anatomicum examen inchiridii...a Thoma Carve. Prague. Typis universitatis Carlo-Ferdinandae in collegio Societatis Jesu ad S. Clementem. 1671

1401Y     Parsons, Robert: A sermon preached. 1680 etc. Not our Persons. Wing P 570-2

Parsons, Robert: see Persons (Robt.)

1402W     Pascal, Blaise: All works listed by Wing as well as Hiscock P 644 + were published under Protestant auspices. Wing P 640-5

1403W     Persons, Robert: A christian directory. London f. Richard Sare. 1699. Hiscock P 566+.

1404W     Persons, Robert: A conference about the next succession. 1681. Wing P 568

1405W     Persons, Robert: The Jesuits memorial. London f. Richard Chiswell. 1690. LFS (Edited by Edward Gee); CN 3 A 2010. Wing P 569

Persons, Robert: Leicester's Commonwealth, see title

1406W     Persons, Robert: Llyfr y resolution. Llundain. 1684. 8vo. L 872 g. 52. Not seen

1407W     Persons, Robert: Llyfr y resolution. Llundain. 1687. (This is the Welsh Protestant version of the Christian Directory)

1408W     Persons, Robert: Parsons his christian directory being a treatise of holy resolution. London f. Richard Sare. 8vo. FSL. Wing P 567

1409W     (Persons, Robert): Severall speeches delivered at a conference. London. Robert Ibbotson. FSL; THC. Wing P 573

1410W     (Persons, Robert): Severall speeches delivered at a conference. London. Robert Ibbotson. 1648. Anr. ed. or variant. FSL P 573a

1411W     (Persons, Robert): Treatise concerning the broken succession. London. 1655. Wing P 574

1412Y   (Petre, Edward): The last will & testament of Father
               Peters. n.p.d. (1688) 4p. Cap. title.
               CN Case 4 A 1853 (This & following are
               satires)

1413Y   (Petre, Edward): The last will and testament of Father
               Petre's. 1688. brds. Wing L 518A

1414Y   (Pinckney, Miles): Treatise of subjection to the powers.
               London. f. Andrew Kembe. 1651. (This
               was written by Thomas Carre, not our
               Thomas Carre, alias Miles Pinckney).
               Wing P 2277

1415X   Plunket, Francis: Heroum speculum de vita Francis-
               ci Tregian. Olisipone. Ex officina Craes-
               beeckiana. 1655. L C 53 h 26

1416W   (Plunket, Oliver): The last speech and confession of.
               Various edd. (Published under govern-
               ment auspices). Wing P 2624-5, 2627

1417V   Preston, T.: The declaration of the Lord General of
               the army of confederate catholicksn.
               n.p. (Kilkenny) 1646. Wing P 3314

1418W   (Preston, Thomas): The tryal and execution of Father
               Henry Garnet. London. Jonathan Robin-
               son. 1679. (This is a trans. of the appen-
               dix of Preston's Supplicatio, A&R 673,
               first published 1616.) Wing W 2087

1419O   The primer or office of the blessed virgin Marie.
               There are two copies of an unidentified
               ed. of this work at Ware, both missing
               tp. 903p. Perhaps same as Wing P 3464 =
               797 supra

1420V   Propositions of the Roman Catholicks of Ireland.
               Waterford. Thomas Bourke. 1644. Wing
               P 3800

1421V   Propositions sent by the Irish parliament. London f.
               I.H. 1647. Wing I 641

1422Z   Protestant rule of faith. London. Henry Hills. 1688.
               Not seen. Wing P 3841

1423W   (Puccini, Vincent): The life of St. Mary Magdalen of
               Pazzi. London. Randall Taylor. 1687.
               OS #2761; O Ashm. 1040; FSL 134513.
               Wing P 4157 = P 4158

1424X   (Pugh, Robert): Excantationis Amuletum. Parisiis.
               1661. O 8° Theta 70 Th.; CN 3 A 2017

1425X   Punch, John: D. Richari Bellingi vindiciae eversae.
               Parisiis. Apud Franciscum Piot. 1653.

1426X   Punch, John: Scotus Hiberniae restitutus. Paris.
           Sumptibus Sebastiani Cramoisy. 1660.
           Walsh #450 (See also Walsh 451-3)

1427V   Queries concerning the lawfullnesse of the present
           cessation. Kilkenny. 1648. C Bradshaw
           Hib. 7.648.9 (-tp). Title is taken from
           Wing and from Peter Walsh's Loyal
           Formulary or Irish Remonstrance which
           reprints it as an appendix. Wing Q 166

1428V   A remonstrance of grievances. Waterford. Thomas
           Bourke. 1643. Wing R 989

1429V   Rinuccini, John Baptist: The decree of excommuni-
           cation...1 Sept. 1646. n.p. (Water-
           ford) 1646. brds. O Carte MSS XVIII,
           414; & LXV, 328. (Also signed by Nich.
           French) Wing R 1521

1430V   Rinuccini, John Baptist: By...a decree of excommuni-
           cation...5 Oct. 1646. (Kilkenny. 1646)
           brds. O Carte MSS LXV, fol. 330. (Also
           signed by Nicholas French). Wing R 1522

1431V   Rinuccini, John Baptist: A decree of excommunication...
           1 Dec. 1646 (Waterford. 1646) brds. O
           Carte MSS lvx, fol. 328

1432W   (Rodriguez, Alonso): A treatise of humilitie. Pub-
           lished by E. D(uncon) Parson sequestered.
           London f. Thomas Johnson. 1654. L
           1544 (2). (This and the following item
           are modified Anglican versions of the
           translation of Sir Tobie Matthew first
           issued in 1631, A&R 734-5) Wing D 17

1433W   (Rodriguez, Alonso): The virtue of humility published
           by E. D. London printed by R. D. 1662.
           (See preceding item) The only known copy
           of this is at Lamport Hall. See 16 The
           Book Collector (1967) p. 441

1434O   S., J.: Catholics are not idolaters. London. Henry
           Hills. 1688. Not seen

1435W   Santa Maria, Fray Juan de: Policy unveiled, or max-
           imes of state. London f. H. Moseley.
           Trans. I.M. (James Mablee). O 4°
           N.16.Art

1436W   Savanorola, Jerome: Truth of the Christian faith.
           Cambridge J. Field. 1661. Wing S 780

1437W    (Scupoli, Lorenzo): The spiritual combat. London f.
                S. Keble; sold by T. Leigh. 1698. O
                Vet A 3 f. 1232. 1 Wing C 1218B

1438Z    A seasonable discourse of the right use and abuse of
                reason in matters of religion. By Philo-
                logus. London. Tho. Passinger. 1676.
                FSL S 2227.5. Not Catholic

1439O    Secrets of the religious life discovered to a devot
                novice. Leige. Chez la v'fve de Boudin
                Brouckert. 1662. (There is a MS copy
                of this book at Lanherne, but no printed
                copy has been discovered)

1440X    Sergeant, John: Clypeus Septemplex. (Duaci) 1677.
                OS #789 & #1882. Wing S 2563. (See next
                item)

1441X    Sergeant, John: Declaratio Joannis Sergeantii circa
                doctrinam in libris suis contentum.
                Duaci. Typis Mariae Serrurier. 1677.
                2 parts. O Vet E 3 f. 54 & Vet E 3 f.
                127 & 8° H 94 Th (imp); OS 790
                (According to DMR "The title Declaratio
                & Doway imprint are on a cancel title
                leaf. In addition is a bifolium (unsigned)
                with a tp Clypeus Semptemplex, errata,
                and preface. Copies are known without
                the cancel title as those quoted in Wing,
                S 2563.")

1442O    S(ergeant), J(ohn): A discovery of the groundlessness
                and insincerity. London. 1665. FSL
                (This is a second part of S 2595). Wing
                S 2564

1443Y    (Sergeant, John): An historical romance of the wars....
                Doublin. 1694. 4to. 88p. CN Case F
                3924.802. Wing S 2570

1444W    Sergeant, John: Informations of... relating to the
                popish plot. London  f. Gabriel Kunholt.
                1681. CN. Wing S 2572

1445Y    (Sergeant, John): The Jesuits gospel. London f. Nor-
                man Nelson. 1679. (This has nothing to
                do with Jesuits. It is an anti-popery
                pamphlet and does not appear to have
                been written by Sergeant). Wing S 2573

1446Y    (Sergeant, John): A letter from a trooper in Flanders.
                London. 1695. (See next item). Wing S
                2574

1447Y (Sergeant, John): A letter from a trooper in Flanders. London. 1695. Hiscock S 2574+. (The copy examined at OC 12 E 61 seems identical with Wing S 2574. It does not appear to have been written by our John Sergeant. )

1448X S(ergeant), J(ohn): Methodus compendiosa. Parisiis apud Andream Cramoisy. 1674. O Vet E 3f. 46 & 8° N 37 Th. Ware; L 1020 c. 16

1449Y Smith, John: The mysterie of Rhetorique unveil'd. 1665 etc. (Does not appear to have been written by our Sergeant). Wing S 2580-4

1450Z Sergeant, John: Sacramental question. 1700. O 1263 f. 105; Not seen

·1451X Sergeant, John: Vindiciae Joan. Sergeantii tribunalibus. n. p. (Duaci) 1678. L 1020 c. 17 (2); O 8° Z 32 G Th

Sergeant, John: Vindication. Wing S 2599, See W., (S) in main list

1452Y A sermon preached by a reverend father in the Jesuits chappel at the Kings-Inn Dublin. London f. R. Baldwin. FSL 142411 (Broad satire written in Irish dialect). Wing S 2636

1453X Smith, Richard: Florum historiae ecclesiasticae. Parisiis. F. Leonard. 1654. L 1229 k. 1; FSL BX 1491 S 6 1654 Cage.

1454X Smith, Richard: Monita quaedam utilia pro sacerdotibus. Parisiis. 1647. FSL 177657; Ware. (Ant. Champney wrote part of this work)

1455Y Spencer, John: Votivae Angliae. England's complaint. London. 1643. (Author is not our John Spencer S. J., but probably the John Spencer who wrote S 4953-5) CN Case C 515. 83. Wing S 4958A

Stapleton, Thomas: see Keynes

1456Z (Stephens, Edward): Asceticks or the heroick piety and virtue of the ancient christian anchorets. Part I. London f. the author. 1696. (Authorship is uncertain and it praises "the good things in Popery," but does not appear to be Catholic). Wing S 5420

1457Z   (Swadlin, Thomas): A Catholick resolution. London.
1668. Y Mhc8. 1668. (This anonymous
work is by the Church of England controversialist). 2 Wing C 1500

1458X   Talbot, Peter: Primatus dubliniensis. Lille. Ex
officina Nicholai de Rache. 1674. Walsh
#544

1459X   Talbot, Peter: Scutum inexpugnabile. Lugduni. 1678.
Walsh #546

1460Z   The temporal and eternal portion of saints. n. p. 1667.
Fry and Davies T 667 A (Not a Catholic
work)

1461X   Terrill, Anthony: Fundamentum totius theologiae
moralis. Leodii. Mathias Hovius. 1668.
DAI

1462W   Theologia germanica or mysticall divinitie. London
f. John Sweeting. 1648. O 8° P 16 (3)
Th BS; Ware. Wing T 858

1463Z   Theyer, John: Aerior Mastix or a vindication of the...
government of the church. Oxford.
(Henry Hall) f. William Webb. 1643.
4to. FSL 161375. (Sometimes counted
a Catholic work, but author was a con-
vinced member of the Church of England).
Wing T 889

1464W   Thomas a Kempis: The christian's pattern. London.
R. Daniel f. John Clark. 1659. CS Yule
collection

1465W   Thomas a Kempis: The christian's pattern. London.
R. Daniel f. John Clark. 1659. anr. ed.
CS Yule Collection

1466W   Thomas a Kempis: The christian's pattern. London.
J. Redmayne & are to be sold by John
Clark. O Vet A 3 g. 40; (This and the
two preceding items plus those listed by
Wing under this title at T 940-7 are
Protestant edd. of the Imitation. They
are lightly revised versions of the
Pinckney translation. )

1467W   Thomas a Kempis: The Christians pattern. London
f. Richard Wellington. 1695. 8vo. This
and the following edition are Worthing-
ton's translation. Wing T 955

1468W   Thomas a Kempis: The Christians pattern. London
Elig. Redmayne. 1699. 24to. Wing T

Wing T 956

1469Z     Thomas a Kempis: The christians solemn vow.
                Edinburgh. 1688. Not seen. Wing T 948

1470W    Thomas a Kempis: De Christo imitando. Canta-
                brigiae. Johannes Hayes impensis G.
                Graves Jun. 1685. Wing T 949

1471Z     A total overthrow of the late pretended plot. London
                f. P. F. Hiscock T 1950+. Not seen

1472Z     Tourville, Anne-Hilarion de Costentin, comte de:
                Declaration of. Translated from the
                french original. s. sh. n. d. p. (1692?)
                <u>TU</u>; <u>CN</u> Case 3 A 1905. Jacobite and
                political.

1473O     Vane, Thomas: Prudence of the serpent. 1652. (This
                is identical with Wing V 89). Wing V 88

1474Z     Vincent, Thomas: An explicatory catechism. London.
                1683. <u>FSL</u> V 436. 2. This and the previous
                edd. of this work (V 432-6) were written
                by a non-conformist divine

1475O     A vindication against Friar Walsh his calumnies
                written by a pastor of the diocese of
                Dublin. (This work is mentioned by
                Talbot in T 116 p. 66, but no copy has
                been found. )

1476Z     W., E.: The death, burial and resurrection of the
                act of 35th of Eliz. (coloph.) London f.
                Nath. Thompson. 1681. Not seen. (There
                is another ed. of this in Hiscock W 15 +.)
                Wing W 15

1477Y     W., T.: A letter from Rome to a friend in London in
                relation to the Jesuits executed. n. p.
                (London) 1679. <u>O</u> C. 10. 6. Th (21). (Some-
                times attributed to Thomas Ward but not
                his. ) Wing W 122A

1478X     Walsh, Peter: Conclusiones theologicae. Romae.
                Typis N. L. Corbelletti. 1651. brds.
                Walsh #644

1479Z     W(alsh), P(eter): A letter desiring a just and merci-
                ful regard. Dublin, reprinted at London.
                1662. Not seen. Wing W 637

1480Y     Ward, Thomas & Evans, Valentine: Two witnesses
                to the midnight cry... by two laymen.
                London. 1691. <u>O</u> G Pamph. 1691 (35)
                (Does not appear to have been written
                by our Thomas Ward)

1481Y    (Warner, John):  A brief discourse of right worship.
London f. the author. 1684. (Not our
John Warner) Wing W 906

1482X    (Warner, John):  Duarum epistolarum a Doctiss. D.
Georgio Morlaio. Auctore N. N. n. p.
1683. Ware; HP; Birrell #16a

1483X    Warner, John:  Duarum epistolarum Georgii Morlaei...
authore Ioanne Warnero. n. p. 1683.
LFS. Birrell #16b

1484X    Warner, John:  Ecclesiae primitivae clericus. n. p.
1686. TU; CN Case 4 A 1873; O Vet E
3 d. 27; Birrell #18

1485X    (Warner, John):  La harangue de monseigneur Guil-
liaume Vicomte Destafford. n. d. p.
(c. 1680). Birrell #15

1486X    (Warner, John):  Harangues des cinq pères de la
compagnie de Jesus. n. d. p. (1680? )
Birrell #11

1487X    (Warner, John):  Lettre escrite de mons à un amy
à Paris. n. d. p. (1679) Birrell #8

1488X    (Warner, John):  Seconde lettre de Mons à un amy
à Paris. n. d. p. (1679) Birrell #9

1489X    (Warner, John):  Vindiciae censurae duacenae seu
confutatio.. authore Jona Thamone
(Pseud. ) n. p. 1661. HP; OS #2278

1490X    White, Alexander:  Schismatis Anglicani redargutio.
Lovanii. Hiernoymus Nempaeus. 1661.
8vo. TU

1491X    White, Thomas:  Appendicula ad sonum buccinae.
n. p. (Paris) 1654. (Ordinarily con-
sidered a part of Sonus Buccinae - see
infra. - but pagination and signatures
are separate) CN Case 3 A 2072

1492X    White, Thomas:  Appendicula tentans solutionem
problematis Torrecelliani. Londini.
1663. (Ordinarily found bound with
Wing W 1841)

1493O    White, Thomas:  Chrysaspis seu scriptorum suorum.
1659. (As far as I know this only exists
in the parts quoted in Querela Geometrica - Q 162). Wing W 1812

1494Z    (White, Thomas):  Chryspapis to querela. London.
1660. O Wood 127; OS #3184. (A purely
mathematical work). Wing W 1813

1495X    White, Thomas: De mundo dialogi tres. Parisiis.
                1642. L 8704 e 5; O AA Art Seld.; FSL
                185777

1496Y    White, Thomas: The dialogues of. 1648 & 1654. See
                Rushworth in main list. Wing W 1819-20

1497W   (White, Thomas): Euclidus physicus. Londini apud
                Joannam Crook. 1657. L 538 a 13; O
                Rawlins. 392 & Radcliffe f. 63. Wing
                W 1822

1498W   White, Thomas: Exercitatio geometrica. Londini.
                1658. O Savile C c 20; L E 1884 (2);
                FSL 185011; NC Smith 513. 1658 W 58.
                Wing W 1825

1499W   White, Thomas: The grounds of obedience and
                government. third ed. London. A. Bald-
                win. d. d. (c. 1700) CS Hh 6. 39 (3).
                Wing W 1828

1500X    White, Thomas: Institutionum peripateticarum..
                Pars theorica. Lugduni. Ex typographia
                Jacobi Rantonnet. 1646. 2 parts. Ware;
                OS #955

1501X    (White, Thomas): Institutionum sacrarum peripate-
                ticis...pars theorica. 2 vols. n.p.
                (Paris) 1652. OS #956; O 8° T 18. 19
                Th. Seld. Wing W 1829

1502X    White, Thomas: Magnifico domino rectori..academiae
                Duacenae supplicatio. n. d. p. (1660).
                L 1019 e 15

1503X    White, Thomas: Meditationes viginti-quator. Parisiis
                apud Georgium Joese. 1651

1504X    White, Thomas: Meditationes viginti-quatuor. Bruxel-
                lis. 1654

1505X    White, Thomas: Mens Augustini de gratia Adami.
                Parisiis. 1652. L 848 c 10

1506Y    White, Thomas: A method and instructions for the
                art of divine meditation. London. By
                A. M. f. Jos. Cranford. 1655. (Not
                our Thomas White). Wing W 1834

1507Y    White, Thomas: A method and instructions. London
                f. Thos. Parkhurst. 1672. (Not our
                Thomas White). Wing W 1835

1508X    White, Thomas: Monumetham excantatus. Rhotomagi.
                1660. O 8° C 318 Linc.; L 1020 k. 15;
                CN 3 A 2078

1509X     White, Thomas: Quaestio theologica. n. p. d. (Paris.
                1652) O 8° V 252 Th. (Imp.); L 848 c 10

1510X     White, Thomas: Sonus Buccinae. Parisiis. 1654. O
                Radcliffe f. 63; CN 3 A 2072

1511X     White, Thomas: Sonus Buccinae. Coloniae. Joann.
                Kinckius. 1659. L E 1877; O 8° W 2 Th
                BS

1512Z     White, Thomas: Tintinnalogia. 1671. Not seen. Wing
                W 1847

1513Y     White, Thomas: Treatise of the power of godliness.
                Not our White. Wing W 1848

1514X     White, Thomas: Villicationis suae de medio animarum
                statu. Parisiis. 1653. FSL 177110; O
                8° C 6 Art.; CN 3 A 2080 (This was the
                original of Wing W 1836)

1515W     (Winter, Sir John): Observations upon the oath en-
                acted. London f. Henry Brome. 1679.
                O Ashm. 993. Wing W 3082

1516O     (Woodhead, Abraham): The Catholicks defence for
                their adoration. Oxford. 1687. (This
                is part of W 3459). Wing W 3439

1517O     (Woodhead, Abraham): A discourse concerning the
                celibacy of the clergy (This is part of
                W 3460). Wing W 3445

1518O     (Worsley, Edward): A discourse concerning mira-
                cles... By E. W. The second part.
                Antwerp. Michael Cnobbaert. 1674.
                (This is part of W 3615. See e. g. OS
                #991). Wing W 3613

1519X     (Wyburne, Edw.): Epitaphium potentissimi et
                nobillissimi principis guillelmi Howard.
                Parisiis. Jo. Bapt. Nego. 1683. O
                Wood 427 (9)

1520X     (Young or Youngson, Andrew): De providentia.
                Lugduni. 1678. Signed "Junius."
                (Newdigate nn.)

# APPENDIX II

Publishers & Booksellers
(Books in Appendix I are not included)

Allestrye, J.　　　London
644, 1072
Bailey, Geo.
964
Bailey, W.　　　London
926
Baker, John.　　　London
998
Banks, A.
1139
Battut, Peter.　　　Boulogne
657
Baudry, Guillaume.　　　Paris
81
Bedel or Bedell, Gabriel.　　　London
213, 676, 677
Belier, John.　　　Paris
397
Beller, Balthazar.　　　Doway
102, 139, 288, 293, 595, 650, 651, 669
Bentley, William.　　　London
202
Bill, A.　　　London
126
Bill, Charles.　　　London
382
Billaine, Jean.　　　Paris
173, 262, 263, 845, 846, 1001, 1002, 1003, 1064
Blagaert, M.　　　Paris
896, 948, 959

Blagaert, widow.        Paris
43, 957
Blaizot, Giles.        Paris
321, 385
Boe, Simon.        Bordeaux
495
Booker, R.        London
864
Boudet, Anthony.        London
301
Bouvet, Andreas.        Louvain
33
Brome, Joanna.        London
1032
Brome, John.        London
1015
Brome, Henry.        London
1014, 1016, 1018, 1019, 1020, 1021, 1022, 1023, 1024, 1034,
1035
Brooke, Nathaniel.        London
918
Brooks, William.        London
18
Brown, D.        London
894, 906
Cadman or Cademan, William.        London
1112
Cadwel or Cadwell, John.        London
1104
Carlier, Ludovic.        St. Omers
714
Carlier, Joachim.        St. Omers
832, 843
Carnius, Robert.        London
719
Chapman, Laurence.        London
1078, 1079
Chapman, Livewell.        London
589
Chrestien, widow.        Paris
738
Christian, Antonie, widow.        Paris
1114
Clavil, Roger.        London
900

Cnobbaert, Michael.      Antwerp
1132, 1133, 1134, 1135
Cnobbaert, John (widow).     Antwerp
639, 640, 797
Cock or DeCock, John.     Bruges
524
Coignard, John Baptist.     Paris
1000
Collins, Thomas.     London
213
Cotes, Ellen.     London
502
Courant, Julian.     Rouen
949
Cousturier, Jean.     Rouen
62
Cramoisy, Sebastien.     Paris
130, 312
Crasbeeck, Paul.     Lisbon
292
Crook, Andrew.     Dublin
329
Crook or Crooke, John.     London
42, 677, 704, 860, 998, 1104
Crouch, Samuel.     London
127
Cruttenden, Henry.     Oxon
308, 920, 988
Dakins, John.     London
32, 155, 196, 428
Daniel, Roger.     London
45, 46, 189, 191, 509, 862, 863, 963, 1006
Danthez, Peter.     Liege
811
Davis or Davies, Thomas.     London
663
Davis or Davies, W.     London
600
Dicas, Thomas.     London
1072
Dod, Edwin.     London
157
Downing, W.     London
1039

English College Press.        St. Omer
16, 17, 23, 69, 89, 136, 187A, 376, 377, 378, 379, 570, 715,
835, 836, 837, 865, 866, 867

Edwards, D.        London
150

Ekin or Ekins, Nathaniel.        London
157

Eversden, George.        London
501, 502

Eversden, Henry.        London
501

Farmer, Thomas.        London
377

Fievet, Thomas.        Doway
71, 72

Flesher, James.        London
1078, 1079

Frere, Daniel.        London
1, 2, 3, 4

Geubels, Thomas.        St. Omers
66, 224, 574

Gilbertson, William.        London
664

Graet, Maximilian.        Ghent
687, 695, 698, 1101

Grantham, William.        London
63, 236, 406, 481

Guignard, Rene.        Paris
48, 421

Guillery, Charles.        Paris
1114

Hales, Thomas.        London
376, 378, 379, 715, 835, 836, 837, 865, 866, 867

Hall, H.        Oxford
839

Harper, Charles
1139

Harper, Thomas.        London
1, 2, 3, 4, 153

Harris, Benjamin.        London
924

Harris, John.        London
126, 875

Helsham, Samuel.        Dublin
329

Herringman, Henry.　　　London
19, 144, 370
Hills, Henry.　　　London
15, 26, 70, 80, 95, 101, 107, 120, 120A, 124, 133, 184, 210,
211, 216, 217, 218, 221, 225, 226, 297, 313, 326, 348, 349,
350, 351, 352, 353, 354, 355, 356, 357, 358, 359, 382, 384,
391, 399, 416, 419, 422, 423, 424, 425, 430, 432, 433, 434,
435, 436, 437, 438, 439, 453, 460, 461, 462, 463, 464, 465,
466, 467, 468, 470, 472, 473, 481, 494, 520, 521, 531, 532,
534, 535, 557, 558, 559, 560, 561, 584, 606, 636, 642A, 660,
661, 662, 666, 700, 737, 740, 741, 746, 760, 764, 765, 769,
771, 783, 784, 807, 822, 828, 830, 841, 850, 851, 852, 853,
854, 855, 856, 857, 858, 870, 870, 876, 877, 889, 923, 933,
971, 1052, 1053, 1121
Hindmarsh, Joseph.　　　London
617, 618
Holden, John.　　　London
587
Holy Rood House.　　　Edinburgh
14, 34, 290, 328, 452, 522, 637, 697, 707, 761, 831, 842,
879, 952
Ians, Christopher.　　　Dublin
621
Jacob, W.　　　London
154
Kellam, Lawrence, the younger.　　　Doway
593, 983, 1007
Kerchove, John van den.　　　Ghent
212
Kerchove, Luke.　　　Bruges
167, 344, 682
LaFosse, Lewis de.　　　Paris
555, 685, 686, 745, 747
Lane, John & Thomas.　　　London
31, 64, 73, 300, 706, 708, 816
Lauren or Laurens, P.　　　Paris
96
Lee, William.　　　London
676
Leigh, Thomas.　　　London
885
Lesteens, William.　　　Antwerp
148
LeTourneur, Nicholas.　　　Rouen
795, 796

Lloyd, Lodowick.          London
499
Lowndes, Richard.          London
55
Mabb or Mab, Thomas.          London
170, 1030
Mairesse, Michael.          Doway
10, 20, 278, 381, 758, 781
Manilius, Bauldwin.          Ghent
77
Martin, John.          London
644, 681, 1072
Maurry, David.          Rouen
569, 794
Mead, Richard.          London
773
Mestais, Jean.          Paris
844
Metcalf or Metcalfe, Ralph.          London
234
Metcalf or Metcalfe, Thomas.          London
885, 891, 900, 906
Mersius, John.          Antwerp
941
Michallet, Estienne.          Paris
712
Milbourn or Milbourne, Thomas.          London
968
Moette, Thomas.          Paris
22
Moore, R.          London
199
Moret, Balthazar.          Antwerp
799
Montius, Jacobus.          Bologna
940
Moutier, Vincent du.          Paris
117, 230, 231, 609, 775, 780, 958
Newcomb, Thomas.          London
382, 587
Newman, Dorman.          London
968
Norton, R.          London
613, 614, 616

Pakeman, Daniel.      London
676
Patte, John.      Doway
71, 72
Pawlet or Pawlett, Robert.      London
526
Ray, Joseph.      Dublin
626
Redmayne, W.      London
891
Redmayn or Redmayne, J. (I?).      London
276, 277
Ridley, John.      London
1092
Roland, Will. Palinggenii.      London
730
Roman, Christian.      Troyes
309, 310
Rookes or Rooke, Thomas.      London
156, 204, 276, 277
Roper, Abel.      London
375, 885, 892, 894, 900, 906
Roycroft, Thomas.      London
615
S. Cong. de Propag.      Rome
742, 743, 744
Serrurier, Christopher.      Doway
984, 985, 986
Sevestre, L.      Paris
909
Sheares, William.      London
209
Shedd, John.      London
134
Stephens, Philemon, the younger.      London
197
Streel, Guillaume Henri.      Liege
602
Targa, Peter.      Paris
254, 318, 364
Taylor, Randall.      London
13, 27, 429, 451, 565, 972
Thompson, James.      Antwerp
639, 797

Thompson, Mary.        London
29, 73, 74, 135, 510, 512, 514, 635A, 673, 806, 814, 816
Thompson, Nathaniel.        London
100, 235, 279, 362, 411, 496, 497, 515, 516, 519, 567, 577,
583, 610, 622, 623, 627, 634, 635, 645, 671, 672, 678, 680,
683, 693, 787, 815, 818, 824, 973, 990, 1041, 1043
Thomson, Jacob.        London
132
Thornton, Robert.        Dublin
220
Tonson, Jacob.        London
326, 330, 331
Tooke or Took, Benjamin.        London
861, 1016, 1017, 1018, 1019, 1020, 1021, 1022, 1023, 1024,
1034, 1105
Tootal, John.        London
418
Tottenham, John.        London
299
Tulliet, Claude Francois.        Aire
369
Turner, John.        London
311
Turner, Matthew.        London
44, 70, 73, 74, 79, 87, 94, 95, 102A, 105, 115, 116, 129,
134, 152, 169, 184, 185, 200, 222, 226, 233, 237, 240, 283,
334, 341, 391, 410, 418, 430, 479, 527, 562, 599, 607, 696,
700, 769, 816, 868, 869, 870, 882, 883, 884, 888, 898, 904,
953, 971, 987, 1005
Twiford or Twyford, Henry.        London
112, 426
Typis Newcomiensis.        London
721
Vere, Thomas.        London
664
Vitus, Robert
720
Walker, Robert.        Ghent
475, 930, 931
Watson, James.        Edinburgh (see also Holy Rood House)
808, 831, 952
Weston, Wm.        Dublin
523
Whitaker or Whittaker, Richard.        London
1081

Wilde, Joseph.          Dublin
388
Williams, John.          London
190, 191, 192, 193, 198, 199, 200, 201, 202, 203, 205, 322,
323, 324, 1075, 1089
Williamson, Anthony.          London
509
Willverval, J. F.          Doway
675
Wingate, R.          London
112
Wood, Ralph.          London
918
Wooks, Cornelius.          Antwerp
25
Wyon, widow (of Marc).          Doway
113, 594, 597, 652, 653, 654
Young, James.          London
426

# APPENDIX III

Chronological Index
(Books in Appendix I are not included)

| | |
|---|---|
| 1641 | 81, 89, 143, 153, 311, 315, 316, 383, 529, 701, 716, 960, 961, 963 |
| 1642 | 23, 113, 187A, 333, 684, 688, 689, 733, 941, 948, 964 |
| 1643 | 652, 734 |
| 1644 | 321, 397, 630, 653, 654 |
| 1645 | 6, 212, 322, 415, 914, 915, 992 |
| 1646 | 674, 723, 774, 991 |
| 1647 | 1, 2, 261, 312, 655, 833, 1065, 1081 |
| 1648 | 3, 4, 189, 317, 320, 385, 478, 658, 659, 676, 844, 974, 993, 994 |
| 1649 | 5, 25, 168, 190, 207, 292, 726, 995, 996 |
| 1650 | 62, 145, 155, 188, 191, 202, 409, 639, 757, 766, 797, 871, 917, 989 |
| 1651 | 45, 46, 50, 287, 380, 587, 798, 862, 863, 916, 1006 |
| 1652 | 49, 51, 52, 53, 54, 142, 157, 192, 254, 318, 319, 375, 413, 484, 502, 639A, 646, 751, 752, 754, 839, 872, 874, 911, 998, 999, 1007, 1101 |
| 1653 | 55, 206, 209, 255, 262, 426, 509, 614, 762, 763, 905, 913, 957, 959 |
| 1654 | 19, 83, 84, 148, 303, 342, 364, 613, 615, 616, 650, 651, 677, 749, 825, 845, 846, 983, 1064, 1067, 1068, 1092, 1102 |
| 1655 | 43, 85, 112, 144, 165, 227, 304, 505, 566, 753, 896, 910, 922, 1078, 1079, 1084, 1095, 1099 |
| 1656 | 213, 305, 687, 873, 1089 |
| 1657 | 71, 284, 285, 506, 508, 555, 591, 594, 596, 597, 644, 685, 728, 729, 745, 778, 897, 919, 939, 954, 1010, 1086, 1093, 1098 |

| | |
|---|---|
| 1658 | 86, 173, 223, 323, 396, 476, 503, 664, 686, 694, 698, 755, 779, 799, 804, 823, 860, 921, 955, 1072 |
| 1659 | 32, 65, 137, 228, 263, 361, 363, 414, 498, 727, 730, 918, 937, 1008, 1066, 1069, 1082, 1083, 1085 |
| 1660 | 42, 172, 360, 374, 427, 428, 477, 589, 592, 598, 601, 702, 704, 767, 819, 901, 965, 966, 1001, 1002, 1080, 1088, 1090 |
| 1661 | 36, 106, 161, 196, 197, 208, 271, 272, 474, 507, 556, 585, 588, 593, 628, 703, 821, 967, 975, 1033, 1063, 1071, 1087, 1094 |
| 1662 | 35, 91, 162, 164, 170, 187, 193, 269, 280, 288, 332, 386, 501, 504, 551, 568, 590, 595, 695, 834, 1027, 1028, 1030, 1036, 1073, 1076, 1077, 1103, 1104 |
| 1663 | 75, 97, 98, 102, 109, 139, 160, 203, 273, 286, 289, 293, 603, 656, 735, 805, 1074, 1091 |
| 1664 | 204, 366, 367, 528, 812, 958, 1031 |
| 1665 | 77, 159, 163, 171, 224, 229, 324, 370, 575, 720, 772, 776, 777, 780, 886, 902, 903, 1075, 1136 |
| 1666 | 180, 181, 182, 775, 887, 997 |
| 1667 | 33, 66, 72, 156, 309, 310, 574, 611, 849, 881, 1116 |
| 1668 | 56, 257, 258, 325, 394, 395, 682, 1134, 1139 |
| 1669 | 68, 141, 230, 243, 346, 387, 648, 667, 721, 794, 820, 832, 943 |
| 1670 | 231, 276, 306, 525, 533, 537, 563, 640A, 647, 657, 738, 843, 847, 938, 949, 1004 |
| 1671 | 24, 166, 619, 631, 640, 890, 942, 984, 985, 986, 1055, 1110, 1114 |
| 1672 | 7, 40, 57, 110, 117, 158, 167, 198, 259, 264, 265, 270, 420, 786, 895, 946, 1003, 1037, 1038, 1100, 1120, 1124, 1125, 1135 |
| 1673 | 111, 179, 244, 266, 281, 307, 344, 388, 499, 552, 602, 681, 724, 768, 800, 880, 950, 962, 968, 1013, 1016, 1017, 1018, 1019, 1029, 1057, 1117, 1122, 1123 |
| 1674 | 69, 82, 175, 176, 177, 260, 343, 393, 400, 482, 485, 486, 564, 569, 570, 573, 641, 838, 930, 931, 935, 936, 970, 1021, 1022, 1026, 1029, 1034, 1070, 1133 |
| 1675 | 60, 147, 238, 239, 389, 390, 392, 487, 553, 571, 580, 604, 609, 632, 649, 756, 934, 944, 1023, 1056, 1111, 1113 |
| 1676 | 88, 103, 104, 131, 335, 398, 475, 488, 530, 722, 743, 976, 1132 |
| 1677 | 17, 41, 421, 489, 526, 742, 1035 |

| 1678 | 48, 146, 154, 205, 490, 576, 690, 791, 857, 893, 940, 1000, 1014, 1048, 1049 |
|------|------|
| 1679 | 30, 37, 38, 39, 47, 67, 277, 372, 402, 511, 550, 578, 579, 691, 719, 732, 750, 785, 792, 1024, 1047, 1050, 1051, 1096, 1126 |
| 1680 | 20, 134, 248, 249, 811, 908, 924, 925, 926, 927, 977, 978, 1054, 1059, 1060 |
| 1681 | 174, 178, 252, 362, 572, 705, 725, 736, 787, 817, 928, 1061 |
| 1682 | 8, 11, 18, 149, 199, 232, 241, 246, 253, 663, 1032 |
| 1683 | 247, 250, 491, 600, 1058 |
| 1684 | 58, 93, 127, 269, 381, 610, 668, 669, 712, 713, 773, 781, 795, 861, 947, 979, 1009, 1015, 1097 |
| 1685 | 12, 59, 59A, 79, 100, 118, 119, 130, 185, 251, 256, 282, 336, 337, 338, 403, 404, 454, 455, 456, 457, 458, 459, 492, 493, 500, 618, 679, 801, 802, 876, 1105, 1118 |
| 1686 | 26, 44, 63, 95, 101, 105, 108, 116, 120, 120A, 121, 122, 124, 125, 128, 133, 140, 194, 210, 211, 214, 215, 216, 217, 218, 219, 220, 222, 226, 242, 313, 326, 339, 340, 348, 349, 350, 351, 352, 353, 354, 355, 356, 359, 368, 384, 391, 410, 411, 422, 424, 433, 434, 453, 460, 463, 471, 472, 481, 527, 531, 546, 559, 561, 562, 581, 599, 605, 606, 620, 633, 642A, 670, 692, 696, 699, 744, 746, 759, 764, 765, 783, 784, 788, 789, 790, 825A, 826, 830, 868, 870, 877, 923, 932, 933, 951, 953, 971, 987, 1035, 1115, 1121, 1137, 1138 |
| 1687 | 15, 21, 34, 61, 64, 70, 80, 94, 115, 123, 129, 152, 169, 184, 200, 201, 221, 233, 235, 236, 240, 279, 290, 295, 297, 314, 327, 328, 329, 330, 331, 341, 357, 358, 365, 382, 399, 405, 406, 407, 408, 412, 417, 419, 429, 430, 432, 435, 436, 437, 438, 439, 451, 452, 461, 462, 464, 465, 466, 468, 473, 479, 480, 494, 496, 515, 516, 519, 534, 535, 536, 540, 554, 557, 558, 560, 567, 577, 582, 583, 621, 622, 623, 626, 627, 634, 635, 645, 660, 661, 666, 671, 672, 678, 680, 683, 693, 697, 700, 706, 707, 717, 718, 737, 739, 741, 747, 769, 807, 808, 813, 814, 815, 818, 822, 824, 828, 829, 831, 840, 841, 852, 854, 856, 857, 858, 875, 878, 879, 889, 898, 904, 907, 952, 973, 980, 990, 1041, 1043, 1044, 1045, 1107, 1112, 1129, 1130, 1131 |
| 1688 | 9, 13, 14, 27, 28, 29, 31, 73, 74, 87, 90, 99, 132, 225, 237, 267, 268, 283, 296, 299, 300, 301, 308, |

         334, 371, 373, 416, 423, 425, 467, 470, 483, 497,
         510, 512, 514, 520, 521, 522, 523, 532, 549, 565,
         584, 607, 612, 617, 625, 635A, 636, 637, 642, 662,
         673, 708, 709, 710, 740, 760, 761, 771, 782, 806,
         816, 842, 850, 851, 853, 855, 864, 869, 882, 883,
         884, 888, 899, 920, 972, 988, 1005, 1011, 1012,
         1039, 1040, 1042, 1046, 1052, 1053, 1108, 1119,
         1127, 1128
1689     107, 418, 443, 714, 981, 1106, 1109
1690     245, 401, 624, 711
1691     495, 513, 865, 909
1692     22, 136, 543, 866, 1062
1693     96, 544, 586, 758
1694     294, 347, 665, 715, 956
1695     150, 278, 376, 378, 444, 445, 446, 827, 912
1696     151, 377, 448, 517, 518, 638, 770, 867, 891
1697     10, 234, 291, 379, 524, 538, 835, 900
1698     126, 274, 441, 447, 449A, 450, 541, 545, 643, 836,
         885, 892, 969, 982
1699     431, 440, 442, 449, 542, 547, 608, 748, 803, 837,
         894
1700     76, 78, 92, 114, 186, 275, 469, 539, 548, 629, 796,
         809, 810, 906
NO DATE: 16, 183, 195, 675, 793, 803A

# APPENDIX IV

Index of Translators, Editors and Compilers
(Books in Appendix I are not included)

N. B.   Cross references given in the main list are not re-
peated here.

A., C., S.J.   909
B., A.   see Everard, Thomas
B., H.   86
B., P.   1139
B., W.   184, 332, 574
Baker, Austin   685
Blount, Walter K.   240, 332, 738, 923
Brook, Basil   196, 197, 198, 199, 200, 201, 206
Burbery, John   476, 477, 601, 644
C., R.   567
Cartor, Richard   288
Caryll, E. or John   809, 810
Chamberleyne, Francis   31, 77
Conny, Bernard   383
Corbington, Robt.   940
Cressy, Serenus   71, 563
D., F.   426
D., J.   987
Darrell, W.   291, 294
Davis, Jo.   129
Digby, Kenelm   19
Dryden, John   132
DuVerger, Simon   153
East, Lewis   113
Everard, Thomas   89
Fitzsimon, Thos.   569, 794, 795
Floyd, John   43
G., F.   475